EDITING FOR TODAY'S NEWSROOM
New Perspectives for a Changing Profession

COMMUNICATION TEXTBOOK SERIES
Jennings Bryant—Editor

Journalism
Maxwell McCombs—Advisor

BERNER ● Writing Literary
Features

FENSCH ● The Sports Writing
Handbook

TITCHENER ● Reviewing
the Arts

FENSCH ● Writing Solutions:
Beginnings, Middles,
and Endings

SHOEMAKER ● Communication
Campaigns about Drugs:
Government, Media,
and the Public

FENSCH ● Associated Press
Coverage of a Major Disaster:
The Crash of Delta Flight 1141

STEPP ● Editing for Today's
Newsroom: New Perspectives
For a Changing Profession

FENSCH ● Best Magazine Articles: 1988

BOGART ● Press and Public: Who Reads What,
When, Where, and Why in American
Newspapers, Second Edition

GARRISON ● Professional Feature
Writing

EDITING FOR TODAY'S NEWSROOM
New Perspectives for a
Changing Profession

Carl Sessions Stepp
University of Maryland at College Park

LEA LAWRENCE ERLBAUM ASSOCIATES, PUBLISHERS
1989 Hillsdale, New Jersey   Hove and London

Lawrence Erlbaum Associates, Inc., Publishers
365 Broadway
Hillsdale, New Jersey 07642

Library of Congress Cataloging-in-Publication Data
Stepp, Carl Sessions.
    Editing for today's newsroom : new perspectives for a changing
profession / Carl Sessions Stepp.
        p.   cm.—(Communication textbook series)
    Bibliography: p.
    Includes index.
    ISBN 0-8058-0325-4
    1. Stepp, Carl Sessions. 2. Editors—United States—Biography.
3. Journalists—United States—Biography. 4. Journalism—Editing.
I. Title. II. Series.
PN4874.S683A3   1990
070.4'1—dc20   89-31412
                                                       CIP

Printed in the United States of America
10 9 8 7 6 5 4 3 2 1

For Laura and my parents

Contents

Preface

I encountered my first editor shortly after I turned 14, on a sparkling June day when I awoke and decided to become a reporter. The local newspaper office sat just around the corner from my home. On many days I had stood in my backyard, spellbound by the sight and sound of newspapers thundering off an ancient flatbed press in the back of the building.

So I didn't have far to go that summer morning. I strode into the newsroom, presented myself as a fresh recruit, and confronted the redoubtable Annie Laurie Kinney, who with her husband Bill owned and ran the semiweekly *Marlboro Herald-Advocate* in Bennettsville, South Carolina.

It must have been a comic scene: a busy editor besieged by a callow, teenage upstart with pencil in hand. But Annie Laurie Kinney didn't laugh. Nor did she patronize me. Instead, she did what came naturally to an editor: She lectured me.

She told me that newspapering was serious business and a public trust. She actually said that "names is news." She reached into her desk drawer and handed me a dusty old paperback—called *The Correspondent*, as I recall—that the Associated Press had once furnished her when she was a stringer.

And she assigned me to cover a baseball game.

On that day, I absorbed my first and perhaps most important lesson about editing: Good editors treat all writers with respect and seriousness, be they prize-winning veterans or quavering greenhorns. That is the backbone of the relationship. And that lesson remains, to this day, one of the inspirations for my career.

What I didn't know then, but soon came to appreciate, was how rare good editors and good editing can be.

Good editors know how to be tough on the copy, but gentle on the ego. They recognize the wild spark that fires the writer-beast, and thrill in the incendiary challenge of inciting it to the creative brink.

As part-time language police and full-time ego massagers, they live in a dual world, shuttling through what may seem a professional mind warp: at one moment, operating in lone-eagle style as sharp-eyed, no-nonsense copy surgeons; at the next, presiding grandly over expansive news projects, marshaling some Machiavellian blend of wisdom, patience, temper and octane to best stimulate the aroused ferocity and fragility of each newshound.

Unhappily, too few editors span these points successfully. In the 25 years or so since meeting Annie Laurie Kinney, I have worked with editors of many flavors. I have become an editor myself. I have studied journalism and taught in a journalism school.

From this all, I have come away fascinated and enthralled by the intricacies of editing, and disappointed and let down by the haphazard, ineffective way too many journalists approach it.

I have had good editors and bad, and I have done good editing and bad. From this experience, nothing thunders more loudly to me than this point: Editing is the essential difference between excellence and mediocrity in journalism. Like movie directors, editors are behind-the-scenes catalysts and coordinators whose efforts fundamentally define the ultimate product.

Yet editing is sadly and inexplicably neglected. In our journalism schools and professional seminars, in the literature and the mythology of our profession, we dwell on writing and reporting, with token tips of the pica pole to editing. We glamorize reporters, but kiss off editors or, at most, dismiss them as glorified proofreaders.

In this book, I seek to help rectify this condition by sharing some of what I have collected and learned about our craft. I hope to encourage others, especially students, to think of editing in new and wider ways.

The book is intended primarily for advanced students of editing, but it may also interest professional journalists who are considering editing or who have, as countless news people do, gone into editing with little formal preparation. I try to cover a range of skills that editors may need over the course of a career, from the fundamentals of line editing to the subtleties of supervising.

Some readers may find material that seems elementary and repetitive; others may find the same passages fresh and eye-opening. That is precisely because we have no standard system for producing editors and no body of knowledge that all editors share. Appointees arrive on the job with vastly differing backgrounds and abilities and, likewise, with differing knowledge gaps and blind spots. No one textbook can serve them all, of course, but I have tried to view the subject and the audience broadly enough to bring many strands of editing together into something coherent.

ACKNOWLEDGMENTS

In writing this material, I think back to Annie Laurie Kinney and to so many other editors from whom I have gained: her husband Bill, who brought a dignity to every story and person; her son, Bill Jr., who shot enthusiasm into both his journalism and mine; Professor Ed Trayes of Temple University, who introduced me to the satisfactions of editing; Bill Fuller, whose gung ho news instincts helped me see the world as editors see it; W. Davis Merritt, who exemplified the meaning of editor—reporter teamwork; Joe Distelheim, the best editor I ever worked for; John Walter, brilliant and inspiring; my teachers at the University of South Carolina, and Laura Sessions Stepp, my wife and also the best editor I ever saw at moving a team of reporters toward the goal line.

And many others: James Batten, Bob Boyd, Ginny Carroll, Pat Carter, Reese Cleghorn, John Curley, Stu Dim, Mark Ethridge, Clark Hoyt, David Lawrence, Luisita Lopez, Walker Lundy, Ron Martin, the late Pete McKnight, Bill Monroe, Rich Oppel, John Quinn, Larry Tarleton, Nancy Woodhull, and so many more.

Because of them all, I believe that editing is vital, it is fun, and we all have much to learn about it.

In addition, thanks go to many current colleagues for assistance and encouragement with this book.

Dean Reese Cleghorn of the University of Maryland College of Journalism gave support from the beginning. My colleague James Grunig directed me toward the publisher, and on its behalf Maxwell McCombs of the University of Texas and Jennings Bryant of the University of Alabama provided helpful early reviews and backing. Robin Marks Weisberg ably edited the text.

At the University of Maryland, my colleagues Jon Franklin, Michael Gurevitch, Ray Hiebert, and John Martin helped shape my original proposal; and Steve Barkin, Maurine Beasley, Alex Greenfeld, Kathy McAdams, and Michael Smith read early drafts and unselfishly offered numerous suggestions.

Friends including Shirley Biagi at California State University at Sacramento, Duncan McDonald at the University of Oregon, Raleigh Mann at the University of North Carolina, Steve Weinberg of Investigative Reporters & Editors, and Roy Peter Clark and Don Fry of the Poynter Institute gave encouragement at important moments.

Many other friends and colleagues played roles, and my students contributed in more ways than they know. My family showed particular patience and love.

I appreciate it all.

One final word should be said about the genesis of many ideas here. Although I have tried to attribute material as scrupulously as possible, it seems impossible to trace many of my views back to original sources. Although I readily take responsibility for all the material I present, I cannot honestly take credit for it.

If I have slighted any sources or seemed to usurp any ideas that others uttered long before me, then I apologize. An editor becomes a different person every day, absorbing lessons and insights from everywhere. I owe especial debts to those who have written about editing before me, particularly in the American Society of Newspaper Editors *Bulletin*, in my view the most helpful magazine being published on editing.

In my evolution as reporter, editor, and teacher, I have been profoundly influenced by innumerable co-workers and colleagues; by practically every editor I ever observed; by my teachers and my students; by books, magazines, newspapers, and lectures; and by presentations at seminars, conventions, and gatherings of all sorts.

Their ideas filled my head, and made me want to pass them on. It is in that spirit, and with thanks to all, that I present this book.

Carl Sessions Stepp

The Changing World of Editing

Of all jobs in journalism, the editor's is perhaps the most misunderstood. In fact, even though *editing* is a central, everyday term in journalism, it is, like *news,* a concept that frustrates easy definition.

Typically, we think of editing as copyreading. We imagine owlish grammarians and wordsmiths poring over articles, sweating out headlines, and penciling in layouts. But the term *editor* also applies in many other ways: to city editors, feature editors, photo editors, managing editors, editorial page editors, and news editors, all with distinct duties. To designers and art directors, who may never touch a reporter's copy. To broadcast editors, who process tape and film. To magazines editors, to whom the term means everything from manager to contributor to reporter.

Editors certainly edit copy. At least many of them do. They also are teachers, counselors, negotiators, schedulers, taskmasters, disciplinarians, ethicists, motivators, ombudsmen, and referees. They are managers and judges, facing the daily idiosyncrasies of human relations and newsgathering . . . and the inflammatory tasks of deciding where new furniture goes in the newsroom and who has to work on Christmas Eve.

Humorist Dave Barry once reflected that "in most newspapers everybody covered by the dental plan is editor of something. You meet people with impressive-sounding titles like Associate Lifestyles Editor, and it turns out their primary responsibility is deciding how many stars to give the Late Movie" (p. 3).[1]

What an editor really does is make decisions (if only about the movies),

---

[1]Barry, D. (1985, March/April). Defining the typical editor: "How Come So Many of Them Tend to Be Geeks?" *ASNE Bulletin,* p. 3.

handle problems, and set rules. More than anything else, editing is newsroom decision making under pressure.

A good newsroom decision maker needs the following three qualities:

First, a knowledge of the substance of issues being decided, such as what makes news or a strong lead or an inviting headline. A good editor should be a good journalist.

Second, the ability to make decisions in an editing environment. A good editor should be a good manager.

Third, the capacity to see that decisions get carried out. A good editor should be a good leader.

Although most people who become professional journalists, whether reporters, editors, or photographers, can be assumed knowledgeable about the substance of newspapering, rarer are those with the last two qualities: the abilities to make editing decisions and to follow them up efficiently.

To make a decision as an editor means acting under pressure, weighing competing priorities, considering others' opinions, understanding a newspaper's policies, respecting the role of precedent, predicting the consequences for the paper and its audience, and gauging risks and benefits. Not every good journalist is a good decision maker under those conditions. Many reporters, for instance, excel at making spot decisions that govern their own work but don't feel comfortable operating in the group setting that faces editors. Others react well instinctively but cannot articulate their reasoning or formulate it in ways that others can follow.

Finally, to see that decisions take hold, an editor must work indirectly, building consensus where possible, motivating others to carry out policies, and following up tactfully but firmly. Again, many perfectly good journalists don't possess such finesse and become frustrated and ineffective when called on to work with and through others rather than simply forging ahead themselves. As, in effect, team leaders, editors succeed only to the extent that they can recognize what motivates each member of the group and then tailor their methods to get the most out of everyone involved.

In this book, we begin by encouraging a modified and modernized view of editing. Instead of pigeonholing editors based on particular duties some may have, it seems wiser to foster the idea that editors form a professional class of journalists whose responsibilities at any one time may be as narrow as writing cutlines or as broad as running a newsroom. In the material that follows, we consider editors as newsroom professionals prepared for decision-making authority over content, graphics, assignments, and personnel. In short, editors are quality controllers.

But quality control is not the role for which editors historically have been prepared. Most frequently, they have been drilled in the mechanical skills of language and style, with an assumption they will absorb the other requisites on their way up the ladder.

Instead of being trained broadly for the range and variety of duties they may encounter, students and novice editors too often are simply instructed in basic copyediting and elementary layout. Incoming professional editors typically are slotted into a first editing job and are forever after left alone to navigate the remaining white waters of the newsroom.

This book is designed to help journalists to better understand the fuller dimensions of editing, with particular attention to assignment editors, those who deal regularly with reporters and photographers. Gary Blonston, national correspondent and writing coach of the *San Jose Mercury News,* summarized the issue this way:

> When reporters and copyeditors become assigning editors, the training they typically receive can be summarized in the following phrase: "Sit over there."
>
> And so they do, spending subsequent months and sometimes years operating mostly by faith, hope, fear and osmosis, a flimsy arsenal for survival in a job that comes with inadequate time, staff and clout; a daily assault from above, below and beside; and the implicit assumption that quality journalism nonetheless should emerge. (p. 19)[2]

In many respects, editors resemble baseball umpires: We notice them only when they blow a big call. On most papers, it is a daily routine to hear reporters growling that "some editor" has fouled up their copy or that the managing editor has sold out to the composing room's demand for earlier deadlines. But how often do reporters offer testimonials to the editor who noticed a careless libel, or inserted a magical phrase that brought sizzle to a lead, or suggested one last interview that yielded the perfect closer quote? Or laud the managing editor for squeezing more columns of space from the ad staff, or the photo editor for battling to get a picture run one column larger and on page 1?

Partly that is because editors, like umpires, are not in the game for the glory. But it is also partly because good editing comes hard, and too much of today's editing is so hurried, careless, and cloddish that, even when it succeeds, everyone ends up too frazzled to notice.

In a journalistic variation of the Peter Principle, newsrooms have a way of moving people into editing jobs because they were good reporters. Yet, as anyone who has done both jobs can testify, the requirements are not the same. Good reporters tend to be fast-moving, aggressive extroverts whose ego gratification comes from the thrill of the chase and the rush of seeing the next

---

[2]Blonston, G. (1988, July/August). Seminars help line editors focus on what it takes to get reporters to write better. *ASNE Bulletin,* p. 19.

day's byline. Good editors, their aggression tempered with patience, are more often introverts, accepting their anonymity and drawing satisfaction from their roles in coordinating an overall team effort.

As a result of a tradition of simply shifting good reporters into editing slots, however, too many editors are forced to learn on the job, relying on hunch and guesswork, rather than proper preparation, to make the split-second judgments required day after day. This tends to produce excellent drill sergeants, but not necessarily the best long-term managers.

Is it any wonder that so much tension separates editors and reporters, or that journalists have the reputation of being hopeless managers? Or that newspapers report that good editors are getting harder and harder to find, and harder and harder to keep?

Few more important long-range problems confront journalism today than the challenge of recruiting, training and nurturing good editors. Unhappily, in too many cases the selection and training of editors takes place through an outdated and inadequate system that no longer produces the quality and quantity of talent needed to handle the complexities of contemporary newsrooms. Too few people want to be career editors, and even fewer people win recognition as good editors. Insufficient attention goes into finding and grooming editors. And inadequate effort is spent on encouraging those editors who do persevere.

Although newsroom training has increased in recent years, too many journalists remain wedded to the outdated notion that defines editing in technical terms without recognizing that the central duties of most line editors today involve administration and judgment.

"So many editors go into it thinking the job really involves making sure the sentences parse and the organization is all right," Flora Rathburn, an editor at the *Pittsburgh Press,* has said. "They're overwhelmed that so much of their time is taken up dealing with human beings and all the problems they have. They're not trained for that. They're taught to write."[3]

My own memories as an editor do not dwell on great leads I helped sharpen or days when my news judgment seemed especially keen or times when I wrote a 1-42-3 headline that fit the first time.

Instead, I remember things like:

- Facing a mother who came to my office pleading that we leave out an investigative story that would, she was convinced, cause her son to kill himself.
- Confronting an agitated reporter who, after working feverishly overnight on a story, had produced only a computer screen full of gibberish.
- Negotiating by telephone with a man who claimed to be an underworld

---

[3]Flora Rathburn, personal communication, August 17, 1987.

figure and wanted $5,000 to provide me with pictures of a prominent local official taking payoffs—if I would join in a cloak-and-dagger scheme involving notes taped to park benches and pay phones at the local library.

I remember, perhaps most vividly, the everyday stresses and strains of supervising people, competing for tight news space, defending stories in news meetings, trying to motivate recalcitrant reporters and rein in overzealous ones, and attacking the scores of daily dilemmas in publishing a newspaper.

And I remember the thrill of the job, tough as it was; the excitement and gratification of being a central participant in moving the paper into print. For all its strains, editing is a powerful and rewarding way of life.

Viewing editing this broadly is not intended in any way to disparage language and grammar skills or to belittle the role of good copyeditors. They are vital, and all too scarce. The point is this: Most editors, including copyeditors, have jobs dominated by the need for intelligent decision making and human relations, but those qualities are not what come to mind in teaching, training, and choosing editors.

At the University of Maryland, journalism students can enroll in a class especially designed for those who hold editing jobs, either on student or off-campus publications. Each week, they bring to class a short report on editing problems encountered on the job. As you can see from the Sidebar at the end of this chapter, the students report on all sorts of issues: editing technique ("When does an editor decide to change the tone of a story?"), logistics ("The entire printing–typesetting system failed at 12:30 a.m."), and design ("The problem this week involved not having enough good quality photographs for the paper before deadline"). But, year in and year out, the dominant category involves problem solving in human relations—how to deal with sources, readers, reporters, publishers, advertisers, and an assortment of other cranks, creeps, and cry babies.

Consider problems such as:

- What you tell a reporter who has gotten a death threat for writing that a local boxer was "a career loser."
- How you edit the weekly column from the local Baptist preacher.
- How you advise a reporter who feels she is being sexually harassed by a local official's dinner invitations and suggestive remarks.
- What you tell an advertiser who pushes to "sponsor" a section of community news.
- How you react when a reporter refuses to interview the relatives of a suicide victim.

These are real-life issues the students have grappled with outside class, some-times to the point of despair. "We spend so much time settling little squabbles between ourselves and among others," one student editor wrote ruefully.

Issues such as these have long vexed journalists. But they have taken on new and ominous dimensions as the newsroom environment has changed in recent years. Editing today is hard and becoming harder, as journalism, society, and individuals evolve.

Editors, would-be editors, and managers can identify several conditions that underlie the dearth of good editing and good editing candidates.

THE CHRONIC SHORTAGE OF EDITORS

Ask any journalism school placement officer: Editors (especially those with design skills) are hot property. Dozens of applications from prospective writers flood newsrooms for every one that trickles in from an editor hopeful.

The shortage starts at the copydesk and spreads throughout the newsroom. In 1986, the American Society of Newspaper Editors (ASNE) surveyed 630 copyeditors around the nation. One key conclusion, said Linda Grist Cunning-ham, chairman of the ASNE's human resources committee, was:

> There is a growing concern among editors that we are rapidly reaching a crisis in finding good copyeditors. The shortage appears to be particularly acute at small and mid-sized dailies, but even larger dailies will be affected if we do not encourage journalists to pursue copyediting as a career. (p. 18)[4]

In a July 1986 article entitled "WANTED: Copy Editors," the *Washington Journalism Review* explored the same issue. It found that newspapers are recruiting part-time copyeditors, luring retirees back to the desk, and offering higher starting salaries to copyeditors than to reporters.[5] A survey cited in the spring 1987 issue of *Journalism Educator* found that copyeditors were starting at $30 a week more than reporters at some large dailies.[6] In short, as Gannett editor Joseph M. Ungaro once said, "The copyeditor is the single most difficult newsroom position to fill" (p. 26).[7]

The problem is not limited to copydesks. "It is very hard to find good line editors—assigning editors who are the first-read editors for reporters," according to Jonathan Krim, metro editor for the *San Jose Mercury News*. "It's hard to find someone who has had reporting experience, is a good writer, can

---

[4]Stein, M. L. (1987, May 30). Rodney Dangerfields of journalism. *Editor & Publisher*, p. 18.
[5]Hill, D. (1986, July). WANTED: Copy editors. *Washington Journalism Review*, p. 8.
[6]Copyeditor advantage grows. (1987, Spring). *Journalism Educator*, p. 19.
[7]Clarke, J. J. (1981, May/June). WANTED: More training programs for copyeditors. *ASNE Bulletin*, p. 26.

see the big picture, and is a good teacher. I have had a devil of a time finding assistant city editor candidates who have that combination of everything."[8]

Indeed, it is a rare youngster who grows up dreaming of life "on the desk." More commonly, it is a youthful yearning to write, to report, to see their names in print, that drives young people toward journalism. It is graceful writing talent, not quality-control skill, that induces teachers to point students toward a journalism degree.

"Most of us are not trained to be executives. We are reporters," A. M. Rosenthal, former executive editor of the *New York Times,* told fellow journalists. "That is how we start out—or, at least, how I did. One day I looked around and I was metropolitan editor. I had never been in charge of anything except a part-time secretary in Japan and all of a sudden I was in charge of hundreds and hundreds of people" (p. 34).[9]

LIFESTYLES OF THE NONRICH AND THE NONFAMOUS

In the lore of the news business, reporters stand as the glamour figures, extroverted energy burners with strong egos lubricated by the sight of their names regularly on page 1. Editors, by contrast, tend to be introverts, carrying out off-stage duties outside the spotlight and without the gratification that accompanies public credit.

Once I asked an editing seminar who could name the two *Washington Post* reporters who won fame by exposing the Watergate scandal. Every hand in the room went up. Then I asked: "Who was their immediate editor?" Pause. A hand went up tentatively; the guess was wrong. Then silence. No one remembered Barry Sussman, Watergate editor.

Yet his role was central. Here's how Woodward and Bernstein themselves describe it in *All The President's Men:*

> Sussman had the ability to seize facts and lock them in his memory, where they remained poised for instant recall. More than any other editor at the *Post,* or Bernstein and Woodward, Sussman became a walking compendium of Watergate knowledge, a reference source to be summoned when even the library failed. On deadline, he would pump these facts into a story in a constant infusion . . . Watergate was a puzzle and he was a collector of the pieces. (p. 51)[10]

It is no wonder, perhaps, that the editor's life is hardly the dream of tender journalists-to-be. While the reporter is at Yankee Stadium interviewing the star

---

[8]Jonathan Krim, personal communication, August 24, 1987.

[9]Keep it moving and fight like hell. (1987, May/June). *ASNE Bulletin,* p. 34.

[10]Bernstein C., & Woodward, B. (1974). *All the president's men.* New York: Simon & Schuster.

shortstop, the editor is bent over the terminal piecing together the agate box score. While the writer is hobnobbing with presidents and rock stars, the editor is rounding up mug shots for the obit page. While the reporter is flying off to foreign wars or dashing to a bus–train fatality, the editor is dozing through the monthly deadline lecture in the publisher's office.

Few would doubt that reporting rather than editing is, to most tastes, the more exciting introduction to the news business.

In fact, the lifestyle of the editor is difficult, and getting more so year by year. Editors are potent figures with decisive influence over every aspect of a paper. But their lives can involve high stress, low recognition, long hours, and tough working conditions, especially in break-in jobs like the copydesk or weekend assigning desks.

For one example, take working conditions: During its 1986 survey, the American Society of Newspaper Editors asked copyeditors about their working hours. To the question, "Do you work the night shift?", 67% replied yes and 31% no. To the question, "Do you prefer the night shift?", the responses flipflopped: 37% answered yes and 59% no.[11] At one morning newspaper where I worked, the building escalators were turned off around 7 p.m., even though the night staff, including a full shift of editors, worked till well past midnight. It was as if normal needs and courtesies did not apply to such a strange breed.

A particular change recruiters must address is the insistence of the new generation of workers on maximizing leisure time and reducing work-related interference with personal life. For single workers, working the weekend and wee hours common in editing offers little hope of a stimulating social life. For young parents, the odd and inflexible hours make raising a family, finding child care, and reading bedtime stories next to impossible. For journalistic graybeards, Saturday night and holiday duties seem an indignity when their peers in, say, the law or medicine are routinely lolling on sailboats and enjoying the material fruits of success.

Beyond status questions, it has become quite common, in today's health-conscious environment, to hear journalists lament the risk of burnout and stress—two all-too-real dangers of the business.

In one survey by the Associated Press Managing Editors, 39% of the editors reported experiencing a health problem that they thought resulted from job-related stress.[12] Members of the Philadelphia chapter of the Society of Professional Journalists heard psychologist Ray Harrison list 12 stress-inducing factors associated with journalism:

---

[11]Cunningham, L. G. (1987, May 6). It is time to bring the newsroom's stepchildren into the family circle. *ASNE Bulletin,* p. 4.

[12]Gloede, B. (1983, November, 12). Stress has a significant presence in newsrooms. *Editor & Publisher,* p. 12.

- long and unusual hours,
- too many tasks to perform in too little time,
- too many decisions to make,
- mistakes becoming known both within and outside the organization,
- job insecurity,
- few opportunities for advancement,
- relentless competition,
- poor and sometimes dangerous working conditions,
- unpredictability marked by periods of both intense boredom and demanding action,
- frequent transfers,
- terrible diets,
- and subjective evaluations.[13]

In 1985, the Rhode Island Supreme Court even agreed that the death of a journalist had been spurred by the odd hours and deadline pressures of his job. *Pawtucket Evening Times* sports editor Edward F. "Ted" Mulcahey had died of a cerebral hemorrhage after covering a pro football game.[14]

Although some stress is inescapable given the hard-and-fast deadlines associated with daily newspaper production, its effects may be aggravated by poor management and by a journalistic lifestyle that shrugs off the potential dangers. "It is more than probable," wrote broadcaster Linda Ellerbee in her book *And So It Goes*, "that too much of this stress is caused by a system of management that chooses not to recognize that an employee is more than the carcass he or she hauls to work" (p. 130).[15] Authors Welch, Medeiros, and Tate, in their book *Beyond Burnout*, pointed out that journalists, like all other workers, work hard and crave appreciation, yet "are in a profession in which such appreciation is most difficult to come by. Their employers seem to provide feedback to them only if the job they do is not acceptable" (p. 239).[16]

It should go without saying here that editors stand on both sides of this equation. As employees, they confront the stress and must work in difficult newsroom environments. But, as *managers*, they bear much responsibility for what the newsroom climate has become. They are, all too often, stress carriers, inflicting damage on others as well as themselves.

---

[13]Chapter notes, Philadelphia. (1987, January). *Quill*, p. 38.

[14]Court concurs: Stress contributed to sports editor's death. (1985, April 6). *Editor & Publisher*, p. 11.

[15]Ellerbee, L. (1987). *And so it goes*. New York: Berkley Books.

[16]Welch, D., Medeiros, D., & Tate, G. (1982). *Beyond burnout*. Englewood Cliffs, NJ: Prentice-Hall.

Whereas in some occupations high salaries may help offset high stress, that hardly applies in newspapering. A survey quoted by the American Society of Newspaper Editors in 1986 showed that about half the editors responding earned under $35,000 a year.[17] The 1987 Employee Pay Scale Survey by Suburban Newspapers of America found that editors averaged $30,280.[18]

David H. Weaver and G. Cleveland Wilhoit, in *The American Journalist*, reported that the median salary for journalists in 1981 was $19,000, a figure that represented $7,000 less in purchasing power than a decade earlier. Weaver and Wilhoit found that pay and fringe benefits were reasons cited most often by those leaving the field.[19]

Although some of these issues hit the supply of editors harder than the reporting pool, there is sobering evidence that the strains of journalism are spread all around. For example, a study at the University of Central Florida found that journalists leaving the business became happier and found better jobs. Of former newspeople interviewed, 53% had expected to make journalism a lifetime career but 75% left within 12 years. Low salaries and bad working conditions were the most cited reasons for leaving. Better working conditions were named most often as advantages of the new job. Forty-five percent mentioned better hours. Seventy-five percent felt the new job was better for them and their families. The authors summarized their study as follows:

> There indeed is life after journalism, and it would certainly appear to be a much richer and fuller life. . . . For the most part, respondents portrayed journalism as a frustrating profession, characterized by low pay, poor management and bad hours. In several cases, respondents said they were left jaded and disillusioned.
>
> Most of these respondents found new jobs with more money, more freedom, better working conditions and real job security. (p. 22)[20]

Certainly, the preceding catalogue of issues is sobering, but it would be unfortunate to let it throw the overall picture out of whack. Editing is a tough business, with its share of tribulations. But, as we see in the following, it also can be enormously satisfying and enriching. The challenge for both potential editors and their employers is to recognize the growing demands of the job, adjust appropriately, and enter the field fortified to overcome them.

---

[17]Youngs, Walker survey samples 171 editors' salaries. (1986, January). *ASNE Bulletin*, p. 29.

[18]SNA salary survey shows highest pay goes to publishers. (1988, February 13). *Editor & Publisher*, p. 34.

[19]Weaver, D. H., & Wilhoit, G. C. (1986). *The American journalist* (pp. 102–103). Bloomington: Indiana University Press.

[20]Fedler, F., Buhr, T., & Taylor, D. (1988, Winter). Journalists who leave the news media seem happier, find better jobs. *Newspaper Research Journal*, pp. 15–23.

THE CHANGING NATURE OF JOURNALISM

As editors advance along the newsroom ladder and as journalism becomes less and less separable from "Big Business," editors find their duties and obligations growing increasingly complex. Their backgrounds and training typically prepare them largely for the technical aspects of processing copy. But as they march from the copydesk to the city desk or news desk, and then penetrate even deeper into management territory, the time spent editing copy diminishes. Consuming tasks become managing people, helping run a business, and making and enforcing policy.

These duties get trickier all the time, as a brief examination of several areas may illustrate.

Journalism As Business. Veteran editor Robert H. Giles described today's challenge in this way:

> Fifteen years ago, editors were editors. Today they are editor-managers. They direct the editing of the newspaper with one hand and, with the other, they are deeply involved in business management.
>
> This editor is expected to carry on in the best traditions of journalistic excellence, but also is expected to share the responsibility for the newspaper as a "profit center." Many editors discovered that this dual obligation created unfamiliar stresses, stresses born of a conflict between the need to be good and the need to be lean. (p. 12)[21]

Concentration is a condition to which we have become accustomed. Ben Bagdikian, in *The Media Monopoly,* has pointed out that 50 corporations control "most major American media—newspapers, magazines, radio, television, books, and movies" and that those 50 firms are partners in such fields as agribusiness, timber, banking, insurance, weapons production, religious instruction, utilities, pipelines, chemicals and microprocessing.[22] The impact of business cutbacks on network television news gained wide publicity during the mid-1980s, but was hardly the only place where cost cutting was supplanting laissez faire as a newsroom management philosophy.

Consider a memo that Time Inc. President Richard Munro sent to all 20,000 employees in 1985. As reported in the *Washington Post,* it contained a message that was simple: Trim the fat. Munro told the Post that his goal was, as the paper put it, "to alter Time's corporate culture by changing the way employees think about spending money" (p. F1).[23]

---

[21]Gloede, B. (1983, November 12). Stress has a significant presence in newsrooms. *Editor & Publisher,* p. 12.

[22]Bagdikian, B. H. (1983). *The media monopoly* (pp. 4–5). Boston: Beacon Press.

[23]Vise, D. A. (1985, November 3). Time Inc. tightens its belt. *The Washington Post,* p. F1.

Once, editors took pride in routinely banning the publisher from the newsroom. No more. Today, the business manager may be a fixture in the editor's office. The editor may also be a corporate vice president whose yearly bonus hinges on advertising revenue increases. Line editors may operate under "management by objective" agreements linking pay and benefits to circulation gain.

The clear effect of this increasing business orientation, of course, is to add even more worrisome areas to editors' portfolios and to raise potential conflicts between journalists' news instincts and their perceived obligation to larger corporate interests.

Richard Duncan of *Time,* recalling former days of editor autonomy, noted how today's corporate culture discouraged such single-handed newsroom control:

> I dare say it's possible that a corporate officer who decides "Damn the torpedoes, let's go in harm's way on this one," could be called to account for shirking his responsibility to the shareholders. I don't think many of the new outside managers of media corporations are expecting their officers to get in there and exercise the First Amendment. (p. 9)[24]

Michael Fancher, executive editor of the *Seattle Times,* noted his deep involvement in three of what he called "marketplace issues" for his paper: deciding where to build a new production plant, expanding zoned editions into the suburbs, and reacting to a competitor's switch from evening to morning delivery. Fancher wrote: "I suppose some editors might read that and groan. If so, the groan is saying, 'I don't want to change.' Sorry, that's not an option. Step aside, please. The future would like to pass" (p. 80).[25]

The Law. It is axiomatic that American society has become an arena for runaway litigation. And editors find themselves on the receiving end of subordinates, readers, advertisers, sources, lawmakers, office seekers, and others who do not hesitate to sue or threaten suit. In an article entitled "Threat of Litigation Casts a Growing Shadow Over Newsrooms," lawyers Judith R. Epstein and John E. Carne wrote in the *ASNE Bulletin:*

> In this era of megaverdicts, one lawsuit can threaten the very existence of a newspaper. . . . Legal planning can no longer begin—if it ever could—when the lawsuit is filed. Whether hiring a reporter, assigning a story, or writing a headline, editors make decisions that affect a variety of legal rights and liabilities. (p. 3)[26]

---

[24]*The cost of libel: A conference report.* (1986). Gannett Center for Media Studies, New York.

[25]Fancher, M. (1987, Spring). The metamorphosis of the newspaper editor. *Gannett Center Journal,* p. 80.

[26]Epstein, J. R., & Carne, J. E. (1985, September). Threat of litigation casts a growing shadow. *ASNE Bulletin,* p. 3.

For many editors, today's concern is not limited to the possibility of *losing* a lawsuit. Many companies, worried about the enormous expenses of merely having to fight a victorious suit, cringe at even the *threat* of a suit. As a consequence, some editors feel pressure to tone down copy to avoid lawsuits even if the paper feels confident that the copy is strong enough to withstand any potential suit.

Editors also face nonstop legal questions short of lawsuits in areas such as equity, labor relations, and contempt of court. The act of firing an employee— once routinely done in whimsical frenzy by one all-powerful boss—now may require extended committee meetings involving several supervisors, the personnel manager, the company psychologist, and a lawyer. Few would contend that the old system was better. After all, newspapers should operate legally and fairly. But today's renewed concern for law and formalities does add pressure on the editor. We examine these issues further in chapter 9.

Ethics and Credibility.   Few topics earn more newsroom discussion these days than ethics and journalists' relationship to the public. More than ever before, reporters and editors find their actions publicized, second guessed, and double checked. A round of surveys during the mid-1980s provided sobering reading. For example, according to one national study commissioned by the American Society of Newspaper Editors, three people out of four had qualms about press credibility and one in five felt deeply distrustful; 42% thought that "sometimes there's too much freedom of the press"; public confidence in the press ranked below that of the Supreme Court, education, banks, the executive branch, organized religion, and Congress.[27]

This leads, naturally, to increased concern about editorial tactics (a development editors may read as increased pressure to do the job neatly and without causing antagonism), not to mention a stepped-up desire to win friends among the readership. As stated in a *Washington Journalism Review* article, "To hear newspapers' top brass talk, it's as important for the current crop of editors and reporters to graduate from charm school as from J-school" (p. 30).[28]

On this issue, as on many, editors stand in a crossfire. The traditional watchdog role of the press requires that newspapers carry out a certain amount of unpleasant snooping and mud collecting. Heeding this mission—and it is a vital one historically—can cause newspapers to rile up their audiences. It can ensure that, at pretty much any given time, some significant part of the readership will be angry. Good editors (and good publishers, too) understand this dynamic and its long-run importance to both journalism and the country. More

---

[27]*Newspaper credibility: Building reader trust.* (1985, April). American Society of Newspaper Editors, Reston, VA, pp. 13, 25, 51.

[28]Franklin, E. (1986, December). Minding your manners. *Washington Journalism Review,* p. 30.

and more, however, the competition in the marketplace builds pressure on the newsrooms to keep consumers satisfied, to appease the audience not antagonize it, and to cooperate in efforts to make newspapers, to use an inelegant modern term, more *reader friendly*. Somewhere in the middle, drawing the lines and fighting off headaches, are the editors.

Yet they need not despair. Although much is changing, newspapers have survived uneasy times before. Educator Everette E. Dennis of the Gannett Center for Media Studies, surveying the current changes, offered some context that can, if not relieve editors of today's burdens, at least offer some solace that good journalists can adapt. Dennis noted that newspapers have responded vigorously to changing conditions, by commissioning market research to better understand their audiences, repackaging content and offering special sections, encouraging new writing styles and reporting techniques, and restructuring operations. Dennis concluded:

> Traditional journalists decried all this, but it is very much a reality today, and not, I think, in the least harmful to freedom of expression. We have little social memory for similar upheavals in the past, including the one that brought us the mass press in the 1880s and 1890s. Then the press became more egalitarian and less elitist as it attempted to lure a new mass audience, and journalists and other critics decried that as a debasing of information. Today just the opposite is occurring, and critics are making similar charges. (p. 4)[29]

Eugene Patterson of the *St. Petersburg Times,* a veteran editor (and board chairman and chief executive officer), also has underlined the importance of the longer view. Patterson sided against what he called "taking a financial approach to a creative enterprise, investing for short-term earnings instead of betting on long-term quality." Patterson offered two supportive aphorisms for editors struggling with today's complexities. First, he quoted Myron Tribus of the Massachusetts Institute of Technology as reminding journalists, "Quality is never your problem. It is the solution to your problem." Second, Patterson offered his own judgment that "quality in newspapers costs less than the long-term expense of ignoring it" (p. 6).[30]

CONCLUSION

For editors, the aggregate impact of all this is clear: A pattern of changing personal, professional, and social conditions has made the editor's life—never easy—more complex than ever. And it has exposed the weaknesses of a system of training editors that is far less than satisfactory in producing the well-rounded talent needed for troubling professional times.

---

[29]Dennis, E. E. (1986, July). A coming of age: Sea changes for the mass media. Gannett Center for Media Studies, New York.

[30]Make an investment for quality. (1987, July 18). *Editor & Publisher,* p. 6.

Lest this chapter seem unduly discouraging, it should be noted that editing remains a desirable, fulfilling, prestigious, and invigorating experience. Rather than being overwhelmed by the job's problems, editors and potential editors need to face them directly and unswervingly. There is a satisfaction, as well as a great deal of fun, in solving them. As the shortage of good editors and good editing worsens, and as the demands intensify, it is important to examine what individual journalists and their organizations can do in response.

SIDEBAR 1
EXPERIENCES IN EDITING

Surprises often await newcomers to editing, who may expect workdays consumed by arcane debate over colon usage or elaborate consultations with reporters on earth-rattling assignments. Instead, editors more likely spend their days absorbed by a variety of duties, many only indirectly connected with copy flow itself.

Over several years of asking student editors to record their experiences each week, I have detected a clear pattern. Issues involving *people* dominate issues involving *copy*. Relations with reporters, colleagues, sources, subjects, and readers preoccupy and often exasperate editors, sometimes to the detriment of their ability to function productively.

The following are excerpts from reports submmitted by student editors, based on their work editing for campus and professional publications:

Reporters and Writers

This week, one of our reporters received a death threat on the telephone because of a story he wrote. The story concerned a boxer who the writer sarcastically said had a "poor taste in footwear" and was a "career loser." The boxer was upset about the article and threatened to rip the writer apart if he ever saw him again. He also said that several other boxers were looking for him. . . . The writer is now afraid to go back . . .

*   *   *

What do you do when you edit a story, can't get in touch with the reporter, do what you consider your best, and then, after the story is printed, the reporter comes back to you and is not at all pleased? . . . I told him as gently as possible that there were too many questions to run as it was . . . I think I finally got him to understand that if he had been available, he would have been able to come in and make the changes himself.

(Continued)

Sidebar 1 (*Continued*)   *   *   *

I don't always feel qualified to tamper with someone else's work, and I especially hate to read stories that need to be completely rewritten. Part of the problem is my shyness; I am not comfortable talking to people about their work, let alone criticizing it. These stories are like a reporter's baby— you don't say just anything about them.

                    *   *   *

When editing a letter to the editor, and the argument within that letter sounds unfocused, and the rambling of a mad man, how far should an editor go to make the letter tight and a cohesive argument? Assume there are no other letters to the editor to use, and the editorial page editor wants to use it.

                    *   *   *

The problem encountered this week involved editing an article written by a Baptist minister. The article was written to go in the religion section of the paper, but it was too long. When I started to edit it for both style and length, I realized that the article was not written in usual inverted pyramid style, but it was written as a regular sermon. . . . The end of the article said, "Remember this is God's word." Can you imagine having the responsibility to edit "God's word"!

Sources and Subjects

A reporter has been on a first-name basis with this official for quite some time and has flirted with him somewhat. I had ignored it partly because she was his friend before becoming a steady reporter. Lately, though, their conversations and actions in public began to bother me somewhat. . . .

The reporter was somewhat naive, especially when it came to this source and his motives. . . . The official first told her he would give her the information on a Friday afternoon. Then the official called her back and told her he would have the information Friday night—after business hours. She told him she was going away for the weekend. They then agreed to meet Monday. On Monday the official came up with another excuse. . . . My advice to her was to start calling the official by his full name in the hopes that he would get the hint.

(*Continued*)

Sidebar 1 (*Continued*)   *   *   *

An article published a little over a month ago contained unemployment statistics for the county and also included interviews with people who had been unemployed. The story had been written four months ago and was held for a later date. . . . Thus, we got a phone call from a man who was upset because by the time the article came out he already had gotten a new job. His boss had seen the article and suspected that the man may be pretending to be unemployed to obtain more money from unemployment benefits.

*   *   *

A recurrent problem is a retired lawyer who shows up at the paper about twice a month. It is true that newspapers must also be their own public relations firms when dealing with the public, but this man is nothing more than a true annoyance. . . . Most of what he wants us to print would land the paper in a court of law on libel charges. But more importantly he is a nuisance and no one really has the time or desire to speak with him about nonsense, and it is hard to hide because he will talk to anyone within earshot.

Colleagues

What do you do when you think you are falling in love with (a colleague)? Or at least like? . . . You work closely with your colleagues on newspapers. This is sometimes bound to happen.

*   *   *

One of the copyeditors I work with does not like me. His whole attitude toward me is condescending and he makes me feel as if I'm not a good editor. He's one of the senior editors so I have to deal with him. I try to be nice but it's difficult when it is obvious that he is nice to everyone but me.

*   *   *

The people I work with regularly go out for a few beers after work. Last week I decided to take one of the writers up on his offer, and five of us headed for happy hour. I felt uncomfortable with them, mainly because I don't know any of them that well, but also because they drank so much. . . .
   Three of my fellow employees left suddenly—probably to avoid driving the fourth home. I was stuck with this man, who I barely know, and had no choice but to take his car keys and drive him home. On the way, he

(*Continued*)

Sidebar 1 (*Continued*)

draped himself all over me and practically made me wreck. I'm engaged, and he's married, so I think he just got out of control. I called him a rather nasty name, and left angry.

I have to work with this man every day. . . . When he sees me, he gets embarrassed and walks away.

Readers

A very angry woman called last Saturday, and I answered the phone. She felt the paper was not giving her daughter's basketball team enough coverage. She seemed to take it personally that there were not enough articles about her daughter.

*   *   *

A decision to stop printing the TV guide was made by management because of the tight financial situation of the newspaper. Now people have been calling in large numbers to complain and to cancel their subscriptions. . . . It is quite depressing to the staff that the only reason people subscribe to the paper is because of the TV guide and not because of the news content.

Stresses and Strains

My problem this week is that the managing editor is having a family crisis, leaving me to handle pretty much all the day-to-day kinds of things, as well as longer term planning. . . . It's difficult to have compassion when you're so exhausted that all you want to do is crawl into bed for about 2 weeks.

*   *   *

My biggest problem with the newspaper has been time management. Where does one find the time?

*   *   *

On Monday a female reporter was accosted in the company's parking lot. The parking lot is dimly lit and is usually vacant after 5 p.m. . . . When I mentioned it to her, her visage appeared to be hiding some misgivings about the assault. I know she is attempting to prove she's a hard-nosed reporter who is not going to be stopped by a little old mugging. But is she being realistic? Is she setting herself up for emotional or physical health problems

(*Continued*)

Sidebar 1 (*Continued*)

later? ... What should management do, other than make the parking lot safer at night?

Down to Earth

My biggest problem this week was that our copying machine broke down ...

*　　*　　*

The problem this week involved not having enough good quality photographs for the paper before deadline.

*　　*　　*

What happened Monday night was something I always feared, but never thought would actually occur. The entire printing–typesetting system failed—at 12:30 a.m.—with 75% of pages 1 and 3 empty. We were lucky. Thanks to the work of our brilliant shop manager, the system was back up an hour later. Nevertheless, the incident made me aware of the fact that we have no type of backup system to bail us out in the event of a mechanical or electrical failure.

One Editor's Understanding

This week's editing problem was one that I had never really had to deal with before. It involved helping a reporter who was hesitant to interview friends and family of a campus student who was murdered last weekend.

The reporter is one who is very capable and very adept at dealing with people. In fact, he is just the person I would choose to deal with people in such a touchy situation. Because he always seems so confident and well-mannered, I was surprised when he told me he was uneasy about going to the victim's dormitory.

The situation really touched me ... because I got a knot in my own stomach just thinking about having to do what I was asking him to do.

As it turned out, I ended up going along with the reporter to talk to the victim's hallmates. Although some hallmates did refuse to talk to us, two girls that lived next door did give us some information. ... I think I subconsciously decided to go because I thought he might need some moral support and because I thought the female hallmates might feel more at ease talking with both of us.

The experience was not as unpleasant as I imagined. ... As an editor, I think it made me feel good to be able to help out a reporter with something that was so emotionally draining.

(*Continued*)

Sidebar 1 (*Continued*)

    This editing problem didn't really turn out to be a problem after all, but it did make me think about what sort of relationship an editor should have with reporters.

The Rise of the New Editor

American newspaper editors have an ink-stained heritage, having begun as printers and writers. Colonial newspapers typically were run by maverick pamphleteers blessed with the typographical know how to raise their voices. Over time, their one-person shops gradually yielded to layered news operations, and the editor's role as partisan editorialist gave way to that of professional news disseminator.

Steadily, over the past 200 years, editors drifted away from day-to-day absorption in writing and processing copy. New responsibilities emerged. Although some editors remained at the typewriter, others removed themselves one or more steps, into news gathering and coordination. Eventually, editors came to preside over ever-expanding, complex organizations whose administrative demands left less and less time for any one individual to attend to writing, assigning, and editing the copy. The editor's world broadened to encompass a full range of editorial and executive duties.

Today's editor, to be fully prepared for a career in the business, requires all the skills of these predecessors and more. Writing, editing, coordinating, producing, and managing all belong in the repertoire of the individual we call the *new editor:* a professional journalist prepared for decision-making responsibility in the modern newsroom.

The new editor does not reside only in the prestigious positions atop the masthead. She or he may be a copyeditor, assignment editor, or designer; in features, news, or photos; a longtime writer enticed into a desk stint, or a career desk person dedicated to the editing track. Over time, most editors will fit more than one of these categories. What should distinguish new editors is not the particular job they hold at the moment. Instead, it is their preparation and capacity for understanding and performing the special duties of editing in today's newsroom.

As we discussed in chapter 1, editors belong to a neglected species. That neglect has given editing something of a bad name and produced misunderstanding about the role, duties, and qualifications of the job. Although good editors always have drawn the respect of their subordinates and colleagues, many journalists exposed to mediocre editing carry away a prejudice disparaging to editors. Multiplied over time, these images of ham-fisted, insensitive tyrants create stereotypes that paint editors negatively.

The result is a kind of spiral. Young journalists do not prime themselves for editing careers or receive sufficient guidance in that direction from management. So, those who are selected for editing often move into the job poorly prepared and lacking confidence. They reinforce the stereotypes. The spiral continues. Coupled with the vast changes taking place in journalism, this syndrome has created serious problems, if not a crisis, in producing the quality of editing that modern times demand.

To address these issues, we first briefly examine some stages editors have gone through historically. The evolution of editors from "writers" to "executives" should appear clearly, even if journalism training and education have not yet quite responded to it. In the final part of this chapter, we further define and flesh out the duties and roles of editors.

In reviewing the origins and development of editing, it is worth noting how each successive phase builds on the past, adding duties, broadening the editor's role, and imposing new requirements. Ironically, as editors increasingly come to specialize, the range of knowledge and ability needed for an editing career (assuming that one will hold several different editing positions over time) increases noticeably.

THE EDITOR IN HISTORY

What Colonial American editors such as Ben Franklin required was mastery of typography, access to presses, and, at least at first, licenses from authorities. Thus equipped, they could spread their messages. Franklin signed on as a printer's apprentice at age 12, composed type for his brother James's *New England Courant,* and eventually rose to editing and publishing on his own.

History remembers that he had a flair for editing: He substituted the word "self-evident" in Thomas Jefferson's draft of the Declaration of Independence that originally read, "We hold these truths to be sacred and undeniable" (p. 105).[1]

Franklin also showed an editor's sensibilities. In his *Autobiography,* he

---

[1]Updike, J. (1988, February 22). Many Bens. *The New Yorker,* p. 105.

boasted of having "excluded all libelling and personal abuse" from his publications, and he cautioned "young printers . . . not to pollute their presses and disgrace their profession by such infamous practices" (p. 119)[2] Despite his wide-ranging accomplishments, Franklin never forgot his origins. In proposing his own epitaph, he called himself "Benjamin Franklin, printer."

These early editors were editorialists more than news gatherers, and their work grew overtly partisan as they associated themselves with specific parties and philosophies. Isaiah Thomas, an apprentice printer at age 6, became one of the young nation's leading publishers by championing the patriot cause against Britain. Noah Webster, best known today for his dictionaries, won fame in his own time by editing one of the country's leading Federalist journals.

It was well into the 19th century before a combination of events, including industrialization, urbanization, and the movement toward mass literacy, produced a new kind of newspaper, the mass press. It was supported not by government contracts, monied patrons, or factional underwriting but by the pennies of popular readers and the advertising support that followed them.

With the mass press came a new breed of editors: men like James Gordon Bennett who recognized the commercial value of relatively straightforward news and who moved aggressively to capitalize.

Bennett's penny-a-copy *New York Herald* opened in 1835, offering unparalleled local, national, and foreign news coverage. Among its innovations was aggressive reporting on sports, finance, crime, and society, everyday topics that quickly won the interest of the burgeoning New York mass audience. Unlike many of his predecessors, Bennett chose the role of news gatherer and disseminator over that of opinion writer. This turning point in journalism produced a model that dominated the 19th century.

Later, editors such as Joseph Pulitzer and William Randolph Hearst responded to political and economic upheaval and led the way into the 20th century by synthesizing Bennett's hard-news model with their updated version of the old partisan evangelizing. The resulting extraordinary aggressiveness in both news gathering and editorial crusading begot the era of muckraking and yellow journalism. As the century turned, newspapers, although increasingly big businesses, had top editors who still could personally oversee news coverage and editorial policy making. But the growing complexity of news operations brought departmentalization and specialization, and gave rise to a new kind of professional editor.

Such a man was Carr V. Van Anda, a brilliant mathematician hired in the early 1900s to be managing editor of *The New York Times*. Van Anda was not the paper's top editor or business strategist (Adolph Ochs was). But he ran the news operation, and stories of his stewardship are legend. It was Van Anda who, based on his own mathematical calculations, decided that the supposedly

---

[2]Franklin, B. (1955). *Autobiography*. New York: Washington Square Press.

unsinkable *Titanic* had indeed sunk, and led his paper with the scoop. On another occasion, he noticed an error in a complicated equation that Albert Einstein had used during a lecture. During World War I, he monitored the movement of armies, dispatching his correspondents to cover expected battles with what David Halberstam called "a surprisingly prophetic instinct" (pp. 212–213).[3]

As the 20th century advanced, editors and subeditors grew increasingly specialized. Newsrooms became small empire. Line editors oversaw routine chores of producing the daily news report. Top editors managed. The higher on the ladder editors rose, the more likely they were to be rewarded for production and executive abilities, not simply journalistic flair. Yet most had begun as writers and subordinate editors, and many felt unsteady and insecure as they climbed from rung to rung, progressively distancing themselves from the kind of work they had initially felt drawn toward.

As we discussed in chapter 1, the modern period has accelerated and intensified these trends, as the newsroom empire, powerful but not autonomous, found itself surrounded by increasingly elaborate corporate and marketing structures. Today, the new editor must build on all this ancestry, and overcome the insecurity. An understanding of writing, reporting, coordination, and production remains vital. But added to it is the need to maneuver in the modern newsroom, a place where journalists increasingly share space and power with publishers, accountants, lawyers, and various other associates from the once-segregated "business side."

In this integrated environment, the new editor remains a decision maker about news, copy, and design. Beyond that, he or she is likely to have expanded duties in making decisions about numerous other issues that may lie outside traditional journalistic and editorial purview. These issues may touch such areas as law, ethics, management philosophy, marketing strategy, and business direction.

Editor Michael Fancher summarized today's condition as follows:

> Change or be changed. That is the choice facing newspaper journalists today. And nowhere is the imperative felt more directly than at the top of the newspaper totem pole—the editor's job . . . . The new technologies, financial environments, and newsroom climates with which newspaper staffs must contend, along with meeting publisher or chain owner expectations and maintaining reader interest, are all part of the challenge . . . . The editor who does not direct the change will be directed by it. (p. 69)[4]

---

[3]Halberstam, D. (1979). *The powers that be.* New York: Knopf.

[4]Fancher, M. (1987, Spring). The metamorphosis of the newspaper editor. *Gannett Center Journal*, p. 69.

These changing times also affect editors beyond those at the very top. Today, it is not unusual for a city editor to have a year-end financial bonus tied in part to the newspaper's overall circulation gains, or for a copyeditor to sit on an interdepartmental committee helping map a paper's 5-year plan, or for a photo editor's work to be monitored by personnel specialists trying to promote company-wide teamwork.

The demand for better and broader trained editors extends throughout the newsroom and is felt in every editing job.

An individual launching an editing career can encounter a path of jobs with diverse responsibilities and requirements. Not every editor will follow this path in a hierarchical fashion. Some, such as a talented reporter chosen to be city editor, begin in the middle. Others, such as a high-powered outsider brought in as editor in chief, may start at the top. More typically, however, editors move through several of the following jobs in a rough progression:

Line editing: Copyeditors, headline writers, page designers, and others work directly with copy, usually on deadline. They need language proficiency, precision, speed, and cool heads.

News editing: News editors, wire editors, and other section editors are gatekeepers who decide what stories will appear and how they will be played. They must have strong news judgment and understanding of their audiences along with the efficiency and copyediting skills to process copy.

Assignment editing: So-called department heads, such as city editors or sports editors or features editors and their assistants, spend less time with copy and more time with ideas, reporters and other editors. They, too, must be accomplished technicians able to edit rapidly and accurately. They also need imagination and the nose for news, the ability to make clear assignments and direct reporters' work, a flair for juggling all the hectic elements of a news day, and sophisticated planning and administrative abilities to effectively deploy their limited resources under severe time pressures. In addition, they must understand their special areas (e.g., sports, foreign news, or graphics) and serve as advocates for the material their staffs produce.

Specialized editing: At about this point, some editors find themselves attracted to various specialities, such as editorial writing or photo editing or production coordination, where particular talents or knowledge may be required.

Managing editing: Depending on the size of a newspaper, several editing jobs may be primarily administrative. The managing editor and various assistants, as well as executive editors, metro editors and others in similar posts, stand one step further from constant involvement with copy or daily assignments. Typically, they handle major stories, oversee page-1 and section-front copy and design, and try to allot time for some hands-on editing. But they also must hire, fire, and supervise; handle matters like scheduling; administer budgets; plan long-term coverage; and frequently serve as liaisons with other parts of the paper such as production staffs. On top of their skills as editors of copy, they must be executives and diplomats, counselors and critics, planners and prodders.

Senior editing: These are editors, editors in chief, senior editors, associate editors, and so on. By whatever title, editors at the peak of all but the smallest newspapers have vast corporate and administrative duties that may, on some days, keep them completely out of the news flow. Whatever their journalistic talents, they must be effective planners, organizers, and overseers on a strategic level.

To cope with the jobs just listed, the new editor needs preparation for a variety of roles, many of them fairly far removed from basic writing and copyediting.

In the following sections, we examine one by one the roles of the new editor. Although not all roles apply to each job, most new editors can expect to fulfill each of the following roles at some time during a career.

THE EDITOR AS BUSINESSPERSON

This is not the most important role, or even the newest one. Early editors, as we have seen, were printers running their own small enterprises. But, as the last chapter explained, concentration and competition have raised the stakes of the business aspects of editing.

Editor David Burgin put it this way:

I don't think editors are as good or as powerful as they were 10 or 15 years ago. The new power in the industry is the marketing director. I want to see more swashbuckling editors. . . . But those days are dead. Now it's target marketing and target marketing and more marketing. (p. 24)[5]

Critic Doug Underwood stated the position even more bluntly:

Welcome to the world of the modern, corporate editor, a person who, as likely as not, is going to be found in an office away from the newsroom bustle, immersed in marketing surveys, organizational charts, budget plans, and memos on management training.

---

[5]Underwood, D. (1988, March/April). When MBAs rule the newsroom. *Columbia Journalism Review,* p. 24.

It's not surprising that, as corporations have extended their hold on U.S. newspapers, the editors of those papers have begun to behave more and more like the managers of any other corporate entity (p. 23).[6]

Editors today can scorn the "business side" only at their peril. They hide from reality if they regard the newsroom as a barricaded bunker protected from the ricocheting flak of market competition. "While from a reporter's perspective, news may remain a public service, increasingly its by-product is profit," Charles Fountain wrote in the *Columbia Journalism Review* (p. 46).[7] The same goes, of course, for the editor's point of view.

A demonstration of this role came when one of the nation's leading editors, Eugene Roberts of the *Philadelphia Inquirer*, was named president of his newspaper and given authority over its circulation operation (p. 76).[8]

It may well behoove newspaper editors to observe changes now fully under way in broadcast news. Broadcast is a younger industry. Its news divisions have traditionally enjoyed somewhat less sacrosanct status than those in the print media, and ratings and profitability have had more direct impact there. Even so, the conditions now facing broadcast, including closing-in competitors, nonjournalistic ownership, and financial belt-tightening, parallel in many ways those affecting print. The resulting pressures on broadcast journalists may signal what could be in store for print.

Critic Ron Dorfman summarized the broadcasters' plight as follows:

- All three major networks have been brought in recent years under "new, extremely cost-conscious ownership or management."
- The networks have experienced losses or lowered profits, even as competitors such as cable-cast "superstations" began doing better.
- Network news does not seem to appeal to young people, the networks' share of prime-time audiences has fallen, and technology now allows local stations to duplicate much of what network news has offered in the past.

As a result, Dorfman reported, "network news organizations are being forced by their new managements to cut to the bone," and executives are talking about "radical restructuring" and even "reinventing" network news (pp. 14–15).[9] Although print is unlikely to face precisely the same consequences, its predic-

---

[6]Underwood, D. (1988, March/April). When MBAs rule the newsroom. *Columbia Journalism Review*, p. 23.

[7]Fountain, C. (1987, November/December). The great ratings flap. *Columbia Journalism Review*, p. 46.

[8]Fancher, M. (1987, Spring). The metamorphosis of the newspaper editor, *Gannett Center Journal*, p. 76.

[9]Dorfman, R. (1987, April). Network news: Keep the big picture in focus. *Quill*, pp. 14–15.

ament does seem similar. The developments in broadcasting may well herald new competitive strains that the new editor must confront.

However, do not misunderstand the editor's role here: It is *not* to serve as a businessperson first, news person second. Nor is it to maximize profit at the expense of quality, nor to abandon news duties in a rush to the boardroom. Newspapers have important social responsibilities that underlie their First Amendment protection. The editor's role is to grow in understanding the corporate culture as well as the news side, in order to have an informed, powerful voice in representing the newsroom, asserting its interests, and sustaining the commitment to social responsibility. With more and more news firms in the hands of conglomerate managers not backgrounded in journalism, editors become more important than ever to insuring that bottom-line mentalities do not crowd out public service and long-term quality.

What has changed is not the editor's values and standards, but the breadth of knowledge and preparation necessary to maintain them effectively and the environment (including financial concerns and potentially less-sympathetic ownership) where decisions get made.

Washington Post publisher Donald Graham addressed the point in a speech:

One of the ultimate questions in any organization is, what yardstick do you measure yourself by? We ought to be familiar with the yardsticks of the manager, of the marketer, and of the public corporation, but the ultimate test comes when the reader opens the door in the morning, looks at the paper and says: "Is there a good story here?"[10]

Charles Bailey, former editor of the *Minneapolis Tribune,* summed it up as follows:

There will always be people around to tell a publisher how he can do things more cheaply, more profitably, less controversially. He needs someone to explain, from time to time, why things have to be done more expensively, less profitably and in ways that create rather than avoid controversy (p. 14).[11]

As an advocate of high standards and social responsibility, the new editor must be able to function smoothly and persuasively in both the business and journalistic worlds.

---

[10]Graham, D. E. (1984, March). New times, old values. *Press-Enterprise lecture series,* University of California, Riverside, CA.

[11]Bailey, C. W. (1983, January/February). Exit lines from a Minnesota editor. *Washington Journalism Review,* p. 14.

THE EDITOR AS PLANNER

I once spoke with a young journalist from Brazil who had spent several months as a visiting writer here. Asked what surprised her about United States newsrooms, she replied without hesitation, "These Americans, they debate *everything!*"

Perhaps it stems from the nonstop growth of journalistic corporations, or from Baby Boom journalists' much-proclaimed yearning for involvement, or simply from society's increasing demands for fuller communication. But editors no longer can get away with barking out unilateral, whimsical orders and expecting underlings to leap to carry them out.

Publishing newspapers today requires as many committee meetings as a busy day on Capitol Hill. It demands carefully plotting everything from long-range marketing strategy to coverage plans for next week's first day of school. It includes meetings inviting subscribers to "talk back" and counseling sessions with staff members in trouble. Increasingly, as we discuss later in the book, it involves marshaling teams of writers, artists, designers, assignment editors, news editors, and copyeditors that cross over traditional turf lines. Building consensus and reducing friction rank high on the editor's duty list. Good planning has priority.

A routine work day may compel editors to look ahead in numerous ways: to decide which of next week's papers will need front-page color, who will cover night cops while the beat reporter attends a stress-management seminar, what comics might be eliminated if budget cutbacks materialize. One of my earliest jobs as the first national editor of *USA Today* was to create from scratch a futures calendar of events covering the entire country.

All this requires anticipation, oversight, and coordination. And those duties fall to editors.

One recent study of how editors spend their time found 32% spent in meetings involving staff and another 15% spent dealing with the public. Ten percent went into planning news coverage. Only about 30% of editors' time was devoted to actually writing, editing copy or designing pages.[12]

Although this survey applied directly to high-level editors, similar demands face editors at all ranks. To take one example, an important new position in many urban newsrooms is that of suburban editor, a job organizationally equivalent to city editor or business editor. This job has been spotlighted as metro newspapers turned increasingly to "zoning the news" by producing regional editions with more local and neighborhood coverage. The goal is to fend off circulation and advertising inroads of smaller publications by better nourishing the readers' local-news appetites.

---

[12]Bennett, D. (1985, Summer). Editors as managers: Their perceived need for specialized training. *Newspaper Research Journal*, p. 28.

For the suburban editor, the job combines fundamental journalism (assigning stories, editing copy, designing pages) with awesome planning challenges. Suburban editors grapple with such issues as how to cover council meetings, school boards, and police and fire departments in 20 or 30 outlying communities. How to deploy bureaus and reporters efficiently (and economically) in a vast geographic area. How to direct these forces on deadline each day. How to assemble copy and illustrations in time to meet inelastic production deadlines that resemble minute-by-minute train timetables. How to keep peace among staffers being asked to record suburban school lunch menus when their true goals are to lay siege to the glamour stories in the "main office."

For some editors, these demands can be maddening. Journalists tend to have driven, can-do personalities, more geared to quick action than to planning, coordination, and direction. In this, as in other aspects of editing, the training and attributes that led a journalist to early success in the trenches can create problems when the individual moves into editing. There, subtlety, discretion, efficiency, and soft stepping may count heavier than individual heroics.

That leads us to the next role of the editor.

THE EDITOR AS MANAGER

You edit people, not just copy. How many journalists have heard that hoary slogan?

But nothing is more important to editors than appreciating that people lie at the heart of the job.

"My job," Kristin Gilger, a *New Orleans Times-Picayune* editor, once said, "is to be calm, reasonable and fair when faced with people who are unreasonable, unfair and not calm" (p. 32).[13]

We commonly think of management, of course, as meaning the direction of people. However, editors also manage in other ways: They manage resources (more and more papers are making section editors responsible for administering five- and six-figure budgets). They manage time, their own and the time of others. They manage reputations, of their staffs and the newspaper.

To many derring-do journalists, few things seem more alien than management. After all, journalists take pride in their iconoclasm. They prize independence, and shout at presidents. What preparation is there in such a life for the moment that often serves as its capstone: appointment to management?

Not much, of course, and therein lies worsening trouble. Given all the changes in newspapering discussed so far, it should be clear that managing has surged higher and higher on most editors' charts. But training and preparation for that role have not nearly kept pace.

---

[13]Stepp, C. S. (1987, December). As writers see editors. *Washington Journalism Review*, p. 32.

The new editor must manage proficiently. As always, good journalism comes first. Without an understanding of journalistic values, a manager—no matter how well trained in personnel policies—cannot master the complex forces of the newsroom universe. So, a key goal for journalism schools and newspaper training programs is to help journalists become competent managers. Otherwise, editors risk finding themselves outmaneuvered and their newsrooms outflanked by deft outsiders better able to manipulate corporate power levers.

Robert Giles, in his book *Newsroom Management,* listed several qualities required of modern newspaper managers. They include the following:

- The need to be effective in running a staff that is ambitious, well-educated, and sophisticated in its expectation of sensitive management.
- The need to be supportive of women and minorities.
- The need to help staffers motivate themselves.
- The need to build a climate of trust.
- The need to let staffers know where they stand.
- The need to help staffers chart career paths.
- The need to understand . . . high technology.
- The need to develop and execute changes in news content and news focus based on marketing and readership research. (p. xi)[14]

In so many ways, editors serve as stewards. Copyeditors are stewards of writers' copy; assignment editors, of the trust and talents of their staffs; managing editors, of the newspaper's ideals and content; directing editors, of the entire organization's resources.

Exercising such stewardship can seldom be accomplished alone. Through thoughtful, sensitive management, the new editor tries to harness the gifts and energies of others. Unified, a newspaper staff is an awesome force. Dispirited, it chugs toward mediocrity.

The difference rests with the management, and the management rests with the editors.

THE EDITOR AS JOURNALIST

In describing the roles of the new editor, we began with the furthest from the daily news operation ("the editor as businessperson") and moved inward toward the center. Squarely at the bull's-eye is the editor as journalist, in the traditional sense. Nothing ranks higher. The first editors knew that, and the new editor does too.

---

[14]Giles, R. H. (1987). *Newsroom management.* Indianapolis: R. J. Berg.

No matter what else she or he can do, the new editor should be a competent journalist. Credibility and authority rise from there.

Just like Ben Franklin and the first American editors, the new editor must come prepared to make productive command decisions day in and day out.

What does this role entail?

Essentially it subdivides into four key categories, decisions about news, content, structure, and presentation.

Making Decisions About News.   Editors represent their publications and have responsibility for generating suitable content. They decide what gets through the gates and into the paper. From the view of the audience, few jobs could be more vital. Every day brings hundreds of potential stories, forcing editors into rapid-fire decisions that govern what kind of newspaper will emerge. Editors, then, must understand their papers' values and expectations, and apply them. That involves understanding what makes news (or features or good photos or whatever the expected product is for a given editor) and demonstrating the ability to supply it.

Making Decisions About Content.   More particularly, editors need skill in analyzing each piece of work and helping make it of the highest quality possible. The best editors think conceptually, helping evaluate whether articles and artwork are accurate; balanced; complete; fair; well-conceived; well-documented; well-organized; and appropriate in tone, taste, and style. From the very conception of a story idea, the good editor serves as a partner in proceeding toward making it reality. As a "copy doctor," the editor needs the skills of an intellectual surgeon *and* the wisdom to know what to leave alone.

Making Decisions About Structure.   Editing requires many gears. As manager, strategist, assigner, or copy doctor, an editor may rev up the engines to top throttle and fly around the ethers of deep thoughts and high ideas. But a crucial duty for many editors is to gear down to low, so to inspect copy word by word and mark by mark. This is fine tuning. It is nitpicking. And it is quality control at its most precise. All editors, somewhere in their careers, must prove their ability to furnish the final product: clear, clean, correct, publishable copy, on deadline.

Making Decisions About Presentation.   Ben Franklin did not have to worry about photographs, and certainly not about pie charts, fever lines, and infographics. The new editor does. Gone is the world divided into "word people" and "the artsy types." Broadcasting, computerization, pagination, and other technological marvels have blurred the old forms. The new editor not only must know what is news, how to get it, how to write it, and how to correct it, but also how to design and display it for maximum effect for a busy distracted audience. Although some editors seem uncomfortable with the new visual world, they should see it as an asset. It presents editors with extremely powerful tools for conveying their messages with greater force than ever. The new editor welcomes that opportunity.

The graphics revolution stands as one highly visible symbol of change, but it is not the only way that the editor's journalistic role has matured.

In making decisions about news, the new editor faces unprecedented questions involving privacy, access, credibility, sources and balance. Competition from television and elsewhere, changing audience tastes, and today's emphasis on trends and depth reporting require a re-evaluation of traditional notions of news.

In content editing, editors no longer wield unbridled, capricious power over copy. Writers demand more sensitive, consultative editing manners. With space at a premium, every story and illustration faces scrutiny. New writing styles, experiments, and risks must be considered.

In structural editing, the emergence of computerized word processing has made the editor the reader-of-last-resort, as copy desks have assumed the role once occupied by proofreaders. Structural editing may now include formatting copy for the production process, running a computerized "spell check," and even using electronic diagnostic programs that evaluate such points as how often passive voice is used and how long sentences run.

In every role, change confronts the new editor.

CONCLUSION

"The role of the editorial cartoonist is to throw bombs," *Arizona Republic* cartoonist Steve Benson once said. "Editors believe their role is to spit on the fuses and throw them back" (p. 9).[15]

That seems a pretty good image for the role of the new editor: a newsroom executive paid for tending to the bombs.

Of course, the job does not necessarily require stamping out the controversial ideas of a reporter or cartoonist. One editor I know thinks today's journalists are too docile and say he fights constantly to goad his staff into stirring things up.

To lob the bomb or to spit on the fuse: That is the editor's question.

The new editor contends with swirling changes within journalism and society. No longer a one-man shop, no more a whimsical individualist, the new editor makes decisions against a backdrop of swift change.

Yet to dwell on the pressures, frustrations, and complications of editing

---

[15]Conrad, P. (1987, March). Op-ed page spot gives cartoonist more freedom. *ASNE Bulletin*, p. 9.

misses a far larger point: The new editor has powers and opportunities like never before. Audiences have never been larger, nor taken journalism more seriously. As executive, manager, planner, and teacher, the new editor derives daily satisfaction from producing a vibrant product with a central role in our information-based society. Editors work daily with enthusiastic, devoted staffs who see journalism as a mission and a calling, not just a job.

One editor's influence extends far further, typically, than any one writer's. Editors touch dozens of stories in a given day. Their vision can embrace every part of the paper: the ideas, the reporting, the writing, the presentation.

Although new editors must make more decisions than ever before, in a more difficult environment than ever before, they also have more help than ever before. Reporters have never been better educated. News has never been more interesting. Technology has enabled editors, almost overnight, to aspire to creative artwork and display unimagined just a few years ago. And for all the financial strains felt in the newsroom, newspapers generally remain healthy, solid enterprises offering editors steady resources and support.

Without a doubt, editing is a complex, frustrating, not always appreciated job. But the best new editors hold true to the spirit of their inky-fingered ancestors. As editors always have, they grow toward a future that is once again changing, broadening, and complicating their lives.

In the next chapter, we examine the people behind the jobs. Given the duties described here, what makes a good editor? What are editors like? What qualities should aspiring editors cultivate?

SIDEBAR 2
DEFINING THE TYPICAL EDITOR:
"HOW COME SO MANY OF THEM TEND TO BE GEEKS?"

By David Barry
ASNE Bulletin

First of all, we ought to define "editor." I say this because, as you have probably noticed, American journalism has become title happy, so that in most newspapers everybody covered by the dental plan is editor of something. You meet people with impressive-sounding titles like Associate Lifestyles Editor, and it turns out their primary responsibility is deciding how many stars to give the Late Movie.

For our purposes, I'm going to rule out these lower level personnel. I'm also going to rule out editors listed on the masthead with titles such as Extreme Exalted Editor, because as a rule these are aged, out-to-pasture coots who wear green eyeshades and refuse to learn how the computer system works, so they use their 1927 Royal typewriters to pound out philosophical op-ed pieces about the change of seasons, only they keep getting the actual seasons out of sequence.

(Continued)

Sidebar 2 (*Continued*)

No, what I'm going to talk about are the REAL editors, the skilled and highly paid upper-level professionals who bear the heavy responsibility of performing the essential tasks of modern-day newspaper journalism, which are:

1. Making up budgets.
2. Telling job applicants that their credentials are very impressive, especially the two Pulitzer Prizes, but due to budget considerations no new people can be hired until at least three current employees retire and then die.
3. Going to budget-related meetings.
4. Deciding that, due to budget considerations, you are going to rely on the wire services to cover the mass slaying in your lobby.
5. Fretting about the Decline in Readership.

So that's what real editors *do,* but who *are* they? What makes them tick? What do they feel, deep inside? How come so many of them tend to be geeks? To answer these questions, we must first understand how these people came to be editors.

Most of them developed their interest in journalism very early. In high school, while the other kids were out playing sports, buying condoms, etc., our young editor-to-be was hard at work on the school paper, cranking out lengthy, dated articles that could be used to sedate hyperactive children. During college, our future editor typically got a summer job as a reporter for a small newspaper with a name like the Buford County Register-Calibrator, where he learned the three basic rules of reporting:

1. Never quote anybody accurately unless you want to make him sound like a jerk.
2. Always describe relatives of plane-crash victims as "grief-stricken." Women who have just seen their husbands reduced to objects the size of cigar boxes in freak trash-compactor accidents are "shocked."
3. If you go to a meeting of the Regional Area Water, Zoning and Sewage Appeal Board Authority Commission, and it lasts three-and-a-half hours and absolutely nothing newsworthy happens, you should engage in cynical, hard-bitten-newsman-style banter with the other reporters about what a waste of time it was, then write a 37-inch story with at least two sidebars.

After college, our editor-to-be gets a full-time job as a reporter with a bigger newspaper, and he quickly realizes that if he moves up to the copydesk, he won't have to talk to the public any more. So he learns the three basic rules of copyediting:

1. Whatever way the reporter has spelled "Caribbean," you should change it to another way.
2. Headlines should always sound as though they had been spoken by Tonto

(*Continued*)

Sidebar 2 (*Continued*)

(REAGAN TO CONGRESS: GIVE ME TAX CUT), and ideally should be completely unintelligible (HOUSE UNIT AIRS SOLONS' PARLEY PLEA).

3. If you are editing a story in which the reporter has risked his life to get an exclusive interview with a machete-wielding, hostage-holding, homicidal maniac, and it is a brilliant piece of deadline writing, a crackling, gripping, tension-filled, firsthand account, you should wait until the newsroom is fairly quiet, then yell to the reporter: "Dammit, Johnson, our style is to use a colon to introduce a complete, one-sentence quotation within a paragraph!"

So our boy gets a job on the copydesk. The problem there, of course, is that according to government figures, working on the copydesk kills your brain cells at the rate of over 4 million a day. So as soon as he can, our savvy editor-to-be makes the move up the ladder to full-fledged editor, with direct responsibility for not hiring people, not spending money, and writing lengthy and vaguely threatening memos to the staff about using the WATS line for personal calls.

If he handles these tasks well, our editor is promoted to an upper level post where, along with his peers, he is responsible for fretting about the Decline in Readership, which is caused by the fact that the average reader buys the paper mainly for sports and the Kmart insert, and pays no attention to the lengthy front-page stories about Lebanon, the deficit, and important meetings of the Regional Area Water, Zoning and Sewage Appeal Board Authority Commission.

Most of this fretting is done in-house, but from time to time our editor will attend week-long Fretting Conferences in warm locales with high-level editors of other papers that are also suffering from Declining Readership. They sit around, day after day, trying to figure out what the hell the public wants, which is not easy because the last time any of them dealt with the actual public in person was back when they were just out of college, and all they can remember is that it seemed to be grief-stricken. Eventually, they decide that what they need to do is humanize the paper, which means use more interviews with Dolly Parton in the Lifestyles section.

What we have in our typical editor, then, is a person who leads a sheltered existence: After about age 30, he hardly ever deals professionally with anybody except other editors. This tends to make him insecure. At home, in his suburban development, he's surrounded by neighbors with real jobs at large corporations that own railroad cars and huge vats of chemicals and entire Third World nations, neighbors who routinely deal with high-level financial concepts such as debentures. These concepts are far beyond the comprehension of our editor, whose only major investment move in his entire life was to join a Christmas Club, in which he lost money.

Oh, our editor tries hard to be one of the guys, to appear as though he has an important job with important problems, just like his neighbors. He starts wearing three-piece suits. He carries a briefcase. He goes out of his way to talk business at cocktail parties. "Bob," he'll say to a neighbor, "how's business?" And Bob will say, "Well, Ed, I had to lay off 67,000 people today, and the division I'm in

(*Continued*)

Sidebar 2 (*Continued*)

charge of lost $3.28 billion in the last fiscal quarter because of unexpected fluctuations in the composite annualized national bond accrual, but, hey, it's nothing we can't handle. How about you?" And Ed says, "Well, we're thinking seriously about dropping 'Dick Tracy.' " And he knows, deep in his soul, that Bob does not view him as a heavy hitter. He knows that if Bob faced a wimpy little problem such as Declining Readership, he would punch some figures into his giant corporate mainframe computer and have it solved before lunchtime.

No, our boy realizes, in the end, that he's an editor, not a businessman. So he trudges back to his cubicle and he looks out across the newsroom at the young, enthusiastic reporters violently pounding out stories, and he thinks: "Maybe it's time I let a new generation take over the tasks of fretting and not hiring. Maybe it's time I slowed down a little, thought a little more about the meaning of life, maybe even did a little piece about the changing of the seasons." Of course, he realizes he must wait until the current Extreme Executive Editor suffers a fatal heart attack while attempting to change his ribbon. Budget considerations, you know.[16]

[16]Barry, D. (1985, March/April). Defining the typical editor: How come so many of them tend to be geeks. *ASNE Bulletin,* pp. 3–4. (Reprinted with permission).

What Is an Editor?

One should fight like the devil the temptation to think well of editors. They are all, without exception—at least some of the time—incompetent or crazy.[1]

—John Gardner

So far, we have concentrated on what editors *do*. Another way to examine editing is to consider what editors *are*, or at least what they *should be*. As we have seen, editors have many jobs and play many roles. Generalizing about them can be risky. Yet it clearly seems important, both for journalists considering editing careers and for managers seeking qualified desk people, to develop some idea of what qualities make for a good editor.

In *The Elements of Editing*, Arthur Plotnik pointed out that "the editorial personality" encompasses "such useful attributes as genius, charisma, adaptability, and disdain for high wages." It must include, he added, compulsiveness, but of a kind that is productive, not disabling (p. 1).[2]

Truly, the editor can be a strange creature. In describing what editors should be, journalists reach for a range of adjectives: creative, energetic, skeptical, curious, challenging, experienced. They apply descriptors that sometimes seem polar: able to write, able to coach; able to teach, able to learn; able to juggle, able to focus; able to stand firm, able to stay flexible; able to lead, able to follow.

No wonder such big game is hard to bag. The gamut of desired editorial

---

[1]Charlton, J. (Ed.). (1985). *The writer's quotation book* (p. 98). Stamford, CT: Ray Freiman.
[2]Plotnik, A. (1982). *The elements of editing*. New York: Collier Books.

qualities runs wide. Just as wide is the range of people who make editing their careers. In examining how editors come to be, it is worth beginning with a review of editor lore. Quite a bit has been written by editors and editor watchers, and sampling that literature offers some intriguing insight into how editors view themselves and are viewed by others.

HOW WRITERS SEE EDITORS

Considering how much power they are supposed to have, editors have never had a very good press. Almost anyone who has spent time in newsrooms can recall sitting through besotted, post-deadline rounds of editor bashing, listening to the disgruntled hoi polloi spin horror tales exposing editors as the literary equivalent of ax murderers.

That so much of the imagery is violent—writer Jon Franklin has said that to edit is "to kill babies" (p. 127)[3]—testifies to the profound, intimate attachment people have to what they write. Writers pour body and soul into their work, and few occasions provoke more naked terror than delivering one's handiwork to an aloof, all-powerful editor who stands like St. Peter, passing ultimate judgment on creative achievement and controlling admission to that journalistic heaven: publication, with a byline.

Consequently, it should not be surprising that writers often come predisposed to view editors as adversaries, or at least formidable rivals for control over what gets published.

In his classic book, *On Writing Well,* William Zinsser crisply set out the basic dichotomy for judging editors: "Are they friends or enemies—gods who save us from our sins or bums who trample on our poetic souls?" (p. 234).[4]

They are, of course, both. Indeed, when one listens to reporters and writers discussing their editors, the conversations tend to lurch from one pole to the other, portraying a love–hate relationship of mutual dependence and battlefield-like tension and exhilaration. Prize-winning Associated Press writer Jules Loh said: "I regard editors as sailors regard the sea. Editors are absolutely essential to my work, but are fraught with peril" (p. 1).[5]

"I want editing," a reporter for the *Louisville Courier-Journal* once told a conference I attended. "I just want the editor to be as good as I am."

What emerges clearly from many such comments is the overpowering realization introduced in the preceding chapter: Editors edit people as much as copy. That is, editors must deal first with human beings and then with their copy.

---

[3]Franklin, J. (1986). *Writing for story.* New York: Atheneum.

[4]Zinsser, W. (1985). *On writing well.* New York: Harper & Row.

[5]Cappon, J. (1985, May 27). Warfare between editors and reporters. *AP Newsfeatures Report,* p. 1.

And it often is the intangibles—such as respect and trust, or the lack thereof—that cement or fragment a writer–editor relationship, and that govern the ultimate quality of copy. This is what writing teacher Roy Peter Clark called "the human side of editing."[6]

For some editors, this feel for people is innate and natural. For others, it must be rigorously acquired and honed. But it is the starting point, and perhaps the most important single ingredient, that charts the direction of writer–editor collaborations.

Madeleine Blais of the *Miami Herald,* interviewed in *NewsTalk I* by Shirley Biagi, spoke of the duality of good editing and poor:

> What you want is an excellent editor, at least one who doesn't interfere with your work if it's good. What you don't want is a bad editor, someone who changes words for the sake of changing words, who isn't paying attention to what you are trying to do. . . . I love good editors . . . If you have readers you can trust, which is what an editor should be ideally—an eminently trustworthy reader of what you do—then you have a helper in your process. I need that, and I think I always will. (p. 100)[7]

"An eminently trustworthy reader of what you do"—Blais has capsuled the writer's longing. There is nothing quite so depressing for writers as those occasions when they recognize that they and the editor have irreconcilable visions of the direction and purpose of a cherished project. And there is nothing quite so thrilling as the synergistic chain reaction that comes from the simpatico teamwork of a writer and editor in synchronization.

In striving for such camaraderie, it is vital to appreciate the different starting points of writer and editors. For the editor, burdened with a range of responsibilities and commonly expected to oversee a thundering herd of writers, working with one reporter's copy may be one single aspect of a complex day's work. For the writer, that one piece of copy is *everything*. No matter that the editor has 15 other articles to move; no matter that the publisher has just called to shrink the news hole by 10 columns; no matter that the payroll report is overdue, the news desk is breathing fire over busted deadlines, the police radio is blaring something about an airliner in trouble, and the company lawyer is on hold to discuss the libel trial. It is the urgent, inescapable duty of the editor to close out the distractions, train full attention on the writer, and approach the copy as if it were a precious, fragile and unique contribution to literary history. Which, of course, it is.

And it is important that the actual moment of copyediting not be the editor's

[6]Clark, R. P. (1987, August). Speech presented to the Association for Education in Journalism and Mass Communications, San Antonio, TX.
[7]Biagi, S. (1987). *NewsTalk I.* Belmont, CA: Wadsworth.

first raw exposure to the reporter's effort. The good editor is prepared for the copy's arrival. He or she will have worked with the writer planning and conceiving the idea, monitored the reporting, and collaborated on possible approaches to the writing.

Occasionally, editors protest that there is not time for such consultations. But in the long run there is not time *not* to have them. To neglect them makes no more sense than for a banker to invest money without regard for the interest rate or for a lawyer to go into court without first reading the depositions. Such preliminary decisions are an irreversible investment in the outcome, and whatever is locked in at the moment of investment determines, to a large extent, the ultimate payoff.

Too often, however, writers and editors regard each other not as teammates but as adversaries, and they may even avoid each other at times during a story's infancy and as it progresses toward production. I know writers who, when they see the editor heading their way, will seize the phone and pretend to be on involved in an important call, just to avoid dealing with the editor.

In a marvelous essay called "A View from the Trenches: The Editor as Enemy?" writer Jim Schutze provided an insightful look at how "editors and reporters actually may live in different worlds." Schutze described his shock as a reporter when an editor appeared angry upon learning Schutze's weather story included information on a record number of snow-related deaths. Schutze, who had been proud of his reporting, relayed his confusion to an older reporter, who explained:

> "The thing is, [the editor] promised a funny story at the morning meeting. Now that your story is depressing, he'll have to explain to the afternoon meeting why he doesn't have a story for the funny hole."
>
> "So what? Who care about the meetings? We're talking about real life here."
>
> He stared at me and then looked off toward the bar as if he hated talking to me worse than anything else on earth. "Look," he said, "what went on out there in the blizzard is your idea of real life. For editors, real life is the meeting." (p. 20)[8]

Such a view of editors—as remote figures drifting into and out of various fog-shrouded meetings—isn't altogether far from reality. As we have seen, editors do far more than process copy: They manage newsrooms, administer budgets, hire and fire and supervise, help run the business, and participate in an assortment of activities that remove them from what writers consider their true responsibilities. These distractions crop up inevitably, but the editor must not let them crowd out discussions with reporters.

---

[8]Schutze, J. (1981, March). A view from the trenches: The editor as enemy? *ASNE Bulletin*, p. 20.

Humorist Dave Barry wickedly captured a similar view of editors in the column reprinted just before this chapter, zeroing in on a hypothetical editor named Ed, whose only contribution to cocktail party talk about "the composite annualized national bond accrual" is to discuss his paper's comic page (p. 4).[9]

Another insightful humorist, Art Buchwald, once described editors as viewed by reporters:

> Editors have two heads, no heart and eyes in the back of their pointy heads. For some reason, which the reporter can't fathom, the editor either ignores the reporter all the time or is constantly on his or her back . . . . The best way to keep your job is to have as few dealings with him as you possibly can. (p. B1)[10]

Writers can be both editors' harshest critics and loudest boosters. Jerry Bledsoe, columnist for the *Greensboro (N.C.) News & Record,* has said that "they're all mechanics and managers. There's no such thing as an editor any more."[11] Pulitzer winner Edna Buchanan of the *Miami Herald,* whose three cardinal rules are "never trust an editor, never trust an editor, and never trust an editor," explains that editors are people "sitting on their rumps doing these awful things to our stories" (p. 40).[12]

Still, according to writer Barry Bearak of the *Los Angeles Times,* "There's nothing a reporter wants more—with the exception of a good spouse—than a good editor."[13]

William P. Barrett, a veteran of three newspapers, the Associated Press and *Forbes* magazine, pointed out that editors' work, each stroke of which may be subtle and nearly invisible, accumulates to become a major determinant of quality. "The difference between a good paper and a mediocre one basically boils down to three assistant city editors," Barrett said.[14]

Writers use many words and images, some of them pejorative, to characterize editors. At worst, they see editors as nagging parents, peremptory drill sergeants, deaf-eared tyrants, unrelenting prosecutors. At best, they see editors as collaborators, teammates and coaches, always tough but also respectful and benevolent.

Underneath the griping and carping, it seems clear that most writers yearn for good editing but fear, as much as anything else in the business, the destructive effect that poor editing can have on their copy and their work life.

---

[9]Barry, D. (1985, March/April). Defining the typical editor: "How come so many of them tend to be geeks?". *ASNE Bulletin,* p. 4.

[10]Buchwald, A. (1985, April). The unexpurgated editor. *Washington Post,* p. B1.

[11]Jerry Bledsoe, personal communication, August 13, 1987.

[12]Edna Buchanan, personal communication, August 12, 1987. See also, Trillin, C. (1986, February 17). Covering the cops. *New Yorker,* p. 40.

[13]Barry Bearak, personal communication, August 17, 1987.

[14]William P. Barrett, personal communication, August 21, 1987.

HOW EDITORS SEE THEMSELVES

Not surprisingly, editors do not always see themselves in quite the same way as others see them.

In his revealing biography *Max Perkins: Editor of Genius,* A. Scott Berg related an anecdote that every editor can appreciate. It took place after Perkins had established his reputation by coaxing classic novels from such writers as Hemingway, Fitzgerald, and Wolfe:

> Mrs. (Madeleine) Boyd worked up the courage to ask Max a question that had long intrigued her. "Why don't you write yourself?" she inquired in a letter. "I have a feeling you could write so much better than most of the people who do write." Perkins delivered his response when they met next. She recalled, "Max just stared at me for a long time and said, 'Because I'm an editor.' " (p. 170)[15]

Journalists become editors for many reasons. Most commonly, perhaps, they move into editing after succeeding as reporters, as A. M. Rosenthal described in a preceding chapter. Because historically editors have earned more money than reporters, turning to editing was an expected career choice for those seeking to advance in status and pay. Others become editors through heredity (their families own the paper), fortune (real estate magnate Mortimer Zuckerman bought the *Atlantic* and *U.S. News & World Report* after making his mint in business), or accident (I became a copyeditor because that job happened to be open when I applied at the *Charlotte Observer*).

Rarer have been those editors, such as Perkins, who through natural selection follow an inner compass that leads directly into the priesthood of the eyeshade. However, as the shortage of editors grows acute, greater attention must be given to identifying potential editors early in their careers and to grooming them in the skills, duties and mysteries of the initiated.

In describing themselves and their work, editors seem to think in lists. Paul S. Swensson, for instance, described an editor as, among other things, "a master craftsman of our language, a generalist on 20th century current affairs and common interests, an expert on readership, a planner, a leader who can sell his news ideas to management, a leader who teaches his staff" and, finally, "a humble person despite this wealth of talent and power."[16] Roy Peter Clark described editors with such phrases as "the offensive line," "the conscience of a newspaper," "champions of clarity," "friends of the reader," and the "seawall" of protection.[17]

For many editors, the variety of the work proves attractive. Editors tend to

---

[15]Berg, A. S. (1978). *Max Perkins: Editor of genius.* New York: Pocket Books.

[16]Swensson, P. S. (1982, Summer). *An editor is . . . .* (photocopied conference handout).

[17]Roy Peter Clark, personal communication, March 10, 1986.

enjoy the power and excitement of dealing with more areas than reporters handle and of controlling more aspects of the news process. Stan Burroway, an editor at the *Los Angeles Times,* put it this way:

> I think I became an editor when I found out you could get your hands on so much more of the news that way. When I got to the copydesk, I found I had my hand on all the big news every day. Excited as I had been to see my byline every day, I lost interest in that.[18]

Thomasine Berg of the *Providence Sunday Journal* magazine conceded that "writers often think editors are nuts for choosing to spend life parked at desks mucking through other people's words." However, she added, "Fact is, editors get to work with the fun part of the whole process: storytelling" (p. 35).[19]

Editors also take satisfaction in teaching others. Working with hungry reporters, often young and eager, is exciting. "I get a kick out of watching people develop as reporters," Flora Rathburn of the *Pittsburgh Press* said. "That to me is as gratifying as getting your name on a byline. I get a real charge out of helping people make a story better—even though maybe nobody but me and the reporter will ever know it."[20]

There is also the lure of authority. *Washington Post* assistant managing editor Milton Coleman has noted, in explaining why he moved from reporting, that "I like putting things together and doing production. I like leadership positions."[21]

It is not only reporters who criticize editors. Editors too quickly point out their profession's own shortcomings, both in terms of language skills and broader issues.

Longtime editor Robert Phelps quoted a colleague's observation that "99 out of 100 copyeditors know how to take a sentence apart and remove the offending part, but only 1 in 10 knows how to put a sentence back together again." Phelps added that the ideal editor "approaches the article with sympathy for what the writer is trying to do but is critical about the execution" (p. 4).[22]

George Edmondson, an editor I worked with at *USA Today,* used to call editors "janitors of journalism," because so much of their job consists of cleaning up.

Kristin Gilger, a bureau chief at the *New Orleans Times-Picayune,* underlined an oft-made point about editors' failings as supervisors. "It's appalling

---

[18]Stan Burroway, personal communication, August 20, 1987.

[19]Berg, T. (1986). Is this stuff interesting? *How I wrote the story* (2nd ed.). Providence: Providence Journal Co.

[20]Flora Rathburn, personal communication, August 17, 1987.

[21]Milton Coleman, personal communication, August 17, 1987.

[22]Phelps, R. (1981, May/June). What makes a good copyeditor, anyway? *ASNE Bulletin,* p. 4.

how bad people managers we are," she said. "It's true at every paper I have ever seen. If you're a bad people manager, you have low morale. And if you have low morale, you have a poor product."[23]

Like writers, editors commonly express an ambivalence about their own work. They recognize its frustrations and their limitations, yet they also see editing's powerful possibilities and cherish the special satisfactions of the job.

WHAT MAKES A GOOD EDITOR

When this issue is addressed within the rather skimpy literature on editing, it tends to turn on qualities of a good copyeditor, reflecting the intensity of our focus on the editor's role as writing coach and language czar.

Kenneth H. Brief, when he was recruiting desk people for *Newsday,* reported that he would search for a professional who:

- Doesn't indulge in preferential editing, knowing when to pick up and when to put down the pencil . . .
- Challenges copy when appropriate.
- Respects good writing.
- Is articulate, well-read and well-versed in current events.
- Is an expert in the use of language, but who doesn't spend hours agonizing over whether to use "which" or "that."
- Can railroad copy in record time but doesn't leave you with a potential libel suit. (p. 12).[24]

Looking beyond the copydesk to the assignment editor, William Zinsser described the qualities this way:

> What a good editor brings to a piece of writing is an objective eye that the writer has long since lost . . . A good editor likes nothing better than a piece of copy that he hardly has to touch. A bad editor has a compulsion to tinker, proving with busywork that he hasn't forgotten the minutiae of grammar and usage. He is a literal fellow, catching cracks in the road but not enjoying the scenery (p. 235).[25]

The flair for "enjoying the scenery," while not losing sight of the need to patch the cracks, is a quality that seems to mark strong editors. Perhaps no one

---

[23]Kristin Gilger, personal communication, August 17, 1987.

[24]Brief, K. H. (1981, May/June). Tips on how to find good copyeditors. *ASNE Bulletin,* p. 12.

[25]Zinsser, W. (1985). *On writing well.* New York: Harper & Row.

has better summarized the daunting requirements of such a super editor than writer Lillian Ross, in the introduction of her book *Reporting:*

> What most writers need is not another writer but an editor—someone to talk to about their work, someone capable of giving guidance and help without getting in the writers' way. A helpful editor should have the following qualities: understanding of and sympathy for writers; the editorial talent to recognize and appreciate journalistic and literary talent; an openness to all kinds of such talent; confidence and strength in his own judgment; resistance to fads and fakery in publishing; resistance to corruption and opportunism, to exhortations from people, including writers and other editors, who are concerned with "popularity" and "the market"; moral and mental strength, and the physical strength to sustain these; energy and resourcefulness in helping writer discover what they should write about; literally unlimited patience with selfishness and egotism; the generosity and character required to give away his own creativity and pour it into a group of greedy and usually ungrateful writers. This kind of editor is a rarity. If you're lucky, you may find one. Avoid the following kind of editor: one who does not like writers. (p. 5)[26]

Most editors begin as writers. How soon some forget! Wherever the careers propel them, editors should never forget several fundamental lessons that help illustrate and separate the roles of editors and writers:

• Reporting is very hard. Editors should have been reporters. They should have been lectured by uppity scientists, threatened by angry police sergeants, yelled at by mayors, and forced to confront an out-of-order pay telephone in the pouring rain after their car battery has died while pursuing, on deadline, a vital source who lives in a part of town they have never been to.

• Writing is very hard. Editors should firmly remember the terror of staring at the blank page and the insecurity of having to prove, time after time, that they still can produce marvelous copy. Writer after writer tells of fearing that, no matter what their prior successes, each new article will expose their weaknesses and unveil them as pretenders. As they move away from daily reporting and writing, editors must hold onto those feelings.

• Editors are not writers. Editors are editors. They help others write. They supervise writers. They often rewrite. And they edit (which involves writing, but doing so unnaturally, that is, in the style of the original writer or of the publication). Editors must do their jobs but leave room for writers to exercise themselves. They must let go.

• Editors are advisers. They are expected to give advice without dominating a project. If a reporter needs to locate a source or document, editors should

---

[26]Ross, L. (1981). *Reporting.* New York: Dodd, Mead.

help. Editors don't have to *know* everything, but they should know how to *find out* almost everything. A good sign of a strong reporter–editor relationship is when the reporter's first thought, on encountering a problem with a story, is to consult with the editor. A bad sign is when reporters avoid their editors.

Short of a saint, what kind of person can have, or acquire, the many qualities demanded of good editors? Are editors born, or can they be taught?

The answer, it seems to me, is that, although some editing talents seem to come naturally or not at all, almost anyone can learn to edit *better*. Surely it helps to have the inborn gift. Some people are natural editors in the same way that others are born ballet dancers or math geniuses or music prodigies. But there is much to learn about editing, not the least of which is sensitivity to the dicey, hair-trigger relationship between editors and those they edit.

No list of desirable traits for editors can be exhaustive, but it can be fruitful to single out several important qualities that seem associated with successful editing.

Attitude. It begins here. Ginny Graybiel, after working as both an editor and a reporter for the *Pensacola (Fla.) News Journal,* cracked the essence of the issue in an article that began, "The Editor Is not the Enemy." It ended, "All these expectations (about reporter-editor relationships) can be summed up with one basic thought: I hope my editor cares as much about my copy as I do" (p. 5).[27]

Good editors care. They respect writers and their copy. They respect the audience.

Intelligence. Editors need to be quick-witted, street-smart, and well-informed. They must, through a lifetime of reading and the instinct of paying attention, display a general familiarity with how things work—from international politics to local zoning to portable computer terminals that fail on deadline.

I once worked alongside a man who had been copyediting for 30 years. He seemed to remember every story he had ever edited, including the time he wrote the headline for the bombing of Hiroshima. His memory was encyclopedic, and the newsroom depended on him. Another editor I worked for had a near-photographic memory. She could recall specific dates and details of news, page numbers where stories appeared months earlier, and the capital of any obscure country whose name cropped in a wire service article.

Curiosity. Editors are annoying buttinskies because they are so curious. Like fidgety children, they want to get their hands on everything. They are

---

[27]Graybiel, G. (1987, May). Let's declare peace in the newsroom war. *Gannetteer: Editorially Speaking,* p. 5.

always tossing off story ideas, meddling in the reporting, tinkering with the layouts, peeping into the wire queues to see what is happening. This can, of course, be irritating but for the most part it is an important quality. Because of it, editors are always stumbling into new and exciting places. "Our best editors," David Halberstam once wrote in reference to Henry Luce, "have always been at least partly hick—everything is new and fresh and possible for them, they take nothing for granted" (p. 100).[28]

Resourcefulness.   Editors get things done. They understand that life consists of a procession of problems to which it is their job to find solutions. Perhaps nothing better defines successful editors than saying they operate as problem solvers rather than problem creators: looking for the most effective solution to the nonstop crises of the news business, without unduly whining about the oppressive deadlines, incompetent staffing, uncooperative machinery, hostile sources, and unreasonable management that bedevil them all.

I recall once slumping into my managing editor's office complaining that we were missing a tremendous story because no reporter with the proper blend of reporting skill and writing sensitivity was available. "Why don't you send the columnist?" the managing editor replied. Indeed, sitting right before my eyes was perhaps the best writer on the staff, our daily columnist, but I had so pigeonholed him as a column writer that it never occurred to me to send him on assignment. I did, and the story worked brilliantly, all because the managing editor was resourceful enough to imagine something innovative.

Analytical Skill.   Before they can solve problems, editors first must have enough analytical ability to recognize and understand the problems.

Mona McCormick has identified seven steps that can help a person critically evaluate information and situations:

- identifying main issues
- recognizing underlying assumptions
- evaluating evidence (by testing claims or checking conclusions against facts)
- evaluating authority (by checking the credibility of sources)
- recognizing bias
- understanding problems of language (such as generalities and cliches that produce misunderstanding)
- and relating information to ideas (to make sure facts contribute to proper conclusions) (p. 220).[29]

---

[28]Halberstam, D. (1978, January). Time Inc.'s internal war over Vietnam. *Esquire*, p. 100.
[29]Ward, J., & Hansen, K. A. (1987). *Search strategies in mass communications*. New York: Longman.

Good editors save time and increase their efficiency by going through these, or similar, steps regularly.

Flexibility.   The editor is a kind of newsroom handyperson, whose dealings over time may skip from managing people to designing pages to conceiving story ideas to editing obits to fending off lawsuits. For most editors, a linear approach—one thing at a time—is fruitless. Editors juggle. They switch from right hemisphere to left hemisphere in the same way modern computers jump from screen one to screen two. This is a ragged and disconcerting way of operating, and it requires good humor and good gears.

One executive editor told me that staff vacancies had forced him to work a double shift for several weeks. During the day, he ran the newsroom, planned coverage, worked on his paper's budget proposals for the coming years, and handled other broadscale administrative duties. At night, he worked on the copydesk rim, fine-tuning stories and writing headlines. His flexibility kept him from drowning in the flood of work.

Good-Hearted Toughness.   Remember Lou Grant, the gruff-but-gold-hearted city editor in the television series? Editors must be skeptics and taskmasters. They cannot be faint-hearted in the ongoing swordplay of newsroom politics. They strive to project a near-the-brink blend of charity and fury that instills just the right touch of fear and affection. But all this must be carried off in a good spirit and without triggering newsroom warfare. I recommend practicing (perhaps in front of a mirror) the ability to smile pleasantly and speak evenly while delivering the most intellectually scathing message.

One editor I know told of waking up in the middle of the night, rehearsing the exact words he would use to tell a reporter who was failing. On another occasion, I worked for an editor who exuded poise and self-confidence in even the roughest situations. One day, just before he was to give a difficult speech, I caught him sneaking off to the bathroom to be sick. On the outside, both these editors were solid anchors for their staffs. Inside, they were just as nervous as the rest of us. Both took special care in handling the tough chores, even to the point of practicing their lines.

Fairness and Diplomacy.   Nobody likes a bully. Editors do not have to win every battle, inside the newsroom or outside, and few things prove more important than knowing when to retreat. Good editors listen to everyone and then try to react judiciously. Of course, staff members will vie for an editor's attention and good will in much the same way children contend for their parents' blessings. Editors need to consciously delegate time to each individual, each duty, each part of the operation.

I remember once being accused of treating some reporters better than others because, on my route to my desk each morning, I routinely stopped to chat with several reporters along the way. It was habit and geography, not favoritism, that underlay my conduct. But after the complaint, I took different routes to my desk each day.

Tenacity.　On the other hand, sometimes editors must display the persistence of the pit bull. This quality sometimes emerges early. As a youth, editor Max Perkins wrote a friend, "I kissed the dickens out of a pretty girl this afternoon. It took about three hours of steady arguing to get it out of her, but finally she gave me permission." After that, editing Hemingway must have seemed like a cakewalk (p. 33).[30]

Energy.　Editors work hard, physically and emotionally. In general, the bitterest newsroom arguments that I have witnessed (and participated in) occurred when people were pushed beyond their capacity to endure. Most editors, like most people, tend to be reasonable and understanding most of the time, but become increasingly churlish, stubborn and itchy-fingered as pressure mounts and weariness sets in. A bit of advice: Watch the eyes. When hard steel replaces the usual twinkle, an editor is overdrafted at the energy bank. Back off. Wait until the next morning to make your pitch for covering the elections in Bermuda.

Sense of Humor.　Special indeed is the editor who, amidst the tensest newsroom crisis, can make everyone chuckle. Few weapons are so disarming as wit, in particular the wisdom to laugh at yourself. Humor and tomfoolery provide important escape valves in many newsrooms.

Eugene Roberts, who led the *Philadelphia Inquirer* to 14 Pulitzer Prizes in 13 years, is legendary for the practical jokes played at his paper. Once, a reporter returning from an assignment in the Mideast walked into Roberts' office with a camel and a goat. Another time, staff members raced motorcycles around the newsroom after the paper produced a series on motorcycle gangs. "Journalists tend to be both creative and insecure," according to Jim Naughton, a Roberts colleague. "They need occasions to laugh together" (p. E10).[31]

Thoughtfulness.　This means basic politeness and respect for others. It also means something else: Editors should think about everything they do. Given the rugged demands of the job, it is tempting to rush through mundane tasks and to plunge through the people and duties of the job as if they were items on a checklist. This is almost always a mistake.

Once when I was a copyeditor, I struggled for hours to polish a major investigative story and to write a punchy headline for it. I went home thinking

---

[30]Berg, A. S. (1978). Max Perkins: Editor of genius. New York: Pocket Books.
[31]Kowet, D. (1988, April 15). Eugene Roberts. *Washington Times*, 1988, p. E10.

I had significantly helped the article but realizing that no one would notice. When I arrived for work the next day, there was a note of appreciation from the executive editor. The copydesk chief had recognized my effort and notified the executive editor, who took the time to relay his thanks. That kind of thoughtfulness is doubly repaid in loyalty.

Concentration. I have heard several good editors refer to their ability to achieve an almost self-hypnotic state, in which they block out noise and confusion and focus 100% on the issues at hand. In my judgment, more editing errors result from carelessness and inattention than from anything else, a point we elaborate on later in this book. Editors certainly have to balance many thoughts at once, but good ones learn how to focus powerfully on one at a time.

Ability. Should this be first on the list, or last? Editors must have a range of skills and accomplishments: knowledge of news, language, style, usage, grammar, graphics, headlines, photos, cutlines; speed and efficiency; decisiveness; carefulness. They must be strong writers, able rewriters, and clinical copy surgeons. They must be, in the usual sense of the word, excellent journalists. These qualities are sine qua non.

But remember: They are the starting point of good editing, not the ending point. Editors who never build beyond these basic abilities will, more often than not, find themselves thwarted and frustrated before very long.

Summary

In summarizing these qualities, it seems fair to conclude that success in editing may be a function of strong journalistic proficiency plus leadership ability. The editor is the orchestra conductor; the writer is the virtuoso first violinist. The editor is the team coach; the writer is the star quarterback.

As team builders and leaders, editors spend their days making and enforcing decisions. In the following group of chapters, we explore how editors make decisions and how they can prepare for the decisions they will face.

SIDEBAR 3
GIFTS

By Charles McCorkle Hauser
Providence Journal-Bulletin

A writer gives, and an editor takes. That's the stereotype.

(Continued)

Sidebar 3 (*Continued*)

Certainly a good writer gives. He gives his all. His creative juices. His heart. His soul.

But the good editor—anonymous, unbylined, unsung, even unappreciated (it goes with the territory)—has a great deal to give, too.

We've spent a lot of time in recent years putting the writer under the microscope—isolating, identifying, labeling and analyzing his attributes. Let's do the same for the editor. While the list of things a good editor gives to a writer is long, I'll focus for the purpose of this short piece on four that I would rank right at the top:

1. The gift of time

Good editing takes time, and the most important time of all is spent not with pencil or cursor, but in conversation with the writer. Sometimes deadlines press, and stories must be railroaded. But when possible, push other matters aside and give the writer your undivided attention.

Yes, I know you have 50 other things competing for your attention, but the story the writer is working on at that moment is, for him, the most important story in the world. Make it, for that moment, the most important story in the world for you, too.

If you really don't have the time, be honest with the writer; don't shortchange him by giving him a quickie discussion and a fast kiss-off. Make a specific appointment for when you do have time.

2. The gift of tolerance

Let the writer make mistakes; let him risk failure. Let him try a different organization, an unusual voice, an unorthodox approach. First person? Why not? Second person? Let's see what happens. Tell the story from an unexpected point of view? Give it a whirl.

We all should have the right to learn from our failures. And sometimes, instead of failing, we succeed handsomely with an offbeat approach.

3. The gift of focus

As an editor, you're sometimes better able to see the true dimensions of a story than the writer, who can be too close to it. But you'll be making a mistake if you say, "No, this is all wrong. I'll tell you what the focus of the story should be." Instead, help the writer find the focus for himself.

The best way I've found to accomplish this is to make a simple request: "Tell me what this story is about." Then listen. In the oral telling, the writer will often zoom in on the heart of the story. You probably won't have to say, "Yes, that's it." He'll know.

(*Continued*)

Sidebar 3 (*Continued*)

4. The gift of empathy

I never had an editor I didn't learn from, and perhaps the finest I ever worked for was Tom Fesperman, managing editor of the *Charlotte Observer* in the '60s. I was his state editor.

I remember going to Tom one day to discuss a Sunday story idea—the emergence of the Republican Party as a new political force in South Carolina. It would take a week of a reporter's time, and I wanted to borrow a particular city staffer for the assignment.

"Why don't you go down to Columbia and do that one yourself?" Tom said.

I began to protest about all the projects I had piled up and the demands on my time, but he cut me off.

"How are you going to be a good editor," he asked, "if you forget what it's like to be a reporter?"

And he was right. Every editor who works with writers should be given the chance now and then to abandon the desk and get his teeth into a story at ground level.

Those are my top four. You may have your own, and you may rank these differently. But if you're an editor, they should be on your list.[32]

---

[32]Hauser, C. M. (1986). *How I wrote the story*. Providence: The Providence Journal Co. (Reprinted with permission).

The Editor As Decision Maker

In some 20 years of working for newspapers, only once did I ever come close to a fistfight. That happened when another editor and I argued irrationally over where new furniture would go in our newsroom.

We stopped short of throwing punches, but the incident stuck with me as an example of how everyday flash points can consume an editor's energy.

As newsroom decision makers, editors regularly confront nasty dilemmas ranging far beyond operational journalism. Tempers flare over who will receive the new computer terminal or which copydesk will win the latest shipment of ergonomic chairs.

On a given day, an editor may spend less time deciding news play than debating how to handle a budding romance between the police reporter and the assistant city editor. Laying out the features page may take second place to placating readers irate about the dropping of one channel from the daily television listings.

Given the highly charged, heavy-stress climate of many newsrooms, these quandaries can be inflammatory and stomach-churning. Invariably, they wind up in an editor's care. When editors complain of being "nibbled to death by ducks," such are the pecks they have in mind.

While doling out the new furniture may provoke the *real* passion, editors also face more orthodox tasks. They make decisions about content, copy, and design. They manage staffs. They make judgments about legal issues, ethics, and policies of all kinds.

Some fortunate editors take naturally to all these tasks, but many find at least some of them daunting.

Having a sense of humor helps. I worked with one editor who gamely espoused the "live toad theory." It holds that if you swallow a live toad as soon as you arrive at work, nothing else that happens can seem quite so bad. On an especially sour day, another colleague of mine left a note in the office mailbox of a late-arriving editor. "Flee while there's still time," the note warned.

Hearty souls though they may be, however, editors also need training and practice at making decisions. Beyond journalistic and managerial skills, editing calls for sound judgment, analytical thinking, and old-fashioned horse sense.

Most of us have these qualities—sometimes, in some quantities—but have trouble displaying them consistently in the face of newsroom crises.

Most editors, I am convinced, have good sides and bad sides. The good sides show at tension's low tide: early in the day after a good night's sleep, or in the local hangout after deadline, or at the podium before a local civic club. In those lucid and relaxed moments, editors can talk eloquently about the stresses of newspapering, the importance of civility, and the necessity, not to mention the cost-effectiveness, of treating people with respect.

But editors' bad sides come slinking from their caves when the pressure needle soars. Eyes darken. Tone of voice turns snappish. Graciousness yields to drill instruction. At these moments, which may come regularly on deadline, episodes that would seem trifling a few hours earlier trigger angry overreactions. Situations that could at better times be calmly reasoned out give rise to testy, forced-march resolutions.

Can we avoid this unfortunate, good side–bad side duality? Perhaps not entirely, given the daily news business. But editors *can*, it seems to me, equip themselves to respond as positively as possible to the duck-nibbles and hair-pullings of life in the newsroom.

In this chapter, we offer an introductory look at how editors can prepare to confront a variety of issues, from substantive areas like libel and news values to policy questions like nepotism and scheduling. Without attempting to solve every problem, we suggest some ways of thinking and planning that can help editors make their own conclusions in the best possible settings. Then, in the chapters that follow, we examine in more detail the editor's role as decision maker in several more specific areas.

MAKING DECISIONS: THE FOUNDATION

Responsible decision making is, of course, partly a function of basic competency. But it can be enhanced by paying attention to the setting where decisions must be made and by studying how decision making works best for each individual.

As just discussed, although newsrooms may never be ideal places for contemplative deliberation, some steps can be taken to smooth out the process. Knowing that the daily nibbles are adding up, editors can institute systems to keep from wasting time and to expeditiously handle arising dilemmas.

At the highest levels, management can help by laying a foundation of support for editor/decision makers. Newspaper people make hundreds of choices a day, many of them under tremendous pressure. So mistakes occur. Under a top management that second guesses too often, editors become gun shy and insecure. Under a top management that never critiques at all, they become lax. To achieve an optimum middle ground, publishers and senior editors can establish fair ground rules and procedures, select staff editors in whom they have confidence, and delegate authority to them to operate within the broad boundaries. Regular reviews should follow, but with a constructive tone and a goal of steady improvement, not finger pointing.

Even with their very tough jobs, editors can thrive in a supportive, team-oriented environment. Without the backing of their superiors, editors run scared, constantly looking over their shoulders. Decision making suffers. This principle holds all along the line: from publisher to top editors to section editors to line editors. At each step, support from above can free an editor to act with confidence and strength.

PROPERLY EQUIPPING THE NEWSROOM

This may seem an odd point to list so early. But having good equipment can save time, raise morale, and keep small issues from flaring into big ones.

Phil R. Currie, a veteran editor and executive for Gannett newspapers, put it this way:

> Don't let bad situations defeat morale and your people.
>
> I once was at a newspaper where some staffers were so concerned about the lack of security in the building at night that they couldn't concentrate on getting the paper out.
>
> I've been in newsrooms where systems, which were supposed to make it easier to get the newspaper out, have become so antiquated that they hinder getting the newspaper out.
>
> What can editors and publishers do about such problems? Fix them! (p. 30)[1]

I worked in one newsroom where making long-distance phone calls required special codes. A vital part of editors' jobs was making sure reporters had priority codes allowing quick phone access on deadline. Otherwise, the reporters were likely to hear a steady drone of busy signals—a sound maddening enough to goad deadline-frenzied reporters into heaving their phones across the room.

---

[1]Currie, P. R. (1984, April). The journalism of mismanagement. *ASNE Bulletin*, p. 30.

Newsrooms need secure work environments and operational phone systems (and *reliable* message takers). They also need such items as televisions, transistor radios, tape recorders, extra batteries, first-aid kits, maps, street directories, and petty cash for pay phones and cab fares. These days, they need working portable computer terminals for out-of-office assignments, and readily available technical help when computerized systems blow out, as they all will do from time to time.

In addition, newsrooms need manuals introducing new employees to the paper (spelling out not just style but also ethics and policies), dictionaries and other basic references, accessible addresses and phone numbers of employees and sources, files and filing systems, and a systematic, complete futures file. They need a good newspaper library, with trained researchers who understand, for instance, how to conduct reasonable, efficient database searches.

Organizing such logistical support *in advance* saves untold headaches in emergencies. If journalists can count on the raw materials to do their jobs, they become far less likely to burden editors with a steady drumbeat of minor crises to settle, to the detriment of more important activities.

STRATEGICALLY ALLOCATING TIME

Time pressures, more than anything else, expose the bad side of otherwise good editors. To make themselves less vulnerable to the inevitable exasperations of deadline, editors can learn some rudimentary techniques for self-organization.

To begin with, many editors install a simple filing system to serve as a reminder about appointments, story ideas and other tasks. It works as follows:

Assemble about 50 manila file folders. Label one "next year," and use it for any long-run reminders and ideas. For example, if after covering this year's July Fourth parade, you are inspired by how you could have done better, then jot down the idea and put it in next year's file to try.

Next, label one folder for each month of the year. Use those folders to store material relevant to a given month. For instance, if, in January, your city hires a new school superintendent, you might put a note in the July file to remind your education writer to take a look at how the superintendent is doing six months into the job.

Finally, label folders with the numbers 1 through 31, one for each day of the month. Use these folders to hold material you need during the current month. Check the appropriate folder daily, and carry over live material from one day to the next. At the end of every month, open the folder for the succeeding month, examine the contents, and redistribute the material as appropriate into your daily folders.

As another major organizational step, a good editor needs a *short-term plan* (for the next day's paper, for instance), a *medium-range plan* (covering the next few days or weeks), and a *long-range plan* (articulating best hopes and visions and how to accomplish them).

To each plan, the editor should set priorities and decide how best to allocate time. Write things down. The act itself helps fix objectives in mind. Obviously, an editor must allow plenty of flexibility and leave room for spontaneity.

A hint: Think of planning your work in the same way you might plan a cross-country vacation. You do not want to lock in every hour's activity, but you do want a general road map and some overall goals. Then, move toward your goals even as you allow room and time for the unpredictable.

Short-Term Goals.   Editors often seem to feel as if they are running on a treadmill, with little control and little progress. Simply coping with a typical day's routine can exhaust the editor's time. One defense is to write out a brief list of goals each day, and let those goals help determine the priority use of time. If at all possible, each day's goal should include at least one thing out of the ordinary: a serious discussion with a writer, one especially memorable headline, the planting of an idea for a great story. Challenge yourself every day.

Middle-Term Goals.   Do not settle for just making it to the weekend. Stretch. Setting modest, reachable goals each week can, over a year's time, for example, produce a body of significant accomplishment. An assignment editor's goal might be one outstanding article for each Sunday paper. A photo editor might rotate a half-day's free time among staffers each week to produce particularly artistic enterprise shots. A managing editor might set aside 2 hours for lunch to rev up an under-used staffer. Be ambitious, but also make your goals realistic ("to produce six excellent projects this year" is a better goal than "to win the Pulitzer Prize"). Good goal are those that you can achieve and that you will be proud of achieving.

Long-Term Goals.   My experience suggests that most editors maintain at least short- and medium-term plans, but many overlook the long term. Football coach John Madden described the value of such planning in a striking way when he recalled a conversation with legendary coach Vince Lombardi:

"What is there," I said, "that separates a good coach from a bad coach?"
    "Knowing what the end result looks like," Vince said. ". . . If you don't know what the end result is supposed to look like, you can't get there" (p. 224)[2]

---

[2]Madden, J. (1985). *Hey, wait a minute.* New York: Villard Books.

Through long-range planning, editors can envision how they want their papers to be and move step-by-step toward their visions. They can consider questions such as how to allocate time, space and other resources (a section editor, for instance, might specify percentages for publishing news, features, profiles, investigations and so forth); set goals for such things as lunching with staff members and sources; identify their two or three most pressing problems, rank them, and set up a battle plan.

Most importantly, by specifying medium- and long-range plans and sticking to them, editors help keep the short-run emergencies from devouring all their time. They also reduce the perennial frustration of "never getting anything accomplished."

Barbara Henry, editor of the *Rochester Democrat and Chronicle*, made the following observation about her first few years of management:

> I've learned that if I'm not organized, I end up not having the time to do the one thing I like doing best—participating in the daily news decisions and planning ways to make the paper better. (p. 3)[3]

Henry listed several suggestions for helping editors use time wisely:

• Plan the day before it begins
• Keep meetings short and to a purpose
• Give yourself deadlines
• Keep a detailed calendar
• Don't put off personnel decisions
• Delegate as much as possible

Notice her reference to *delegation*. Delegating is not something that comes naturally to all editors. As we have noted already, most journalists have personalities more suited to immediate, individualistic action than to sharing responsibilities, and their early years in the ranks serve to underscore that tendency. The typical reporter, for instance, prefers to work on a major story alone than to share it with colleagues. Journalism, especially the writing aspect, is inherently private. So incoming editors often lack the habit of delegating, and consequently overload themselves with work. Although in the short run this can seem to set a good example, in the long run it leads to burnout and ineffectiveness.

---

[3]Henry, B. (1986, July). Using time well means reader wins. *Gannetteer: Editorially Speaking*, p. 3.

Delegation does more than relieve the person doing the delegating. It also shows trust in the staff member receiving the delegation, serving to challenge and teach that person.

SETTING A TONE FOR GOOD COMMUNICATIONS

Walk into some newsrooms, and you instantaneously sense bad vibrations. Hostility and alienation leave a glow, almost an odor, that few people miss. In other cases, newsrooms seem warm and relaxed. Newcomers quickly spot these qualities, and old timers never forget them.

Ironically, considering that journalism depends on communication, editors often show remarkable insensitivity to problems in their own domains. As an editor, especially a beginning one, do not underestimate the importance of the tone you set. The best editors nurture a demanding but pleasant atmosphere that encourages free communication and that keeps channels open, even in the throes of deadline overload.

Editors can act in several ways to foster better newsroom communications. One way is by scheduling occasional meetings at which staff members can determine the agenda, question managers, and make suggestions. Another is by having open bulletin boards where staffers can display anything they like, from examples of good work to anonymous cartoons poking fun at management. A third idea is to distribute a newsletter every month or so, to which all staff is invited to contribute praise, criticism, and general discussion of newsroom matters.

Rule one is to make communication easy. Rule two is to make it happen. As an editor, you should:

• Communicate up (to your bosses), over (to your peers), and down (to your subordinates) every single day. The more you know about what people in the newsroom are doing and thinking, the better armed you are for helping them (and yourself) through the rough spots.

• Be clear about expectations—yours and theirs.

• Avoid surprises. Keep your superiors informed, and insist that staff members keep you informed.

• Debrief each other after a day's work or a tough assignment. Learn from successes and failures.

• Cultivate the idea that handling crises should be a team effort, not an individual burden.

• Know where you can turn for help, and who is likely to call on you.

• Strive toward consensus rather than conflict. Reward cooperation *and* constructive disagreement.

Sniff the air. Monitor the tone. In a divided, divisive newsroom, small complaints fester and decision making pays the price. In an open, team-spirited newsroom, petty irritants get swept aside, and even tough decisions come easier.

SHAPING A PERSONAL DECISION-MAKING MODEL

In the cooler moments, when the good side prevails, editors should think through how they like to make decisions. Most of us have some scheme, whether we articulate it or not, that helps us resolve dilemmas. With some reflection, editors may be able to identify theirs and to isolate its stages.

The more familiar they become with the steps in the model, the easier the model is to apply under fire.

Here, broken down into steps, is a simplified model for working through tricky issues.

A Decision-Making Model

1. Collect information and listen to all points of view. If possible, remain open-minded during the fact-finding stage.

2. Analyze the information. Isolate and focus on the central issues. Set aside the secondary ones. Consider motives, values, and consequences. Try to summarize the issue in a way that gets as close as possible to its heart.

3. Weigh all options, in light of your goals and values. Do not think only in extremes (for example: whether to front-page a gory news photo or leave it out altogether). Consider possible middle courses as well (whether to crop the photo and reduce the gore, to display it inside the paper instead of on the front, to run it a column smaller than your first instinct, and so on). Try to think creatively, looking at problems from all sides in search of solutions.

4. Solicit advice. Research the question as time permits. Others may have suggestions or experiences that apply. Sharing the problem also gives others a stake in solving it and, once a decision is reached, in making the decision succeed.

5. Make a decision, and specify the reason for it. Clarify to yourself and others the basis for your actions.

6. Explain and carry out the decision as positively and flexibly as possible, without trampling on people you may have overruled. A tendency arises at this stage of the process, especially when the decision may be unpopular or have taken long negotiation, to become impatient and gruff. By now, you will be tired of the process. But try to speak evenly, tolerate a suitable amount of

dissent, and avoid acting self-righteous or as if your decision is divinely inspired. This is a crucial stage, both in determining how enthusiastically the decision will be effected and in affecting whether people will remember your actions as fair and judicious or as arbitrary and divisive.

7. Follow up. Gently but firmly make certain the decision goes into effect and is carried out (even if not necessarily liked) by the staff.

8. Move on.

In summary, the steps are to *collect information, focus on the problem and consider the options, get appropriate help, make a decision, explain it, implement it, follow up* and *move forward.* By giving thought to their individual decision-making methods, editors can grow more comfortable with using them under pressure and can bring a consistency to their problem solving.

CONCLUSION

In my view, the *substance* of journalism should outstrip the *process.* That is, what matters most is what gets published and presented to the reader, not the gyrations journalists go through to produce their newspapers.

It need not concern readers that a computer malfunction required reworking a front-page headline at the last minute. All the readers notice is the unintelligible headline. It does not matter that the sports editor and the football reporter had a yelling match about how to handle the game story. All the reader expects is good, clear copy.

Results count. Therefore, I do not mean to overly encourage editors to lose themselves in the dynamics of decision making at the expense of concentrating on good journalism. Making plans, setting goals, and following models can, carried beyond moderation, generate unnecessary paperwork and create artificial impediments to a natural working style. No editor wants to spend all day shuffling paper and filling in forms.

But ignoring the process can carry high penalties. Good editors, generally not trained in making decisions and managing time, can save themselves terrible tribulation by understanding how and why decisions take hold. A small percentage of their time devoted to planning, thinking through objectives, and systematically attacking problems can keep an editor focused on the most important targets. If so, then time will actually be saved.

Of course, being prepared to make decisions does not necessarily produce wise choices. It can, however, dramatically reduce the stress and battle-zone nature of operating on deadline. Better substance should result.

In the next few chapters, we further explore the editor's role in reckoning with the full range of newsroom issues, beginning with the most pervasive of all: working with people.

SIDEBAR 4
HUMAN PERVERSITY

Editor & Publisher

Out of the goodness of his soul a newspaper man of our acquaintance bought a handsome ambulance and proceeded to operate it, in the name of his newspaper, for the benefit of suffering humanity of his town. Any sick or injured person could call for this ambulance and get a free ride. It was a beautiful charity, but soon there were complications.

A certain type of citizen, seeing the gilded chariot of the newspaper dashing through the streets on errands of mercy, would remark: "That's another way to get free advertising." One day a "regular subscriber" called up and wanted the ambulance in a hurry. The car had gone some distance into the country to bring into the hospital a woman near to death. This excuse was not satisfactory and the subscriber demanded that a taxi be sent to his house at the newspaper's expense, though he only had a stomach ache.

Another influential subscriber insisted that the ambulance call for him daily, though he was able to pay taxi fare to the hospital where he was being treated; indeed, he was found to be able to walk the short distance.

Each day brought a crop of complaints—but few evidences of public appreciation. The circulation department heard of a number of stops, due to the indignation of persons dissatisfied with the ambulance service.

The publisher has now turned the ambulance over to a hospital for operation. One learns much about human nature in newspaper work.[4]

---

[4]Human perversity. (1984, March 31). *Editor & Publisher,* p. 189. (Reprinted with permission.)

Making Decisions About People

5

For many editors, nothing consumes more time, energy, and emotion than the endless challenge of dealing with people. Every move an editor makes, from hiring a trainee to launching an investigation, to rewriting a lead, can ripple far into the newsroom and even into the community.

A moment of brilliance, often even unwitting, can transform a person's life. I once received a letter profusely thanking me for "saving the career" of a young man years earlier because of a chance remark (which I had by then forgotten) that inspired him to rededicate himself to journalism. Yet a careless misjudgement, or just bad managerial luck, can bring trauma to talented staff members, their families, and the newspaper.

Editors deal with all sorts of people: subscribers, advertisers, sources, subjects, applicants, subordinates, superiors, and many others. In this chapter, we limit our examination to two areas that seem especially relevant to the career editor: managing people in the modern workforce, and leading other journalists.

The first aspect involves management in the largest sense, hiring and firing, and training and supervising, and so on. The second involves management in a more localized sense, helping fellow writers and editors produce the best possible journalism.

MANAGING IN TODAY'S NEWSROOM

Not all editors manage, but most do. And the ability to manage—specifically, the ability to manage other *journalists*—stands among the most widely prized, yet difficult to come by, qualities in modern journalism.

As prior chapters have described, today's newspaper managers confront

64

ever-more-complex circumstances. In part, that stems from changes involving journalistic institutions (centralization of ownership, a sense of losing ground in the competition for people's time, greater scrutiny of finances, and the pressures that ensue), and in part from changes involving people (the so-called "yuppiefication" of the work force). James S. Ciavaglia of the *Asbury Park (NJ) Press,* cited two principal reasons for the changes. For one thing, he said, within the past decade newspaper owners have become more inclined to cut costs and push for efficient business operation. Second, "Attitudes have changed. We not have people in the business who are more attuned to financial rewards, fringe benefits, career goals and long-term planning. Managerially and administratively, more expertise is needed than ever before" (p. 11).[1]

John Epperheimer of the *San Jose Mercury News* observed, "The day has passed when you could give orders and expect that everyone would obey them without question" (p. 16).[2] Writing in the *Washington Journalism Review,* editor Susan Miller concluded that the "young and the restless" generation, roughly defined as those journalists in their 20s, stresses creativity, leisure time, and personal concerns, often at the expense of careers. She quoted *Chicago Tribune* editor James Squires as saying of this group, "The biggest management problem is motivation. They don't want to work overtime. They don't want to work bad hours. There's less determination to be first, because other things, like the quality of their time off, are important" (p. 36).[3]

Even without the contemporary complications, journalistic managers have never exactly won acclaim. In an excellent book entitled *Newsroom Management,* veteran editor Robert H. Giles recalled noticing throughout his career that "we put out pretty good newspapers, but we don't give much thought to managing people." By now, according to Giles, the problem has become excessive:

> Insensitive management has driven thousands of talented, bright, hard-working journalists from daily newspaper jobs ... Publishers and senior editors were slow to recognize the features of newsroom life that were creating the talent drain: high stress, low pay, lack of opportunity for growth, uncaring management. (p. x)[4]

One panelist told a Society of Professional Journalists audience that bad management had driven more people out of journalism than poor salaries (p. 68).[5]

---

[1]Tadie, V. (1984, February). Management: Editors changing their tune, *presstime,* p. 11.

[2]Stein, M. L. (1987, February 7). The "yuppiefication" of the newsroom. *Editor & Publisher,* p. 16.

[3]Miller, S. (1985, October). The young and the restless. *Washington Journalism Review,* p. 36.

[4]Giles, R. H. (1987). *Newsroom management.* Indianapolis, IN: R. J. Berg.

[5]You say you want a revolution? (1987, November). *The Quill,* p. 68.

Evidence of disaffection at the editing level emerged in a 1986 study of copyeditors by the American Society of Newspaper Editors. Among the findings were the following: 53% felt they did not have adequate time for editing; 45% felt the desk lacked clout in the newsroom; 29% felt senior editors did not support the desk; and 80% labeled their feedback as only "occasional" or "rare" (pp. 4–8).[6]

In the survey, copyeditors offered testimony to some of the frustrations of desk work. Among their comments were the following:

Copyeditors need more clout and more backing from management. All too often, they are looked upon as gadflys and irritants, and their judgment is constantly overruled. We are treated as little more than spelling checkers or proofreaders.

Supervisors must learn copyeditors are not all broken-down, tired reporters who wish to spend their last few years before retirement at the desk. There are people who have chosen this job and who spend time trying to improve their skills. (pp. 18–19)[7]

Under these circumstances, managing a newsroom would challenge even the best-trained executives. Journalists, however, tend to advance with little training in management, human relations, and organizational skills. Not even the current popularity of advanced business degrees solves the problem, because what is most needed is journalists who can manage, not managers who can learn journalism. Journalistic values and skills remain the most fundamental qualifications for editing. The task for the coming generation is to systematically add to those basic values a working appreciation of the techniques and subtleties of managing other news people.

Where does an editor or aspiring editor begin in learning to manage?

Editor Janet A. Mittelstadt listed three essential management traits: "(1) communications skills (questioning, listening, oral,written, interviewing, and meeting leadership); (2) problem-solving and decision-making skills; and (3) coaching skills (p. 26).[8]

Robert H. Giles, in his previously mentioned book, identified five general principles at the heart of a philosophy of newsroom management. They can be summarized as follows:

---

[6]Cunningham, L. G. (1987, May/June). It is time to bring the newsroom's "stepchildren" into the family circle. *ASNE Bulletin*, pp. 4–8.

[7]Mittelstadt, J. (1987, November). If I were managing editor. . . . *ASNE Bulletin*, pp. 18–19.

[8]Mittelstadt, J. A. (1985, October). Even editors can learn—and improve—management skills. *ASNE Bulletin*, p. 26.

1. All people are different.
2. There is no best way.
3. Behavior can be changed but personalities cannot, and editors must deal with a variety of personalities.
4. Perfection with people is impossible.
5. Natural motivations (such as the drive to achieve) are more powerful than artificial ones (p. 9).[9]

Building on such overall understandings, editors then must develop their own styles and strategies for coping with the range of management obligations in the newsroom such as recruiting and hiring, supervising and evaluating people, and dealing with stress.

We examine some of these issues more closely in the following sections.

Developing a Management Style

Trust Yourself

Managing, like so many other activities, begins with that Emersonian injunction. Like it or not, your management style will in all likelihood reflect your personality. So build on that. Be yourself, and operate in a way that comes naturally.

Take charge. Make the tough decisions. Have the confidence and security to behave as though you actually believe you should be the boss. But do not become consumed or obsessive. Keep your sense of humor. Remain flexible. Do not bully others. Admit mistakes. Do not get your ego so engaged that every issue becomes a psychological tug of war.

Robert M. Stiff, a veteran Florida editor, once summarized his management style as follows:

I have no philosophy of management but I have a golden rule.

I try to manage with sensitivity and treat my staff as I wanted to be treated when I wasn't an editor. I praise in public and criticize in private—and do both frequently. The staff needs to know I read every section regularly.

My door is always open and even if it means staying very late to finish what I'm doing, if a staffer says, "Do you have a minute?" I always do.

I seldom lose my temper, insist on staffers having fun at their jobs, take a personal interest in them, keep them informed about what is happening, never lie to them, try to treat them fairly, try to pay them what they're worth within budget

---

[9]Giles, R. H. (1987). *Newsroom management*. Indianapolis, IN: R. J. Berg.

constraints and let them know they have disappointed me deeply when they screw up. (p. 6)[10]

A key concept in management is simply *respect,* for yourself and those persons around you. "Talk to us regularly," responded a copyeditor to the 1986 American Society of Newspaper Editors survey. "The worst thing about editing is its invisibility—and when you're invisible to the big boss, too, it's doubly frustrating" (p. 19).[11]

Editors have much to gain by remembering the proverbial golden rule of managing: Treat your employees as you want your boss to treat you. However, following that rule raises the obvious question of what today's journalists want from their employers.

What Do Journalists Want From Employers?   Typically, they want respect; trust; challenge; reasonable working conditions; clear direction; candid feedback; some say in schedules and assignments; and a sense of working someplace special. They want better pay and opportunity for advancement. They want more stability than newsrooms have traditionally afforded, so that they do not feel compelled to move on to a bigger paper every 2 or 3 years or to drop out of the profession when it comes time to pay children's college costs. And they want greater appreciation of their professionalism and less exploitation of their commitment to working 50- and 60-hour weeks without extra compensation.

Managers may or may not deliver on all these desires, but they should begin by understanding them and taking them seriously. Editors in particular often feel that they are invisible (unless they make a mistake). Simply being listened to and noticed will help. In turn, managers have the right to their own expectations, and employees must respect and appreciate them.

What Do Today's Managers Want From Staff Members?   They want commitment to a profession whose relentlessness leaves little margin for error or slack. They want hard, fast, accurate, thoughtful work. They want people who are both tenacious and flexible, creative and open to direction, tough and fair, individualists when appropriate and team players when necessary.

Nobody who has ever worked in a newsroom remotely expects utopia, of course. But editors must face up to this hard-headed fact: Newsrooms can be managed more effectively than in the past and, whatever the obstacles, it is the responsibility of editors to do it. Whatever management problems exist in a newsroom may stem from inadequate resources, prima donna staff members,

---

[10]Musings from editor-managers on their management styles. (1981, March). *ASNE Bulletin,* p. 6.

[11]Mittelstadt, J. (1987, November). If I were managing editor. . . . *ASNE Bulletin.*

lack of support from ownership, or a host of other sources beginning with the unflinching dailiness of the job. But, as the newsrooms' problem solvers, editors have the duty of analyzing whatever problems they find and then working as constructively as possible to relieve them.

Take Responsibility

So, if the first rule in management is trust yourself, the second is take responsibility. Forget pointing fingers or looking for scapegoats. Set aside, as much as possible, the excuse, "I didn't have time." Figure out what your goals are and what you can change or control to move toward them.

Here are some additional suggestions for managing effectively. They apply whether you are the assistant features editor or the managing editor or head of the three-person Bumpkin County Bureau:

• Forget both dictatorship and democracy. Today's highly educated, self-aware journalists would not stand for old-fashioned authoritarianism, but they do not like drift and wimpiness either. They accept the authority of the boss, as long as they feel heard and respected. Make it clear that you are in charge, but that you need and want their help.

• Promote teamwork. Cultivate the idea that everyone is in the game together, for the same goals. Harness collective energy, for example by convincing copyeditors and reporters to be collaborators not antagonists. Or by giving employees a chance to help set policies on such things as weekend scheduling or how to allocate new newsroom positions.

• Explain and discuss. Have you ever, in jobs you have held or classes you have taken, felt you knew as much as you wanted to about what your boss or teacher was thinking? Neither has anyone else. Few management sins are as universal as underestimating how important a few words from the boss can be.

• Praise people; criticize work. Writing coach Roy Peter Clark often asks groups of journalists, "How many people here think they get *too much* praise?" I do not think anyone has ever raised a hand. At the same time, most journalists thirst for constructive feedback. For the manager, the most effective course can be to personalize praise and to depersonalize criticism: "*You* wrote an excellent headline yesterday," but "I'm not sure this lead is as effective as *it* could be."

• Play fair. Listen to complaints, and recognize that people encounter personal problems. In your newsroom, try to set a humane tone. But keep an appropriate distance from staff members and make clear that you expect professionalism on the job.

• Stay close to the action. Be visible, and talk privately to find out what is on people's minds. It is often said that one primary rule of managing is to get out of your chair.

• Do not neglect "managing up," keeping your superiors informed. Follow the "no surprise" rule and insist your staff follow it, so that everyone is kept informed about major developments, changes, and decisions. Nothing makes top editors' blood boil hotter than to get flooded with complaints about stories they did not even know about. Nothing riles reporters faster than not being informed of major rewrites before stories get published.

• Watch the details and the little things. Is the parking lot well lighted? Does the company snack bar close before the copydesk goes home? Does anyone ever put notes on bulletin boards praising good writing, clever headlines, intrepid work by a photographer?

• Watch the big things. Does the city editor play favorites? Does a key staffer have a drinking problem? Is sexism tolerated in the newsroom? Has your pay scale been the same for 5 years?

• Give people an opportunity to influence you and your policies. As editor Walker Lundy has written, "Give an employee's ego a way out of every discussion" (p. 3).[12] If you and a staff member disagree, for example, explain that he or she may be right but you are not yet convinced. Transfer to the staffer the burden of providing evidence to convince you.

• Do not go it alone. Consult with subordinates and superiors about key decisions. Use available resources such as company personnel specialists or psychologists, people with relevant experience in other newsrooms or elsewhere, outside experts such as university people.

• Do not play God. Do not try to convince subordinates that superior wisdom and infallibility underlie every decision you make. They will not buy it. A common management error, especially in newsrooms, is to phrase issues in terms of "right" and "wrong": "Your story is written all wrong, and I'm going to show you how to make it right." Instead, acknowledge that journalism is often subjective, and explain that you take your responsibilities seriously and are doing what you believe to be best. Enforce your decisions, even unpopular ones, because that is your job. But don't presume that your decisions are necessarily any smarter or righter than anyone else's.

Coping With Newsroom Problems

In any enterprise, journalism included, the range of potential problems may be unlimited. However, we can identify several newsroom issues that are universal and fundamental enough to merit individual consideration here. They include recruiting and hiring; supervising and evaluating; and handling the inevitable stress of the business.

---

[12]Lundy, W. (1981, March). How should managers manage managing? *ASNE Bulletin,* p. 3.

Recruiting and Hiring. Not all editors participate in formal recruitment or hiring, but almost all can or should have some say in those processes. Whether it is in attracting an individual to the newspaper itself or deciding which two reporters to pair on a special project, editors need the knack of appraising and positioning people. Here are some observations that may fit editors' needs.

- Make recruitment an affirmative process. Do not just wait for wonderful applicants to come to you. Create a network and work it regularly. Visit key journalism schools, read college newspapers, track the best students, encourage them to stay in touch with you. Cultivate contacts in other regions and work the grapevine to learn who the best journalists are at papers just beneath your own. Keep clear, complete files of good candidates.

  In addition, and this is often overlooked, make sure you know the aspirations and abilities of existing staff members, who often make excellent candidates for other jobs. Take special pains to identify prospective candidates for which you may have a special need, such as members of minorities or potential female managers.

- Always be ready to take advantage of an opportunity. Despite your most systematic exertions, hiring often is a matter of timing and luck. One day a reporter quits, and the managing editor cannot decide whether to fill the position or to use the money to buy new computers. If you have an appropriate candidate already in mind and have done the preliminary screening, your readiness can determine whether you get or lose the position.

- Be thorough. When considering an applicant, read clips, check references, ask nonreferences who might know the candidate. Ask staff members for advice. Involve several people in the interview process and value their impressions. Give tryouts wherever possible. Hiring someone can be a lifelong, hundreds-of-thousands-of-dollars decision, and it should seldom happen merely because an applicant makes a good impression over lunch.

- Make job interviews revealing. You want to get beyond stock answers and predictable situations. Sandra Rowe of the Norfolk, Virginia, papers recommended such probes as "What kind of situation most often makes you angry? Describe a recent failure. What accomplishment are you most proud of? What type of person do you have the most difficulty working with?" (p. 17).[13]

- Hire brains. Editors have an endless list of qualities they seek in applicants.

---

[13]Rowe, S. M. (1984, September). "We are too squeamish about asking questions" on personality, background, behavior. *ASNE Bulletin*, p. 17.

But few are more important than hiring smart people with a demonstrated commitment to journalism.

- Listen for "bells." I do not know whether this accords with orthodox personnel theory, but it used to work for me. More often than not, outstanding candidates will in some way set off special "bells" in your head, by the quality of their work, the excitement of their minds, or just some intangible measure of personal electricity. Good applicants should somehow make a strong and arousing impression. Don't settle for the mundane. If you do not have a candidate you feel excited about hiring, keep looking, and listening.

Supervising and Evaluating. Veteran *Newsday* reporter and editor Bob Greene once said that managing journalists is like herding goldfish. They are slippery little devils with cantankerous, independent natures. Managers who value journalists for their tenacity and skepticism outside the newsroom should not flinch when those same traits arise within it, often aimed squarely at management. To supervise such people requires what often has been called "tough love": thick-skinned editors who set firm standards, push relentlessly for excellence, relish the give-and-take of intellectual combat, know when to intervene and when to leave alone, and understand as if by instinct when to exhort and when to mollify.

The following advice is aimed at helping editors with motivation and oversight of subordinates and staff members:

- Try to understand each staff member's goals and needs. David McClelland has identified three fundamental motivations for workers: the need for achievement, affiliation, or power (p. 37).[14] Recognizing which drive is motivating a particular individual can help you tailor a successful management approach. The adage, "Treat everybody alike," certainly holds in terms of fairness, but it remains important to remember that each individual has different strengths, styles, dreams, and fears.

- Listen carefully. Whether you are making a photo assignment, revising a reporter's lead, setting a story's length, or transferring someone from one bureau to another, the person involved will probably have stronger feelings than you expect. Listen to those feelings, think about them, put yourself in the employee's place. Many editors are so itchy to dispose of an issue and move on that they fidget, scowl, interrupt, and react in other ways that reduce their ability to listen. Try not to reveal your own feelings until the staff member has finished. Then respond. Even if you stand absolutely firm, sent employees away thinking they have received a fair hearing.

---

[14]Sohn, A. B., Ogan, C. L., Polich, J. (1986). *Newspaper leadership*. Englewood Cliffs, NJ: Prentice-Hall.

• Set clear goals and offer regular evaluations. Think of this point in both short-range and long-range terms. In the short run, you should make clear assignments and give employees routine feedback so they know how well they meet your expectations. Over the long run, you should provide periodic formal evaluations, in private, in which you review the standards and the employees' performance. Be specific, candid, and constructive, using examples to document both praise and criticism. Do not be cruel and do speak softly, but make certain that employees, including those who are failing, know where they stand with you and, vitally, what they can do to improve in your eyes. Most employees are willing to modify their work to better please their bosses, but they cannot make those changes unless they know what the boss wants.

• Remember the 14th Amendment. That's the one that stresses "due process of law" and "equal protection of the laws." Treat all employees equally and fairly. And follow an orderly process of dealing with problems. The two worst things you can do if people are not meeting your standards are, first, nothing (a festering problem only worsens) and, second, overreaction (such as firing without warning). Instead, devise your own systematic due process. Discuss the problem; develop a plan and timetable for improvement; offer assistance and monitor the employee's progress; and then, after a reasonable period, decide whether further action is needed.

Managing Stress. In chapter 1, we saw evidence that newsroom stress can breed high tension, early burnout, and serious health problems. A 1983 survey for the Associated Press Managing Editors, quoted in the *Newsroom Management Handbook* published by the American Society of Newspaper Editors, identified three basic aspects of stress for editors: (a) the environment in which editors work, including relationships with boss and staff, company values and policies, and their range of authority and control; (b) editors' personal vulnerability to stress, encompassing factors such as age, self-image, physical and mental health, and experience with stress; and (c) actual stressful situations, such as work load, time pressure, staff problems, lack of recognition, responsibility versus authority, conflicting demands, and confrontation (pp. 2–3).[15]

In addition, as we noted in chapter 1, editors can also induce stress in others, through their management styles. Author Bob Baker listed several ways in which subordinate writers and editors can experience such anxiety: unpredictable overtime, night work, distrust of editors, lack of leadership or direction from editors, inability to meet or understand expectations, pressure for productivity at the expense of quality, boredom, and the need to play office politics in order to advance (pp. 188–189).[16]

---

[15]Giles, R. H. (1985). Burnout and stress. In *Newsroom management handbook* (section 17, pp. 2–3). Washington, DC: American Society of Newspaper Editors Foundation.

[16]Baker, B. (1981). *Newsthinking: The secret of great newswriting.* Cincinnati: Writer's Digest Books.

Given the inherent pressures of the job, editors will never banish stress from the newsroom. In fact, a certain level of stress helps account for the exhilaration and excitement that makes journalism so satisfying. What the good editor can try is to contain and manage stress, to keep it within reasonable limits, and to help others cope as well.

The further away I have gotten from daily newspaper editing, the more destructive and inexcusable the high-stress newsroom environment has seemed to me. Although newspapering is inevitably pressurized, some editors pour on unnecessary fuel by condoning Stone Age management styles: cutting remarks; macho city-editor crudeness; contempt for family and free-time needs; and petty battles over space, time, and assignments. Good editors can do a great deal to reverse much of the inattention and misplaced priority that aggravate the naturally high stress levels.

Writing in the *Washington Journalism Review,* Michael Wines offered the following sobering view of the effects of stress in the newsroom:

> The most visible results of job pressures are early deaths, alcoholism and drug abuse and even occasional suicides, but stress-related illness among both reporters and editors is far more widespread than those extremes would indicate, therapists say.
>
> Some of them say journalists seem prone to certain kinds of mental problems linked to stress: depression, self-destructiveness, marital problems, difficulty in switching from the objective deadpan of the newsroom to the intimacy of personal life. One expert even blames stress for that bane of the writing craft, hackneyed phrases. "It makes you write in cliches," he says. "You get desperate—it actually affects your choice of words." (p. 35)[17]

Because of their roles as decision makers, editors can be both victims and inflicters of stress. They need to fortify themselves with precautions against both spreading and absorbing it. Some suggestions, which editors can apply to themselves and recommend to others, include the following:

- Live a balanced life. Eat and sleep properly. Set aside time for relaxation, family, and social events. Exercise regularly. Develop a hobby. Steal a few minutes from a busy day to take a brisk walk, make a personal phone call or listen to some music.
- Share. Do not bottle up anxieties and frustrations. Do not feel responsible for every mistake and dilemma in the newsroom. Communicate. Delegate. Consider yourself part of a team, not the Lonesome End.
- Never lose your sense of humor.

---

[17]Wines, M. (1986, May). Burnout in the newsroom. *Washington Journalism Review,* p. 35.

- Set reasonable goals, and work toward them systematically. Do not constantly over pressure yourself.
- Solve one problem at a time. Break large problems (the publisher's criticism of your news coverage) into a series of smaller problems that you can tackle one by one (setting new goals for the city desk; adding one new enterprise story a week; improving coverage of high school sports).
- Imagine how you want things to be in 1 year, 5 years, or 10 years. Then, as Thoreau said, move toward your dreams.
- Get away from journalism and journalists. Have a separate social circle. Eat lunch with someone new. Take a course in religion or physics.
- Be positive. Accept your own anger and failings and those of others. Do not compromise your standards or settle for mediocrity, but keep life in context, expect some adversity, focus on what you can control, and do not dwell on the past.
- Have a long view. Perhaps some problems *do* deserve major-league fretting (the $10-million libel suit filed because you misedited a story). But most do not. Journalists spend a great deal of time worrying over whether paragraph 6 should be paragraph 11, or whether a story should be 12 or 18 inches long, or whether the managing editor likes the city editor better than the features editor, or whether my lead is better than yours. A managing editor I once worked for would periodically cruise through the newsroom saying, "In a hundred years, we'll all be dead." That did help put things into perspective.

Management, in Summary

Overall, management can be considered a weak point in many newsrooms and for many editors, but it also provides opportunity to dramatically influence people and improve journalism.

Editors who want to improve as managers can take to heart this good overview, quoted from the *Scripps Howard News,* which concluded with three fundamental facts of management:

- Management consists of achieving things through other people, not doing things yourself.
- To the extent that there is satisfaction in management, it comes from helping other people improve their performance.
- The best predictor of success for a manager is a group of employees who believe their manager cares about them and wants them to succeed (p. 2).[18]

---

[18]Can you confess to these management sins? (1987, February). *The Editors' Exchange,* p. 2.

LEADING OTHER JOURNALISTS

Editors do not manage in a vacuum; they manage in a newsroom. And although journalists have much in common with all other workers, today's reporters and editors also inherit a special tradition. By that tradition, they exalt First Amendment values of independence and idiosyncrasy, elevate individualism, resist corporatization, and regard affiliation with the paper as a kind of loose confederation of kindred free spirits rather than a synchronized workforce under central command. They are not easily managed, but—crusaders and missionaries at heart—they stand ready to be led.

The editor tossed into a leadership role should remember two general (although not universal) qualities of the contemporary journalist:

1. The typical journalist chose the business for reasons that are nonmaterial. While compensation and working conditions play a growing role in career calculations, most journalists are, underneath it all, reform-minded writers who feel they have something important to say and who appreciate help in saying it.

2. Journalists do not see newspapering as only a business, or even as primarily a business. They see it as a public-spirited enterprise with special social responsibility, in the words of A. J. Liebling "a privately owned public utility" (p. 31).[19]

As we saw in chapter 3, editors enter this equation at some peril, generally experiencing bittersweet relationships with the reporters, photographers, and others they supervise. Officially, they must carry the corporate mandate and the corresponding power to act as boss. Unofficially, having not forgotten their own rank-and-file sensibilities, they must captain their unruly shock troops with a deft combination of empathy, exhortation, and example.

Because journalists increasingly see themselves as professionals, they expect to have a large say in their duties. Rather than hired hands to be ordered into action at an editor's whim, they prefer being considered specialists to whom editors turn for needed expertise.

Most often, this scenario plays out in terms of individual editor–writer relationships. Therefore, we now examine how editors can bolster their capacity to lead their colleague/subordinates.

---

[19]Liebling, A. J. (1961). *The press*. New York: Ballantine.

Helping Versus Hindering

In an extraordinary helpful volume called *How I Wrote The Story,* writing teacher Donald Murray and staff members of the *Providence Journal-Bulletin* shared their insights into what editors should and should not do in trying to help writers.[20]

They suggested that editors listen open-mindedly to writers; ask questions and stimulate ideas; let writers know, without nagging, that the editor is available to help; suggest approaches without demanding them; challenge writers' assumptions; help locate holes in stories; and change copy only when change is needed.

"Remember," they wrote, "that psychologically bad editing is far worse than technically bad editing. An editing mistake may be remembered by the writer for a week; a mistake in handling the writer may be remembered for a lifetime."

They also pointed out actions by editors that hinder writers. Among the problems cited were inflexibility in assignments, unrealistic deadlines, overly preconceived story ideas, failure to listen, unnecessary tinkering with copy, condescending or defensive approaches to the writer, mistakes inserted into copy, and editing without conferring with the writer.

Heeding some of these suggestions, the Providence staff members concluded, could help at "achieving a lasting truce between these natural enemies of the newsroom."

Similar words could be written about the relationships editors have with other constituences: subordinate editors, designers, photographers, and others. Utmost concern must go toward establishing positive bonds.

Coaching and Teaching

Roy Peter Clark and Don Fry, two sensitive and thoughtful writing coaches at the Poynter Institute in St. Petersburg, Florida, have become fervent apostles of what they call "the human side of editing."[21] Donald Murray, in a similar vein, encourages what he called "consultive editing" (p. 33).[22]

All three equate the editor with the "coach," an apt metaphor conjuring the image of a stern but loving teacher and taskmaster.

---

[20]The quotes and suggestions in this section are taken from Scanlan, C. (Ed.), (1986). *How I wrote the story* (pp. 15–18). Providence, RI: Providence Journal Co.

[21]Clark, R. P. (1987, April). *The editor as writing coach.* Paper presented at the American Society of Newspaper Editors convention, San Francisco, CA.

[22]Murray, D. M. (1986). Consultive editing. In C. Scanlan (Ed.), *How I wrote the story* (p. 33). Providence, RI: Providence Journal Co.

The image of the editor as coach-teacher is appealing, but it is interesting to note how differently editors and reporters may come to it. Editors tend to feel they already do a great deal of coaching. Reporters tend to want much more.

In a study reported in 1987, researchers asked the same questions to a group of reporters and editors. The results were instructive. When asked whether "editors understand the importance of their teaching role at my newspaper," 39% of editors said yes, but only 15% of reporters agreed. When asked to rate dialogue between editors and reporters, 42% of reporters said there was little or none, compared to only 17% of editors. And when asked how much "positive criticism" editors offered, 60% of reporters replied little or none, compared to 29% of editors (pp. 21–22).[23]

Although widely acknowledging the importance of coaching, writers and editors may differ on how much is enough. Based on the study just described, as well as conversations with numerous editors and writers, it seems fair to conclude that editors believe they coach more than writers give credit for and that writers want more feedback than they now get.

Clark, Fry, Murray, and others offer useful advice on how to improve coaching, beginning with the idea that writing and editing are collaborative processes. The opposite view, of the editor as tyrant, was grippingly expressed by Heywood Broun in a 1920s column reprinted by *The Guild Reporter*. Broun wrote of covering a small story, writing it painstakingly ("as I settled down to my machine playing it as some of the masters play Chopin"), and then turning it over to "the big man at the desk":

> The copy reader took out a long, keen knife and sharpened several pencils . . . . Yawning slightly, he got to work . . . . He lingered over this opening sentence. I wondered why . . . Finally, the man drew his thickest pencil and throwing all the power of his back and shoulders into the stoke he slashed my copy. Probably it was my ears alone which heard the horrid sound of blood dripping to the floor. . . . 'I did it for *The World*,' I murmured and fainted quietly upon my desk. (p. 7)[24]

Today, the good editor operates quite differently, of course. But, as Broun's column vividly conveys, editors should never forget that every writer feels a trembly, sweaty dread in relinquishing beloved copy to an editor's foreign hands.

Much of this fear can and should be offset by early reporter-editor consultation. In later chapters, we discuss making clear assignments and monitoring

---

[23]Gaziano, C., & Coulson, D. C. (1987, August). *Effect of newsroom management styles on journalists: A case study of two newspapers*. Paper presented at the Association for Education in Journalism and Mass Communication, San Antonio, TX.

[24]Broun, H. (1975, October 24). The copy reader . . . sharpened 7 pencils. *The Guild Reporter*, p. 7.

reporters' progress. For now, we can summarize by citing Murray's astute advice that editors consult with reporters at six points: at the assignment, during the reporting, before the first draft, at delivery of the draft, after reading the draft, and after publication (p. 34).[25] Such close communication helps insure that neither reporter nor editor will be surprised as the process plays out.

It is important to note that reporter–editor conversations can take place quickly. Extended, sit-down discussions, although sometimes helpful, are not at all required. A 30-second dialogue focused on a specific problem ("What's the point of your story?" "Can you help me with this second paragraph?") can pinpoint key issues and align the thinking of both parties.

Roy Peter Clark advised editors to confer quickly (in what he calls "30-second, 90-second, 5-minute bursts of activity"). He also recommended that they isolate the biggest problem and help solve it; ask questions to identify problems but turn responsibility for changes back to the writer; be predictable, asking key questions over and over; and insure that no evil consequences flow from reporters' sharing with editors.[26]

Through such continuing conversations, editors and writers develop mutual trust, make each other's lives easier, reduce strains, and lower the likelihood of error or misunderstanding. They build the bonds that can last far beyond today's passing story.

None of this advice is meant to lessen the editor's responsibility to be in charge, to be the boss. For all the sensitivity that editors need, they also require decisiveness and determination. Not everything is negotiable. Entrusted with responsibility for all or part of important business activities, they cannot shirk the burdens of production and performance. Inevitably, editors will disappoint, anger, overrule, and overpower others. But others in the newsroom recognize this imperative, and they respect it.

It is not *that* an editor must lead that is at issue, but *how* the editor does it. Like good coaches and teachers, good editors realize they are not operating democracies, but they strive to execute their responsibilities with respect and appreciation for their colleagues.

CONCLUSION

In this chapter, we began by considering management in a rather broad sense: What are some strategies for the supervision of employees by a designated superior? Then, we added some particular considerations for managers within a newsroom: What makes journalists peculiarly hard to manage, and what methods help?

---

[25]Murray, D. M. (1986). Consultive editing. In C. Scanlan (Ed.), *How I wrote the story*. Providence, RI: Providence Journal Co.

[26]Clark, R. P. (1987, April). *The editor as writing coach*. Paper presented at the American Society of Newspaper Editors Convention, San Francisco, CA.

Effort has intensified over recent years to remedy some longstanding news-room management problems, but much work remains. Surveying the record on the topic, Professor Gerald Stone concluded:

> Although research has documented journalists' desire for greater feedback from supervisors, more involvement in decision making and better access to methods of attaining job growth (continuing education, for instance), there is little evidence these roads to job satisfaction are being adequately provided. . . . Recent interest in newspaper management is certainly a good sign, but it is unclear if these developments will be sufficient to fill the near-void in newspaper management that has existed. (pp. 98–99)[27]

Consequently, developing strong management techniques can give any editor an important head start and can clear time and energy for the more enjoyable aspects of the job. As a good manager, however, the aspiring editor is only partially equipped for duty. As important as people skills are, nothing substitutes for strong journalistic skills as well. The new editor must suitably combine an ability to manage with competence at the many other demands of the business.

In the next few chapters, we examine how a full understanding of news, copy, and design can help round out the development of the editor.

SIDEBAR 5
EDITORS MUSE ON THEIR MANAGEMENT STYLES

The *ASNE Bulletin* asked several editors to describe their styles of management. Two interesting contributions came from Neal Shine of Detroit and James Squires of Chicago:

Neal J. Shine, *Detroit Free Press*

I've long felt that management skills and management style are quite different. Skills are things you find in the American Management Association catalogue. Go—on company expense—some place nice, like San Francisco, to acquire them.

Style, on the other hand, is not an acquired skill. It's genetic. The management styles we've got—for better or worse—are the ones we were born with. Style's a function of personality; it's not easy to change either one.

(Continued)

---

[27]Stone, G. (1987). *Examining newspapers.* Newbury Park, CA: Sage.

Sidebar 5 (*Continued*)

In 30 years, I have worked under a number of management styles: "The Head Coach" ("It's first and 10, team, so let's move the ball!"), "The Cheops Foreman" ("Unless we all pull harder, people, we'll never put this baby together") and "Murder Inc." ("The next sonofabitch who writes a lead like this is a dead sonofabitch!").

And many more.

I'd call my management style Celtic Contemporary. An approach that combines the best of St. Patrick and Brendan Behan. Under this style, it's important to have an office big enough for a conference table. If people hold a lot of meetings in your office and staffers use it for interviews and to eat lunch and watch TV and to call their friends from a phone where the religion writer can't overhear them, then you've solved the problem of access. After all that, you haven't got an office, you've got a day room—and that's good.

This style requires instant availability and undivided attention for problems of alienation, frustration, personal finance, domestic turmoil, career and/or identity crises, and afflictions based on the real or imagined fear that the copydesk is out to get you. It calls for dealing not only with the walk-ins and referrals, but making desk calls a few times a week to reach those who don't reach you.

Like most other editors I know, I'd rather edit than manage. Managing produces the same emotional rewards as ritual scarring. But both editing and managing are vital, and good management is really nothing more than the soft side of editing.

James D. Squires, *Chicago Tribune*

Our newspaper is big on training and development in management techniques—most of which I've found valuable in advertising, circulation and production but totally useless in trying to manage reporters and editors. Therefore I have developed my own. It's called "flexible."

My management style was born in self-defense when, at age 25, I became city editor of the *Nashville Tennessean* and realized I had no idea what I was doing. I took the coward's way out and asked the staff what I should do.

It worked. The same "let's-all-get-together-and-do-my-job" approach has stayed with me through several positions for which I've been similarly unprepared.

My staff has helped me manage because I needed help and asked for it. I hate arbitrary decisions and will go to great lengths to avoid anything resembling autocracy.

I prefer to work as the member of the team who has the final say but never has to exercise it. I try to forge a consensus that becomes clear to an overwhelming majority.

(*Continued*)

Sidebar 5 (*Continued*)

Of all the so-called "management schools," I prefer the touch system which dictates a completely open-door, candid approach that touches all employees and treats them as equals—but which also keeps me in trouble constantly.

I try to stay visible and active at virtually every level, not for the purpose of looking over a manager's shoulder but of keeping myself informed. This is viewed as meddling by some. But I have never been able to condition myself to be surprised by what I read in our paper.

I spend my time trying to get the best possible people in place and working alongside them in a common effort. The result usually takes care of itself. The key to success is the quality of the people being managed. I try to attract the best and then make sure they all talk to each other—and to me.[28]

---

[28]Anderson G. (1981, March). Musings from editor-managers on their management styles. *ASNE Bulletin*, pp. 5–6. (Reprinted with permission.)

Making Decisions About Coverage

If one views a 48-page newspaper or a 22-minute newscast from afar, it may seem like a bottomless well, with plenty of room for everything and with another opportunity tomorrow for material that cannot be included today. Closer up, however, editors stare at a grimmer reality: Every issue or program confronts finite, inflexible space and time boundaries that require editors to make constant, sometimes brutal priority decisions among volumes of material competing for inclusion. It is no exaggeration to say that a huge (and, to the audience, invisible) part of editing is deciding what not to publish.

In this way, editing may seem like murder. Every day, editors must kill ideas, half-done stories, finished copy. Functioning like triage officers at a disaster scene, editors reach rapid-fire verdicts about which story tips to pursue and which to dismiss, which reporters to count on and which to suspect, which projects to accelerate and which to drop, which articles to publish and which to delay or withhold.

Typically, we call this *gatekeeping,* or the exercising of *new judgment.* Bear in mind that not all editors deal in news in the strict sense. Some manage feature desks or sports sections or editorial pages, where content definitions differ. In all such editing jobs, however, the gatekeeping responsibility remains the same: Editors must understand the demands and standards of their part of the publication and then make choices that most likely will produce copy that complies.

To exercise gatekeeping authority effectively, editors should refine both their decision-making and decision-enforcing skills. Neither ability suffices alone.

The following attributes help put editors in position to make and apply gatekeeping decisions.

- knowledge of what news *is,* both in general and as specifically defined by their sections or publications.
- knowledge of what news *is not,* of what reasons may require that some apparently worthy material be rejected.
- capacity to organize and direct staff efforts to find, cover and present the content expected of the publication.

WHAT NEWS IS AND ISN'T

Practically everyone has tried to define news, and practically no one has succeeded completely.

Author and teacher Ken Metzler offered this textbook definition: "News is a prompt, 'bottom-line' recounting of factual information about events, situations, and ideas (including opinions and interpretations) calculated to interest an audience and help people cope with themselves and their environment" (p. 23).[1]

Other definitions tend toward the droll. "News is anything that makes the reader say, 'Gee, whiz,' " according to one editor (p. 21).[2] One of my favorites, attributed to longtime Knight-Ridder editor Creed Black, is that news is anything that happens to or near publishers and their friends.

Most commonly, when stuck for a satisfactory definition of news, we resort to characterizing it. Most reporters and editors will be familiar with the following standard list of some attributes of news: timeliness, proximity, prominence, conflict, magnitude, unusualness, and human drama.

Most editors I know can confidently and competently recognize news when they see it. What often distinguishes the best editors is an ability to make discriminating judgments between various grades of newsworthiness and to recognize, and efficiently dispose of, material that does not merit publication. Determining what to kill, and when and how to kill it, calls for more rigorous judgments than simply knowing how to reflexively follow the trail of a valid news story.

For example, I was editing copy on deadline one day when one of my best reporters phoned in breathlessly. He had been standing by at the courthouse while a grand jury considered whether to indict a prominent public official. As he waited in the corridors, the jury room doors had opened, grand jurors strolled out for a coffee break, and several began discussing the case openly and loudly. My reporter had ambled over, without identifying himself as a journalist. Apparently thinking he was a court official, the jurors talked on,

---

[1]Metzler, K. (1986). *Newsgathering.* Englewood Cliffs, NJ: Prentice-Hall.
[2]Metzler, K. (1986). *Newsgathering.* Englewood Cliffs, NJ: Prentice-Hall.

revealing specifics about evidence in the case and their desire to indict the official. Eventually one juror blurted out, "That man ought to be in prison." What a story, my reporter exclaimed to me: grand jurors outraged by the conduct of a public official.

The story had all the attributes of news: timeliness, proximity, prominence, conflict, unusualness. Yet it never ran.

Why not? Our reporter's information had come under ethically ambiguous circumstances, involved sensitive private opinions not being offered knowingly for publication, and would most likely, if published, compromise a complex case and require disbanding the grand jury. In the editor's judgment, the price was too high for a little juicy, careless conversation.

In short, the story fell into several categories of what might be called *disqualifiers* of news, attributes that make information less likely to be published even though it appears to meet the requirements of newsworthiness. The following section discusses categories of disqualifiers.

Legal Problems. Editors may withhold information for a variety of legal reasons: because it raises potential libel or invasion of privacy problems, because it involves stolen documents or national security, because it could provoke a contempt of court citation. As discussed elsewhere in the book, editors should not be intimidated to the point of knuckling under to every legal risk. But legal considerations do apply and they sometimes result in decisions not to publish interesting material. In 1986, *Washington Post* executive editor Benjamin Bradlee wrote that his paper had withheld information from "more than a dozen stories" that year for national security reasons (p. F1).[3]

Ethical Problems. Often, editors choose not to run material they consider incomplete, one-sided, unfair, tainted by improper news-gathering methods, or otherwise in violation of professional standards of conduct. Information can be contaminated in many ways. Most newspapers, for example, decline to pay sources for information. Editors usually reject stories if they know reporters have lied or misrepresented themselves to get them. A reporter who based an article on stolen documents would face a heavy burden to convince most editors to publish the material.

Taste Problems. Particularly with photographs, editors often decide that good taste rules out running material on high interest; gory disaster scenes, bodies from car wrecks, shots containing nudity or obscenity. Written copy, too, often generates questions of taste, especially those involving use of explicit language.

---

[3]Bradlee, B. C. (1986, June 8). *The Post* and Pelton: How the press looks at national security, *Washington Post,* p. F1.

Privacy Problems. Here, we should distinguish between the legal notion of invasion of privacy and a broader ethical concern that can be called *disregard for privacy*. This involves the publication of material that may be perfectly legal to use but that seems unduly intimate, personal or private. Many arguments occur over such issues, simply because they become quite subjective. But examples abound. Many newspapers do not publish the names of victims of sex attacks, for example. Suppose you learn that the married mayor is having an affair, or once had an affair, or is involved with someone 30 years younger, or is having a homosexual affair. Is any of that news? None of it? Clear guidelines remain elusive, but nearly every editor will at some time invoke a standard of compassion and privacy to withhold otherwise newsworthy material.

Danger to Individuals or Groups. My phone rang on deadline once and I heard a federal law enforcement official asking me to kill a story that, he said, would unmask an informant in a drug case and almost certainly result in the informant's death. In such cases, editors face an anguishing calculation: to publish and risk harm, or to withhold and fail in their obligation to bring the truth, whatever its consequences, to the audience. Here, editors consider such issues as the value of the information to be published, how widely it already is known, whether it involves public officials or the public trust, and whether it will emerge elsewhere. They also must evaluate the risk, knowing that some threats are deadly serious but that others are bluffs or manipulative attempts to stifle legitimate coverage. Editors also should look for reasonable alternatives to the stark poles of publishing as is or killing. There are other choices: delaying publication, taking precautions to avert the danger, or under some conditions, "trading" for a better story. For example, in the case just described involving a drug informant, we agreed to withhold publication for a few days in exchange for an exclusive interview with the informant when he was out of danger.

In these and other ways, editors regularly must weigh the apparent news value of information against a range of potential disqualifiers. What results are journalistic cost–benefit analyses in which editor's personal qualities of judgment, compassion, experience, courage, and discretion play every bit as important a role as their professional understanding of news and audience interests.

In addition to the predispositions of editors themselves, what qualifies and disqualifies material for publication can be affected by social, institutional, and organizational factors.

Sociologist Herbert J. Gans, after studying how several national media assemble news content, isolated what he called eight enduring values reflected by the American press at large.[4] He defined them as "values which can be found in many different types of news stories over a long period of time; often, they affect what events become news." As identified by Gans, they include the following:

- *Ethnocentrism:* the tendency to elevate this country and to evaluate other countries on how well they live up to American ideals.
- *Altruistic democracy:* the notion that democracy is superior to dictatorship and that ideal domestic conduct pursues public service and the public interest.
- *Responsible capitalism:* an optimistic faith that people and businesses limit their pursuit of personal gain and try to behave as responsible citizens.
- *Small-town pastoralism:* a stress on the virtues of the small and rural.
- *Individualism:* the idealization of the rugged individual struggling against adversity.
- *Moderatism:* the discouragement of extreme or deviant conduct.
- *Social order:* the value placed on order and, in news stories such as disasters and scandals, the concern for restoring order.
- *National leadership:* the celebration of the availability of moral, competent leaders.

Although these factors do not directly define news, they contribute to how the press in general, and editors in particular, view society and set expectations regarding news. They also underline a central point: News is not an absolute, objective phenomenon, and news coverage does not in some miraculous way precisely reflect reality. News is a product constructed and reconstructed by journalists and sources, based on a range of values, expectations, motives, and ideals. All these issues influence editors as they go about activating their newsrooms in the search for the desired content.

ORGANIZING COVERAGE

Assume that you, as an editor, have developed a working familiarity with what coverage is expected. Now you face the duty of searching each day for real-life examples of news within your area.

Where do you start?

Let's consider three aspects of the process:

---

[4]Gans, H. J. (1979). *Deciding what's news* (pp. 39–52). New York: Vintage Books.

- organizing to gather news
- making assignments
- coordinating the flow

Organizing to Gather the News. Beginning reporters learn that there are only three ways of finding out anything: seeing it yourself (or *observation*), hearing about it from someone else (*interviewing*), and reading about it (*documents research*). Editors can put this truism to use in organizing their newsrooms or departments to seek news.

First, much of the news is predictable and observable. Reporters can be assigned to see for themselves such events as baseball games that begin at 7:30, city council meetings every Thursday, or theater openings and rock concerts on specific evenings. Second, reporters and editors can hear of news by plugging themselves into various beats where news can be expected to occur and by developing a broad network of sources willing to supply news tips. Third, journalists can use a host of written sources, both predictable (e.g., lawsuits filed each day) and unexpected (e.g., a reference in a magazine to a new product being manufactured in your area).

In a pioneering work on news gathering, sociologist Gaye Tuchman examined how journalists' routines and patterns of organization influence the product. She concluded that news, whatever its definition, "is a product of specific ways of organizing newswork" (p. 104).[5] The following sections summarize some of Tuchman's insights dealing with place, time and sources, as presented in her book *Making News: A Study in the Construction of Reality:*

- *Place:* Where journalists are influences what news they produce. For example, if an editor assigns a reporter to Suburb A and does not assign one to Suburb B, then Suburb A is likely to get more coverage than Suburb B. That does not necessarily mean more news actually occurs in Suburb A. It simply means the newspaper is *better organized* to find the news there.

Typically, editors assume that readers have high interest in news from specific locations (Suburb A), from specific institutions (city hall), and about specific topics (sports). So they disperse their staffs accordingly by *geography, specialty,* and *topic* in order to acquire this high-interest news. As a result, readers are more likely to get news from these established, predictable zones than from elsewhere. They are less likely to get news that isn't territorial or beat-specific, that is intangible or abstract, or that falls between the boundaries.

- *Time:* When events take place influences whether they get coverage. For

---

[5]Tuchman, G. (1978). *Making news: A study in the construction of reality.* New York: The Free Press.

a morning newspaper or an evening television newscast, the earlier in the day something happens, the better its chances of appearing. News that happens on weekdays, when staffs are at full strength, is more likely to be noticed than events on weekends.

In a much broader sense, time favors the coverage of events over issues. Events (a trial, a ball game) have discrete, observable beginnings and endings. They are easy to find and to cover. Issues (sexism, falling educational standards) evolve, without necessarily falling into what Tuchman calls the "news net."

• *Sources:* Whom you ask determines what you learn. In the conventional news net, journalists routinely turn to centralized sources (celebrities, bureaucrats, industry spokespeople) more often than to sources not as easily located or encountered within the news net (neighborhood leaders, rank-and-file workers). The result is a kind of legitimization of the status quo and a potential overrepresentation of middle-class, professional values in the news.

For editors, one important goal is to cast the news net as widely and as fairly as possible, bearing in mind critiques such as those by Tuchman and Gans. A key function becomes assessing how best to organize their staffs to achieve this goal.

Simply recognizing the power of routines and patterns can help. Among other steps that editors can take are:

• *Creating beat systems that look beyond the obvious:* As Gans and Tuchman have pointed out, under most beat systems news will be gathered reliably from such places as the state legislature or city hall. Editors, then, must take special steps to acquire news from places where reporters are not regularly stationed, such as a university research lab or a tiny ethnic neighborhood. Designating beats such as "research" or "neighborhood issues" can fling the news net beyond the usual topical and territorial boundaries.

• *Matching beats and lifestyles:* Try to define beats in ways that overlap with how people live rather than defining beats by institution. For example, a beat described as "recreation" will produce broader coverage than one described as "Department of Recreation." Defining "workplace issues" as a beat, instead of "labor unions" or "Labor Department," will do likewise.

• *Expanding sources:* As we have seen, a paper is more likely to rely on bureaucrats and officeholders (who have accessibility, a certain legitimacy and are thought to be in positions to know things) as sources than private citizens or interest-group leaders (perceived as biased or untested). Consequently, coverage tends to favor established groups and to neglect newcomers, fringe groups, or others outside the mainstream. Try to offset this tilt by suggesting that reporters develop sources from all segments of society and by making sure that official sources don't dominate your copy.

• *Reading your own paper and the competition,* including the ads, looking for new ideas or stories that need follow-ups.

• *Monitoring local news on television and radio stations.*

• *Interviewing reporters and other staff members* about interesting goings-on in their lives, neighborhoods, clubs, schools, churches, and other social groups. Quite often, even your own staff members will neglect to mention something interesting because they assume editors already know about it.

• *Checking wire services and the national media* for stories that may have local angles or for trends that your community may be a part of, or, perhaps more interestingly, an exception to.

• *Reading the mail:* Most newspapers get bagloads of mail each day, most but not all of it dull.

• *Reading the microfilm* in your library of papers from last year or 10 years ago to see what was going on then. Surprisingly often, you will notice something worth checking on now.

• *Doing your own reporting:* Develop your own source networks, both informal and formal, and work them diligently. Call friends and acquaintances. Find out who the area's best (and most reliable) news gossips are. Locate the best-informed people about the areas your paper covers and stay in touch with them. And get out of the office. Have lunch with a source (preferably a new one) once a week. Drop in on meetings, events, activities. Make sure you and your reporters are chasing the news, not waiting for it to announce itself.

• *Encouraging sources to come to you:* Make it easy to find your phone number. Pay stringers and correspondents for usable tips. And, crucially, make sure that your and everyone else on your staff (especially people who answer the phone) react with courtesy and appreciation to callers with story ideas, even when the ideas seem nutty.

• *Reading and insisting that staff members read,* everything from popular magazines to the trade journals in each beat area, from alternative publications to house organs, from municipal budgets to inspection reports on local restaurants, from the minutes of meetings you can't cover to every incident report at the local copshop.

The bottom line is to make the search for news an aggressive and generative process, not one that is passive or locked into stale and predictable routines.

Making Assignments.   As any editor can tell you, selling yourself on an idea does not insure it will see print. Editors do not write stories. They work indirectly, through others. So the hardest work often comes in selling those others on the idea. I can remember countless times when what I thought was an inspired vision for a wonderful story came back mangled and unrecognizable because I failed to effectively convey that vision to a reporter.

In making assignments, strive for:

• *Clarity:* Be clear about the idea and about the ground rules of the assignment. Most of the time, it is advisable to give a reporter as much autonomy as possible. If you want a feature story on this year's Christmas parade, select a good reporter, talk through your own ideas, offer suggestions, and help the reporter see the end product you have in mind. but leave as much room as possible for the writer to put his or her mark on the assignment.

On some occasions, however, you will have reason to insist on a particular approach. If so, make sure the reporter understands what you are asking, and why and how you want it done.

• *Helpfulness:* Be an editor that reporters count on for help. Reporters can tell the difference between an editor who bullheadedly dominates every point and one who offers steady counsel and useful suggestions. Offer your ideas and the wisdom of your experience in a constructive, not a patronizing, way. Be ready to suggest sources, documents or other steps that can help get a reporter unstuck.

• *Flexibility:* Try to avoid clinging to preconceptions that aren't borne out by reporters' research. Some reporters, of course, will dawdle on unwanted assignments and find countless reasons to pooh-pooh them. Learn to distinguish between a bad idea and an unmotivated reporter.

• *Balance:* Most newspapers operate on the cafeteria model, trying to present a little something for everyone, from nutritious entrees to luscious desserts. Editors call this a good mix, and achieving it generally requires an openness to ideas from others (including ideas not to your personal taste).

• *An overall strategy that sees beyond the daily grind:* Related to balance, this point involves making sure your assignments go beyond the next issue of the paper. Make sufficient short-range assignments to cover the news, of course. But do not neglect medium- and long-range needs also. If possible, make sure that a portion of your resources is always devoted to medium-range projects (such as a weekender looking into hiring practices in the mayor's office) and long-range ideas (such as a look at the health effects of the local nuclear-power plant.)

Coordinating the Flow. You have flung your news net, snared some nifty story ideas, and crisply assigned them to your crack staff. Time to relax, check out the comics, and wait till the golden prose flows in?

Not exactly.

Far from relaxing, the editor is now more likely to resemble a harried police dispatcher, routing units from one scene to another, analyzing each situation to determine where resources are needed most, juggling false alarms, unexpected bulletins and logistical logjams. Here, again, an ability to make swift, defensible decisions under fire separates the successful editors. Like quarterbacks calmly surveying downfield receivers as 300-pound behemoths lunge maniacally toward them, editors must bring knowledge, experience, hunch, and luck together to make a procession of snap, all-important judgments.

In so doing, the editor will benefit by bearing in mind the following points:

• *Monitor reporters' work:* Consult at several key points of the reporting process: at the time of assignment, during the reporting, before the first draft is written. You do not want to hover pantingly over a writer's shoulder or to butt in every few minutes. But good editors keep abreast of how stories are developing, in order to offer suggestions at timely moments and to avoid being taken by surprise by a finished story that turns out much different from expectations.

• *Think graphics:* Make clear, complete *art* assignments at the same time you assign a story. Then, as stories rise and fall during a cycle, coordinate art and photo needs with other relevant editors. Good art takes no less time than good writing, so start early and plan carefully.

• *Think space:* At the point of assignment, give the writer a preliminary idea of what kind of treatment you have in mind, from a one-graf brief to a lead-the-paper package. Then, constantly re-think space needs as you monitor variables such as how the story actually develops and what competing demands for space may be. Ask the reporter to alert you immediately if the preliminary idea seems unworkable, and for your part keep the reporter posted on any changes in newsroom plans for the story. Avoid the kind of newsroom anarchy that results when every reporter writes to a self-chosen length heedless of what others are doing or planning. It is much easier to write a coherent 10-inch story if you conceive and organize for 10 inches to begin with than if your craft a 20-inch article and then have to cut it in half.

• *Coordinate with others in the newsroom:* This may call for a range of political, diplomatic, and negotiating skills. Keep superiors informed about sensitive stories or those needing unusual treatment. Try to avoid overlap among reporters or duplication with other sections. Pass on tips that may be relevant elsewhere in the newsroom. Lobby when necessary for the extra time or space or handling that key projects deserve.

CONCLUSION

In the interval after articles are assigned but before they arrive for editing, paying attention to the details of art, space, coverage, and flow can have dramatic effect. It can help the editor keep ahead of careening news processes, anticipate problems, and smooth the way for what comes next: editing the copy and designing the pages.

SIDEBAR 6
SURE WAYS TO BECOME THE WORLD'S WORST EDITOR

By Carl Sessions Stepp
ASNE Bulletin

I once worked for an editor who started rolling a fresh sheet of paper into his typewriter whenever he saw me coming with copy.

He would leap to redo my story, and it is true his leads always outshone mine. But how was I to learn, or to care, if he did all the writing?

Later, as a reporter-turned-editor myself, I discovered how difficult it is to resist bludgeoning your staff into doing a story just the way you would have.

Realizing that the editor's role is not to DO the reporting and writing, but to HELP others do them, is one of editing's hardest, and most central, lessons. It is one of many precepts in how-not-to-do-it that I learned, mostly through my own sins, over the years.

My list of sure ways to become the world's worst editor would also include:

• *Going it Alone:* The worst editors make reporters feel like adversaries; the best excel at teamwork. In this process, working with people becomes at least as important as working with copy. An editor and reporter working as a team produce far stronger copy than each trying to overpower the other.

• *Revising it Yourself:* It is certainly faster that way. But you are usually better off letting the reporter do any necessary rewriting. To reporters, the idea of an editor's moving in on their copy is the equivalent of an art teacher growling to Leonardo da Vinci, "This painting ain't bad. Just a little work on the smile, and I'll have 'er ready to hang."

• *Editing Without Reading:* The bad editor loves to plunge right into the copy, making immediate marks that brand the copy as part his or hers. A better way: Before lifting a pencil or depressing the keyboard, read an article all the way through, open your mind to the logic of the reporter's approach, and offer at least minimal courtesy to the professional who has dripped blood for it.

• *Changing Without Consulting:* What reporter has not had the disgraceful experience of having to explain to an outraged source that the article carrying the reporter's byline was actually botched up by some nameless clod of an editor? Writers organize stories for reasons; wording is often shaded in precise ways to insure accuracy, preserve nuance or tiptoe around unseen landmines. Editing without asking can destroy this delicate literary ecology.

• *Going Out of Style:* The truly bad editor is tone deaf to the mood and rhythm of copy, and as a result will edit words in or out in a style inconsistent with the writer's. I once wrote a story in which a congressman accused a bureaucrat of "trying to purify the race of boiling off some of the dross." Trying to be helpful, an editor inserted the words "impurity or waste" in

(Continued)

Sidebar 6 (*Continued*)

parentheses after "dross," a well-meant gesture that thoroughly clunked up the quote.

• *Playing Bully:* On more than one occasion, I have heard myself speaking to reporters in the same tone I use when my children put rocks in the washing machine. An editor–reporter conversation should, however, sound like two equal adults discussing an issue with mutual respect. When you overrule a reporter, don't drone on about who's right and wrong; explain your decision evenly, acknowledge there can be other views, and point out that you are empowered to decide and are doing your best.

• *Bogging Down in the Stylebook:* Of course every good editor must master grammar, spelling, style, and usage, but some editors bog down there. The best ones also edit for organization, theme, focus, thoroughness, and accuracy. They evaluate the overall story—raising concrete question about logic and conclusions as well as about sentence structure. They consider what is strong, what is weak, what is missing, what is wasted, and offer specific suggestions in a positive, nonaccusatory way.

• *Overplaying Your Hunches:* A hallmark of bad editing is making changes for which you cannot cite a rule or offer succinct explanation. ("It just does not sound right" does not count.) Correcting obvious errors should be unchallengeable, of course, but make sure you're right. If you hit a stalemate, don't be afraid of consulting a referee. This is a subjective business. You don't have to win them all.

Of course, if you want to win, common horse sense sometimes helps. I remember an editor who argued with one of his best reporters over the lead on a major story. After they yelled at each other for a while, he suggested that the reporter go home for the day and relax. A few hours later, he phoned the reporter, who by this time had mellowed out in front of the fireplace with a drink or two. Guess who won the argument?[6]

---

[6]Stepp, C. S. (1985, June). Sure ways to become the world's worst editor. *ASNE Bulletin*, pp. 8–9. (Reprinted with permission.)

Making Decisions About Copy

What problems do you see with the following lead for a news article?

School supt. Audrey Smith took the witness stand Monday and said that, despite conflicting advice from school board members, she plans to implement a new bussing plan for city schools next Fall.

An alert copyeditor quickly can spot several problems: failure to capitalize supt., improper capitalization of Fall, misspelling of bussing. But those are the easy catches. They do not capture what is most wrong with this lead: It is off base and out of focus.

First, it is long, cumbersome and loaded with fuzzy words like "implement" and "plan." Second, it backs into the point. And, third, it offers superfluous information, such as "took the witness stand," at the expense of what the audience truly needs to know.

A lead I prefer:

School Supt. Audrey Smith promised Monday to enforce school busing next fall "even if it costs me my job."

If you are like many editors to whom I have shown this and similar leads, your attention may have locked immediately onto the style and usage problems. Given what *Miami Herald* reporter Edna Buchanan called their "itchy cursor fingers,"[1] editors often plunge right in and begin correcting such obvious errors.

---

[1]Edna Buchanan, personal communication, August 12, 1987.

Too frequently, however, they overlook more important, but less glaring, deficiencies in an article's basic message or focus.

To avoid such problems, many editors find it helpful to subdivide editing into two stages—editing for content and editing for structure. Content means substance: the facts, images, and ideas, and their selection and arrangement. Structure means form: the language, usage, grammar, spelling, punctuation, and style.

Each stage requires a different style of editing and a different way of thinking. Trying to do both at once produces incomplete, inconsistent editing, the kind of headachy blur that would result if a scientist kept bobbing between the microscope and the telescope.

For many editors, content editing raises more difficulties than structural editing. With structure, editors have well-defined rules and styles to follow. A paper's style is either to capitalize the word "fall" or not, and editors can look it up. But content editing requires dealing with intangible qualities such as fairness and thoroughness or with subjective measures such as taste and literary merit. These areas are trickier, rooted less in memorized regulations than in professional judgments and experience. They are negotiable and disputable.

So too many editors begin and end by concentrating on structure, with perhaps a passing gesture toward content.

Whereas previous chapters have stressed that editors perform a range of duties besides processing copy, it is inescapable that, ultimately, the ability to edit copy is a defining, touchstone quality of editors. Few will succeed without it. The editor who gains a reputation as a helpful "copy doctor"—able to take copy apart, examine it and put it back together without the writer seeing anything amiss—will win the allegiance and trust of a staff. The editor regarded as a "butcher" faces resentment and resistance.

In this chapter, we first discuss content editing. Then we turn to structural editing. That is the suggested order for editors as well: The editor should look first at content and take whatever steps are appropriate to help writers tailor it to fit their intentions for the audience. Then, it is time to edit for structure.

There are three reasons for this order: First, if you meticulously edit the structure before dealing with content, and then your content editing produces major revisions, you will have to repeat the structural editing anyway. Second, content and structural editing, as distinct processes requiring different ways of thinking, are best done sequentially rather than simultaneously, moving from broad conceptual thinking (content) to fine-tuning (structure). Third, editors who begin with structure may wind up spending all their time on it, never getting to content.

Editors, like writers or chefs or football coaches, develop personal work habits ranging from the cerebral to the idiosyncratic to the weird. Although you will find considerable variety in how editors operate, what follows is a brief model that sketches how an editor can effectively proceed through a piece of copy.

A MODEL FOR EDITING

1. *Prepare to edit.* Remember that you are handling the copy of a fellow human being, a writer who is probably both proud and nervous about the work. Respect the effort. Make yourself concentrate fully. Whenever possible, consult the writer before making any except the most mundane changes. As an editor, you have responsibility for the story, but it does not belong to you.

2. *Read the copy completely* before editing anything, to get its overall effect and to see how it strikes you, cold, as a reader.

3. *Think about the copy and the writer.* Try to understand the goals and intentions. What was the assignment? Who is the audience? What special circumstances surround the story? What does the writer seem to be attempting? How will the story be played? Has it already gone through another editor?

4. *Focus on the lead and the basic outline.* Is the lead clear, interesting, and pegged to the most compelling possible point? Does the body of the article flow logically from the lead in an order that seems considered and appropriate?

5. *Edit for content.* Check the story for accuracy, fairness, clarity, consistency, logic, taste, thoroughness. Are sources named and reliable? Is evidence adequate? Does the piece pose legal or ethical problems? Is something important omitted? Is the copy interesting? If you encounter questions or problems, discuss them with the writer. If major changes are necessary, try to give the writer responsibility for making them.

6. *Edit for structure.* Inspect the grammar, punctuation, spelling, style, and usage. Guard against wordiness and muddy writing. Think of style in its literary sense. Strive for polish and sharpness. To the extent you can, make your editing consistent with the writer's style. Finally, let the writer see the finished copy.

7. *Re-read the story, for final effect.* Is there anything at all whose accuracy is in question? Is anything crucial missing? Will you vouch for this story?

Although following this model might seem to require large chunks of time, that is not necessarily the case. The key point is that, using whatever time is available, the editor should attend to each step in proportion to its relative importance. Thus, a rough schedule might go as follows: *Preparation* (steps 1 through 3), 10% of available time; *content editing* (steps 4 and 5), 50%; *structural editing* (step 6), 30%; *conclusion* (step 7), 10%. Such an allocation works if the editor has 10 minutes or 10 hours for a project. And it gives precedence to content, allows time for structure, and leaves room for a good beginning and a clean finish.

Now, we can examine the model in more detail.

Preparing to Edit

Editing taking time and concentration. But by the nature of their jobs, many editors must juggle numerous thoughts and duties. Often I have caught myself putting my brain in a kind of editing autopilot while I also pondered some separate issue. This, however, is no more advisable for editors than it is for air traffic controllers. Far more editing errors, in my view, stem from inattention and carelessness than from incompetence or stupidity. For rookie and veteran editors alike, few steps will produce better payoff than training themselves to devote total attention to the project at hand.

Many editors devise elaborate warmup rituals for this purpose. Although green eyeshades are vanishing from newsrooms, old-timers still may carefully sharpen five fat copy pencils and line them up just so before even glancing at the story. Computer-trained editors adjust the contrast button painstakingly, then set the cursor to go down the left side (or the right side, or from word to word, or from paragraph mark to paragraph mark). Others will inspect their chairs, carefully raise or lower the height, slide a favorite pillow underneath, limber their fingers like a pianist, and then, at last, peer in at the copy. Others simply stare into space for a few minutes, clearing the mind. One editor I knew would roll up his sleeves, wring his hands, and walk around the newsroom saying, "Scrub me up, nurse."

At best these rituals, whether products of rational planning or black magic, serve to bring editors into something akin to a state of self-hypnosis, allowing intense concentration.

Thus prepared, editors should spend a moment contemplating their task. Read through the story. Consider the writer, the assignment, the circumstances. Is it news, or feature? A story alone, or a package including photos, charts or other graphics? Culmination of a 6-month project, or a 15-minute phone job on deadline? Intended to convey some specific message to the reader (such as tomorrow's weather forecast), or open to experimentation (such as how area farmers are coping with a season-long drought)?

The editor's goal here is to become oriented to the story and everything that has preceded it, from conception, through reporting and writing, to any judgments already made by other editors. All this can happen in just a few seconds or minutes, but it is important. The more that editors know of this history, the more sensitive they can be in handling the copy and sidestepping potential land mines.

Editors should never forget a central difference in point of view between themselves and writers: To the writer, the turned-in copy represents an *ending*, the finished product of a creative professional. To the editor, it may seem the point at which work *begins*.

Although the reporter may view the story as the equivalent of perfectly grilled steak ready for the palate, editors may see it as raw hamburger meat, available for shaping in the hands of a master. At this point, some common courtesy is called for. The writer should understand that editors are charged with taking a broad view and that it is duty, not simply their itchy trigger fingers, that compels them to scrutinize, challenge and sometimes rework copy. Editors, on the other hand, should respect the writer's work. Nothing is gained by patronizing writers. Instead editing should be the time for two professionals to have a constructive, respectful conversation about work in which both have an active stake.

Before plunging into detailed word and content editing, the editor should address the *overall impact* of the copy. Does the story make sense? Is it of value? Will it leave the reader saying, "Who cares?" or does it make a significant point? If the editor has fundamental questions about the overall tone, direction or quality, now is the time to iron them out, through positive give-and-take and before either the editor or writer gets too invested in specific approaches.

Beginning at the Beginning

A good lead is like ice, so slick that before they realize it readers find themselves sliding flat on their backs into the middle of a story. Nothing else (except the headline) comes close to the lead in having the power to sell readers on a story or send them fleeing.

Thus, the lead is the logical place for an editor to begin hands-on editing. It is a crucial starting point, and, for too many readers, the quitting point as well.

In reviewing leads, it is wise to remember how people read newspapers. In fact, viewing their audiences as "readers" may be less pertinent to journalists than imagining them as "scanners." Typically, they read rapidly, scanning everything, turning pages quickly, making hasty and cut-throat decisions about what to read and what to ignore. They read while watching television, eating breakfast, fussing at their families, or sitting in the bathroom. They may take only 3 or 4 seconds to decide whether to read an article that a writer has spent weeks preparing.

However, this harried speed reading may not be the setting being imagined as the writers go about crafting their articles. Instead, writers are more likely to envision an idealized audience of attentive, hungry news devourers, ready to drop everything in order to read to the very last word of every story.

Previously, we mentioned the different perspective of writers and editors. How easy it also is to forget the differing perspectives of writers and readers. Writers begin to write at the point of peak interest in their stories, after hours or days or even weeks immersed in discovering what is interesting in the lives and events of their subjects. Readers, by contrast, begin to read at a point of relatively low interest, without knowing (as does the writer) how the story will come out, without the context to quickly grasp the relevance of every description or foreshadowing anecdote.

A problem, then, is that writers, knowing what is to come, may want to build to their climax, as an organist builds toward a crescendo. But readers, not knowing or even necessarily caring what is to come, may be unwilling to stick around past a slow-moving prelude.

Into this equation comes the editor, who must help writers reconcile their literary aspirations with the knowledge that so many readers are skimmers who must be hooked quickly or not at all.

Where does the editor begin? Although leads can be classed into many different types (such as the summary lead, the single-element lead, the narrative lead, and so on), it is less important to dwell on classifications than to consider how a lead can best carry out the writer's intentions.

Every writer aiming for a mass audience should begin by asking two question: "What is my purpose, and who is my audience?" These questions also offer a place for the editor to start.

Purpose.   Most often, a newspaper writer's purpose is to inform (via a news story), to tell a story (via a feature), or to do some combination of the two. If the purpose is informational, then a simple, direct statement of the most important point is almost always the most effective lead. The mission is simply to convey the point from one place (the writer) to another (the reader), as efficiently as possible. The inverted pyramid structure works quite well: Begin with the most important point and proceed with points in descending order of importance.

If you are standing at an office window and see a tornado approaching, for instance, you would not turn to your colleagues and say, "Today dawned bright and sunny over the city but before long the clouds began to roll in. . . ." You would say, "A tornado is heading this way and we'd better take cover."

For such stories, an old saw generally works: Base your lead on what you would say if you were summarizing the story for your mother.

If the purpose is narrative, then the direct statement may not work best. In storytelling, the idea is not necessarily to rush to the ending as quickly as possible, but to create the best dramatic effect using characterization, plotting, scene, description, emotion, and other such devices. This process is akin to telling a joke: You do not begin with the punchline, nor do you drag out the story to such elaborate lengths that the audience loses its edge.

The editor, therefore, must understand the writer's purpose and help analyze whether the lead best serves it.

Audience.   A second key point is the audience. At whom is the story directed? If the article is aimed at the mass newspaper audience, then, the writer must keep in mind the distracted, heterogeneous nature of the group, and must write accordingly. Clear, simple, direct language, focusing on the point of greatest interest to the average reader, is paramount.

On the other hand, if the article has a special focus—say, the weekly chess column—then certain assumptions about the audience can be made. Or if the piece is designed for the Sunday magazine section, then the writer can presume the audience is prepared to devote more attention and time, and a more leisurely, essay-style approach may be suitable. Again, the editor's duty is to help ensure that the writer, in choosing a lead and basic framework, has tailored them to the appropriate audience.

Having done all this, the editor can then ask a series of questions that help evaluate the interest level of the lead:

- Is the lead focused firmly on the most compelling point of the story? Has the writer chosen the most effective possible way of interesting readers in the topic?
- Does it make the audience want to read on? Does it offer enough tension, irony, drama, or seductiveness to promptly engage the reader's curiosity?
- Is is clear? Nothing besides accuracy is more important.
- Is it vivid? Does it use direct, concrete words and images that readers can readily visualize?
- Does it answer the questions "Who cares?" and "So what?" Does it demonstrate, through the power of fact or narrative, why the overall story is important enough for readers to care?

In some ways, writing an article for the public is a supremely arrogant act. Writers dare the audience, in effect, to stop everything else, to reject every possible alternative use of time, in order to read what they have written. Consequently, a heavy burden falls on writers (and their partners, editors) to make readers consider this sacrifice worthwhile.

It is not possible or even desirable to promote any precise lead-writing formula, but it may be useful to offer some general observations about leads. In my view, good newspaper leads should:

- Take less than 25 words and fit into one sentence.
- Express a single thought. Roundups, overgeneralized summaries and leads that try to skip through several elements confuse readers. Given that readers are in a hurry, the best way to seize their attention is to begin with the single most tantalizing point and write it crisply.

• Be direct. Go to the heart of the story. Usually, the subject and verb of the lead sentence should reflect the main figure and the main action of the story.

• Use active voice and action words. Stories should be dynamic. They need movement. If they stand still, so does the reader. By the end of the lead, something should have *happened* or *changed*.

• Avoid the verb "to be" and passive introductions like "There is."

• Place the dominating idea—the single most crucial point—as near the beginning of the lead sentence as possible.

• Avoid the nonessential. Leave out extraneous circumstances ("took the witness stand today and said. . ."), acronyms, jargon, unnecessary titles, names of government agencies, unless they are required for clarity or accuracy. This material can come later.

• Give the reader some worthwhile new fact or feeling or image, in understandable, easily pictured terms. Consider the lead: "A local man is a hero tonight after rescuing his wife from an auto accident." What does the reader see here? What man? What is a hero? What kind of rescue? What kind of accident? Instead, substitute stronger words and say, "A 76-year-old local man dragged his paralyzed wife from their flaming car tonight, seconds after a tractor-trailer rammed it on Fifth Street." In your mind, you can see the difference.

Of course, the editor's job is to help the writer, not to replace the writer. So the role remains to analyze and evaluate, then to discuss feelings (and the reasons for them) with the writer. If revision is needed, editors can point out why they think so, and then, wherever possible, let the writer do the revising. If the lead seems splendid, point out why, and leave the writer feeling good.

Other Content Issues

Based on our editing model, the editor by now should have become acquainted with the copy and the writer, considered its overall impact and scrutinized the lead. Now other content areas await.

Central Logic.   Stories are more than their parts. Early on, an editor should look at the story as a whole, and make sure it is internally and externally logical. At one newspaper where I worked, we frequently invoked the "2-minute-mile rule," which held that if someone makes a claim that is too good to be true (such as having run a mile in 2 minutes, half the world-record time) then it probably is not true. Had that rule been followed, the *San Angelo (Texas) Standard* might not have had one of its corrections featured in *New Yorker* magazine: when it mistakenly attributed a cooking contest victory to the "Whorehouse Chili Team" rather than the "Orehouse Chili Team" (p. 150).[2]

Organizing Principle. Does the body of the story flow smoothly from the lead? Try to outline the story. Typically, you should find a lead that introduces the main theme, followed by about three secondary themes, covered in some logical and orderly way. If you cannot detect an outline or order, then the story may well ramble or seem blurry. The equivalent of turning the focus knob on a television set is to ask a writer to reexamine organization to make sure it flows smoothly.

Purpose. Read a newspaper sometime and notice how easy it is to find stories that never directly demonstrate why they exist: articles about obscure cabinet changes in faraway places or subcommittee haggling inside Congress or microscopic fluctuations in business indices. Unless a story's importance is inherently obvious (such as when a plane crashes and 75 people die), I think copy needs a concise, straightforward statement of meaning. Often, it comes in the second paragraph. The lead expresses the newest or most dramatic development. Graf two puts that development into perspective.

Papers have many words for such a graf: the billboard, the key-shit graf, the nut graf, the catholic graf. My favorite description is to call it the "why-are-we-at-this-party" paragraph. If you cannot find one, ask the writer the age-old question: How would you sell this story to me in one sentence? That sentence, quite often, can become the telltale graf.

Accuracy. Nothing is more important than accuracy. The editor should make sure (and this can be surprisingly tedious) that every assertion or fact is sourced and documented. Look for careless errors, hasty conclusions, unwarranted assumptions. Do not hesitate to ask the reporter, "How do you know this?" *Chicago Tribune* reporter Jim O'Shea tells of dealing with a skeptical editor:

> I remember an editor said to me once, "Jim, I got only one problem with this story. I don't believe it." Well, we went through the whole thing. By the time I was through, I had convinced him. but he made me put in enough so he could see it was true, and the reader could too.[3]

Sources and Documentation. In checking for accuracy, the editor should independently consider whether sources and documentation are authoritative, adequate and reliable. Many editors invoke the "two-source rule," popularized

---

[2]Inadvertence in San Angelo (1979, September 10). *New Yorker*, p. 150.
[3]Jim O'Shea, personal communication, August 18, 1987.

during coverage of the Watergate scandal in the 1970s, which requires separate confirmations of any point that may be disputed. Reporters, in their haste and eagerness to locate someone willing to talk, may exaggerate the importance of a source or whether a source is truly in a position to know. A red flag for the editor should be phrases such as "a Defense Department employee" or "a company executive." Even when such sources are named, it does not necessarily follow that they are authoritative. Similarly, sourcing should be especially solid on material with a high potential for embarrassment.

Consider a 1984 *Washington Post* article that ran shortly after NBC's Roger Mudd grilled then presidential candidate Gary Hart in a television interview. At a subsequent dinner, according to the Post, "Hart and Mudd . . . were introduced together. One observer said Hart sat down quickly while Mudd kept taking the applause and 'wouldn't sit down.' Finally he did."

Should the phrase "one observer" have signaled trouble? Probably. The next day, the Post published the following correction: "The *Washington Post* reported incorrectly yesterday upon the length of Roger Mudd's acknowledgement of applause at the Gridiron dinner, which is closed to coverage. According to several sources Mudd was introduced, stood and promptly sat down" (p. E2).[4]

In short, sources should be clear, named, and dependable. Readers should know, from the story, where information came from, how the writer got it, and why the sources were in a position to know it.

Completeness.   Stories need context, background, and definitions of unfamiliar concepts. I can remember as a youngster reading news articles about the Vietnam War and wondering who was fighting whom and why. While it is not practical to give detailed explanations in every story, it is important that sufficient historical background be present so readers can comprehend each story. And it is worth remembering that new readers (newcomers to town, young people, people who usually read the competition) constantly enter the news flow without the same frame of reference journalists have. The obsessive fear of repetition is a journalistic bugaboo that should be laid to rest.

Omissions.   The editor not only must critique what reporters have written, but also what they have not written. What pertinent questions have not been asked? What information is missing? What angles are not covered? What arguments or points of view have been slighted? What alternative approaches might work better? For some, editing what is not there proves the hardest editing of all, because it requires imagination and distance, two elusive editing qualities.

---

[4]Correction. (1984, March 27). *Washington Post,* p. E2.

One simple, time-tested technique is to explicitly search for the five Ws and the H in every story. You may surprise yourself at how often one is missing.

Another method is to compare the existing copy against an imagined ideal, and see how close the two can be made. This is one area where dealing with the writer can get dicey. An editor who insists on new material is directly challenging the reporter's thoroughness. So move cautiously here, but do move. Instead of demanding, "Why didn't you call the defense lawyer?" try saying, "What if we added a quote from the defense lawyer?" Instead of complaining, "This is a one-sided story about pit bulls," try saying, "What would you think about calling the dog's owner?" In almost every case, reporters recognize a good suggestion and are eager to add material that will improve stories, if they do not have their backs up because of the editor's style of challenging.

Fairness. Unfairness creeps in many ways: in choice of what sources to interview and what material to include, in the judgments of reporters and sources alike, in the ignorance or distortion inherent in sources' and reporters' points of view, and in word selection, among others. As a relatively impartial reader, the editor tries to sniff out unfairness or apparent unfairness, and to inform the reporter when it seems present.

A common example occurs in police stories, where officers assume the guilt of an arrested suspect and announce something like, "This arrest clears up 47 burglaries in the northeast of town." Too seldom do we hear the position of the accused, or of his or her lawyer. A good guideline is to see that any people criticized in an article are given a chance to offer their very best defense *within the same article*. Saving that for a follow-up story is not fair.

Another fairness problem occurs when writers adopt the terminology used by one side of an issue (using words such as "pro-life" in the abortion debate, or "tax reform" in the political arena).

Stereotyping. Stereotyping, as when racism, sexism, or ageism finds its way into copy, can be blatant or subtle. Many papers still, in obituaries for example, refer to women by their husband's first name, as in "Mrs. John Smith died Saturday. . . . " Ask yourself whether it is pertinent to, as a television reporter did in 1984, mention that vice presidential nominee Geraldine Ferraro wears a size 6 dress.[5] Be careful of racial identifications. In descriptions of suspects for instance, do not fall into the trap of signaling that people are assumed to be White unless you tell the reader otherwise.

Double Entendres. Nobody has dirtier minds than journalists, except perhaps readers. So an editor must watch for both the dirt that almost every reporter will at times try to slip by and for the dirt that no one notices until it

---

[5]deView, L. S. (1984, September). Test your bias IQ. *ASNE Bulletin*, p. 18.

is too late. Beware of obituaries of the sort that begin, "Florence McGuff, 54, died Saturday shortly after assuming a missionary position." Watch headlines, where the devil seems to get loose most often. Everybody enjoys reading *Columbia Journalism Review*'s "lower case" collection ("Pastor aghast at First Lady sex position"), but no one wants to personally contribute to it.

Taste. Sex. Nudity. Blood. Gore. Death. Violence. Profanity. Blasphemy. Taste issues abound, in copy, headlines, and especially in photos. A Pennsylvania state official calls a press conference, produces a pistol, and shoots through the top of his mouth. Do you publish photos? The Federal Communications Commission bans a list of dirty words from the airwaves. Do you itemize them?

Although this issue is covered in more detail elsewhere in the book, its applicability to content editing is obvious: In most such cases, the editor's job is not necessarily to impose taste decisions on reporters, but to raise them for discussion. Different publications will have varying standards. What is most important is for editors to regard themselves as early warning signalers, programmed to respond when they see a potential taste issue, so that the ultimate publish-or-not decision is reasoned and deliberate.

Law. This subject, too, is dealt with elsewhere in the book. But it cannot be overlooked in the context of content editing. Few duties surpass the editor's responsibility for producing legally sound copy. The editor must look for potential libel, invasion of privacy, contempt of court, plagiarism, and trademark or copyright violations. As with taste questions, the editor may not be a lone decision maker and should not simply reflexively snip out any potentially offending item. Instead, the editor should trigger whatever procedure a publication has (and every publication should have one) for deciding legally troublesome questions.

Having listed all these categories, I find myself wondering what kind of paragon will have the time, judgment, and brain capacity to police them all. Clearly, so much can go wrong with stories that not even the world's best editor can possibly guard against everything.

How do editors deal with this problem? Some editors, like those reporters who always seem to be nearby when the big story breaks, do it with instinct, with some sixth sense that nudges them about an approaching defect in copy. Part of that intuition, I think, comes from a life of constant reading and writing. Eventually they come to sense good and bad work, in the same way that, after years of listening to music, one can tell when a record is warped or an instrument is out of tune.

Other editors do try to question everything, cross-examining reporters with one indiscriminate question after another with no sense of priority. I think this approach is a mistake. The best editors do not simply think of every possible question and then suffocate reporters with them all at once. Instead, they *rank* their questions, asking the most crucial ones first and moving down the line as time and reasonableness allow. Most questions fall into one of four categories:

Fatal: These are questions that must be settled or else the story cannot be published. Example: in an investigative story on corruption in the mayor's office, what to do about possibly libelous material not adequately attributed or documented.

Important: Questions that need answering, and must either be settled or written around. Example: in the mayor story, how to resolve a conflict on the spelling of a source's name.

Marginal: Questions worth settling if there is time, but of less consequence than the above. Example: background information on what previous mayors have faced investigations.

Picayune: Questions of very esoteric interest or little interest at all, which suggest an editor is simply showing off an ability to ask *something.* Example: what the mayor was wearing when interviewed for the corruption story.

Overall, one good rule is to consider what is most likely to go wrong and what areas have the potential for most damage. Then, pay priority attention to these areas. On my list of code-red areas would be the following:

Identifications: Names should be checked and double-checked. Errors here ruin stories, destroy credibility and invite lawsuits. Once—following the rule that, in controversial stories, full identification is best—my newspaper published a story about Maurice H. Wilson Jr. The next morning, I heard from the *other* Maurice H. Wilson Jr. in our town.

Be careful and be consistent. Make sure stories and cutlines match. A *USA Today* article talked about Jodi Rupe; its cutline said Rube.[6] Make sure stories and ads match. The *Washington Post*'s movie review mentioned Kristy McNichols; seven pages later, the movie ad called her McNichol.[7]

Numbers: Face it. Many journalists turned to writing only after they realized they could not pass math. Always double-check numbers. Make sure stories and headlines are internally consistent. A headline read, "19 Men Are Arrested At Shopping Mall on Homosexual Charges"; the story listed 16. All over the area, people wondered who was left out, and why.[8] Triple-check phone numbers. An editor I know was once assigned to go answer the nonstop calls coming

---

[6]Lurie, G. (1986, April 21). Victim's daughter sets up bounty. *USA Today,* p. 3A.

[7]*Washington Post,* weekend section, November 16, 1984, pp. 21, 28.

[8]Fishman, C. (1984, July 21). 19 men are arrested at shopping mall on homosexual charges. *Washington Post,* p. B3.

into a local bank, after her paper mistakenly listed the bank's phone number as the place for citizens to call to request the city's fall leaf pickup.

Something of a mathematical furor followed a *Milwaukee Journal* report that a faucet leaking one drop per second would waste 2,300 gallons a year. Readers and, later, editors turned to such sources as the *Joy of Cooking* and *Popular Mechanics* and arrived at varying answers. "The point of all this," wrote Ruth Wilson, the paper's reader-contact editor, "is to illustrate the need for editors to question unsubstantiated figures. If they don't, some reader surely will" (p. 13).[9]

Claims: Recognize that people take special glee in trying to catch the press in errors. So verify any special claim such as a superlative (the county's biggest tomato ever, the largest drug bust in state history, the first woman to hold a certain job) or historical citation. The *New York Times* reported that no Nobel Prize existed in math because gossip had it that Alfred Nobel's wife had been involved with a mathematician. Subsequently, a reader informed the Times that Nobel was a bachelor.[10]

Editing for Structure

A schoolchild became upset after discovering a pea in his milk. Rumors flew, and reports hit the Chicago media: Urine had been found in pupils' milk.[11]

A pea or *pee?* As the message was passed along, the absence of language's tiniest word turned the meaning inside out. So it goes often in the process of communicating. Success rests on sustaining the fragile bond between writer and audience, a bond possible only if both parties heed the structural conventions of language.

Once content editing is done, editors enter the structural editing stage. Where content editing calls for viewing copy broadly as through a telescope, in structural editing calls for viewing copy broadly as through a telescope, in structural editing editors slide copy under a microscope, analyzing each mark on the paper or dot on the screen. Every comma, period, and space; every word, phrase, and clause; every sentence, paragraph, and page requires scrutiny. Clarity, accuracy, and precision compel the pickiest attention to this fundamental architecture of writing.

The good editor finds it axiomatic that "there's no such thing as a small error." Consider the headline that forms the title of the *Columbia Journalism Review* collection of press missteps: "Squad Helps Dog Bite Victim."[12] Here, all meaning hinges on the humble hyphen.

---

[9]*Quill,* September 1984, p. 13.

[10]Gleick, J. (1986, August 24). 3 awarded prestigious prize for breakthroughs in math, *New York Times,* p. A13, and Blomgren, T. (1986, August 24). Nobel's wife. *New York Times,* p. 20E.

[11]Copperud, R. H. (1986, November 8). Editorial workshop. *Editor & Publisher,* p. 4.

[12]Cooper, G. (Ed.). (1980). *Squad helps dog bite victim.* Garden City, NY: Dolphin Books.

Or take an example cited by editor Roscoe Born: "Use a *which* for a *that*, and your readers may have to have their stomachs pumped." He illustrates with the following sentence: "If you eat ashtolaka nuts which come from the groves of the Portmanteau Islands, you may die within hours, for they are deadly poison." Are all ashtolaka nuts poisonous, or just those from Portmanteau? The answer lies in whether the clause is restrictive (essential to the meaning) or nonrestrictive (incidental), and therefore in whether it needs commas and should be introduced by *that* or *which*.[13]

Such hairsplitting necessarily occupies at least some time of most editors, and often dominates the work of copydesk rim people. As the last news people to see copy, editors stand responsible for ensuring the clarity and correctness of everything that is published, down to the finest details.

Why does structure matter?

First, structure affects meaning. Language is a code that depends on consistent, mutually obeyed rules.

Second, structure affects credibility. The audience includes people who understand structure, and they rate the press. Sloppiness in structure breeds suspicion and mistrust that can compromise the overall integrity of writing.

Third, structure adds convenience for the reader and writer. It provides a consistent model. It gives writers some helpful substitutes for the voice modulations, facial expressions, hand gestures, and other techniques that complement spoken language.

Finally, structure contributes to artistic value. The late John B. Bremner became a legendary wordsmith, labeled by the *Wall Street Journal* as an "itinerant evangelist on behalf of grammar, logic and rhetoric." After conducting more than 50 seminars over several years, Bremner concluded, "The need is great. I see it in the sad state of the language. I'm trying to remind people that newspapers are a literary endeavor, to rekindle the fire" (p. 19).[14]

To begin structural editing, editors should take time briefly to adjust their vision. Inspecting each individual item requires utter concentration.

And still, no editor will see everything. So, as one essential element in structural editing, good editors try to cultivate an instinctive awareness of the danger zones where defects most likely lurk. Then they pay extra attention there.

Among the most common danger zones are spelling, grammar, punctuation, style and usage. We discuss them briefly here (and more detail is provided in the Appendix).

Spelling. Andrew Jackson once supposedly snorted, "It is a damn poor mind indeed which can't think of at least two ways to spell any word" (p. 154).[15]

---

[13]Morton, J. (1987, March). Wit and wisdom of a word-watcher. *Washington Journalism Review*, p. 60.

[14]Simison, R. L. (1984, July 23). Bremner's golden rules for editors. *Wall Street Journal*, p. 19.

[15]Mencher, M. (1987). *News reporting and writing* (4th ed., p. 154). Dubuque, IA: William C. Brown.

What's worse, for writers and editors, is what we might call the Journalist's First Law of Spelling: The longer you stare at any word, the less certain you are whether it is spelled correctly.

While the occasional genius arrives on the rim knowing how to spell *will-o'-the-wisp,* most of us struggle to sort out *principle* and *principal.* Doubtlessly, much can be done in school to improve spelling, and perhaps study would help clarify why Webster's Third New International Dictionary lists *buckshot* as one word and *bird shot* as two, or *boyfriend* as one and *girl friend* as two. But, given the infinite aggravation spelling inflicts on almost everyone, I prefer a purer, quicker method to wipe out most spelling errors: Buy a dictionary, and use it *any time you are not certain a word is spelled correctly.*

Carry it in your pocket. Set it on your desk. Open it 25 times a story. Looking up dozens of words takes only a few minutes, and it replaces countless semester hours lost in memorizing "i before e except after c" rules that do not apply to *seize* in the first place.

One caution: More and more newsrooms these days use computerized spelling checkers. These programs search through copy and match words against those in a computerized dictionary. They then highlight words that may be spelled incorrectly. Although these programs can assist the editor, they do not substitute for careful copyediting. In particular, they may not recognize misusages such as "it's" for "its" or "principal" for "principle," where the error involves a variant that might be correct in other circumstances.

Grammar and Punctuation.   You cannot remedy grammatical problems by owning a dictionary, but you can and should attack them systematically. Grammar can be mastered. It usually takes about one year's tough drilling. For some, that comes in Mr. Smith's or Mrs. Whitner's ninth-grade English course. Others are not so fortunate. If you still find yourself spending excessive time struggling with grammar, then act promptly. Take a demanding grammar course. Buy a grammar handbook. Use a computer for self-guided grammar tutorials.

As a teacher and editor, I find some grammatical issues crop up regularly and sometimes can be headed off early. Among the most common are subject–verb agreement, noun–pronoun agreement, comma usage, and punctuating quotations. These are worth checking faithfully in each piece of copy. (For further review of these problems, see the Appendix.)

Style.   Journalists use the word "style" in two ways. Broadly, it refers to the literary qualities of writing, as when we speak of the "spare, potent style of Hemingway." More narrowly, style designates journalists' policies governing recurring matters of abbreviation, capitalization, and usage that formal grammar may not cover.

Newspapers, magazines, wire services, and others adopt style rules for several reasons. Style contributes to consistency, credibility, and clarity. It provides standard guidance for the thousands of tiny issues that arise daily. It settles endless questions that linger over such issues as whether to abbreviate the word "Street" in addresses, or whether to use numerals or words to indicate someone's age.

But keep in mind that while knowing and enforcing style is an important beginning point for the editor, it should never become an obsession or an ending point. I have known some editors so compulsive about style trivia that they get consumed by questions such as whether "coroner" is an occupational title (and therefore not capitalized before a name) or a formal position (and therefore capitalized).

Rather than memorizing a particular stylebook that might or might not be used on the job, it is preferable to learn to *think* about each potential style issue and to enforce whatever policies hold sway within an organization. What matters is not whether one capitalizes the word *president* but whether one recognizes the editor's duty to understand and enforce some reasonable style.

Few newsrooms would suffer (and, I suspect, readers would gain) if editors spent just a bit less time mulling over matters like whether "5-foot-7" should have hyphens and more time editing for content, logic and clarity.

Usage. Read the following statements (adapted from an exercise I first encountered from William L. Rivers[16]), and then answer the questions that accompany them. Give one *specific* answer for each question, reflecting as best you can what image comes to your mind.

1. "Mayor Smith won re-election by an overwhelming majority." What percentage of the vote did the mayor receive?
2. "She comes from a well-to-do family." What is the family's annual income?
3. "I watch an average amount of television each week." How many hours do you watch every week?

When I pose these questions, students often express surprise at the extraordinary range of answers. For Question 1, answers have defined "overwhelming majority" as everything from 50% to 90%. For Question 2, estimates of the family's annual income range from $30,000 to $300,000. For Question 3, average television watching is listed as anywhere from 2 to 40 hours a week.

Students quickly grasp the point: If a group of relatively similar students does not have common understanding of such everyday terms as "overwhelming," "well-to-do," and "average," then imagine how much more difficult

---

[16]Rivers, W. L. (1983). *News editing in the '80s* (p. 99). Belmont, CA: Wadsworth.

communication becomes when journalists present far more subtle material to a heterogeneous mass audience.

For that reason, questions of *usage* have far more riding on them than one might at first think. *Usage* refers to how we use words. As journalists, our object is to move a message from sender to receiver, maintaining the meaning as precisely intact as is humanly possible. We falter in the mission with every example of vague, fuzzy, distorted, imprecise, ambiguous usage.

Writer know what they intend, and this knowledge taints their ability to read their own copy dispassionately. Their intentions ride piggyback on their words. Writing is not sharp.

It falls to editors, then, to guard against problems such as excessive use of prepositional phrases, weak verb constructions, tag-along words ("thunderstorm *activity*"), redundancies ("past experience," "12 midnight"), and euphemisms (an amusement park's use of "protein spill" to describe an occasional occurrence—when people throw up on the roller coaster).

In addition, readers can be not just annoyed but thoroughly baffled by use of jargon, gobbledygook, and their fellow travelers.

For instance, political scientist James David Barber once surveyed a single evening newscast and listed 31 words and phrases he felt would stymie many viewers. Among them were allocation formula, consumption levels, surcharges, most-favored-nation trade status, tariff concessions, cold shutdown, wage-price guidelines, cottage industry, pork-barrel legislation, long-range facility plan, and Republican conference leader. As Barber sagely observed, "Viewers who cannot understand the words will turn off the set" (p. 19).[17]

As an editor, consider yourself a translator. Remember the wise advice of editor Jim Gannon: "If you can't simplify, you don't understand (p. 156).[18] Take the wordiness, insider terms, and circumlocutions and turn them into plain English. Then publish the English.

Caution: In all these matters, editors should tred cautiously, for hasty or sloppy editing too often introduces errors. A study by Gilbert Cranberg found that of 680 stories, 128 of them (just under 19%) had inaccurate headlines or contained errors evidently introduced during editing.[19]

To reduce the chance of errors, good editors approach copy with firm knowledge of the rules, regulations, and policies. But they need other qualities as well: An "ear" for good writing, a sensitivity to individual style, and a judicial carefulness.

---

[17]Barber, J. D. (1979, September). Not the *New York Times:* What network news should be. *Washington Monthly*, p. 19.

[18]Teel, L. R., & Taylor, R. (1983). *Into the newsroom.* Englewood Cliffs, NJ: Prentice-Hall.

[19]Cranberg, G. (1987, March/April). The editor-error equation. *Columbia Journalism Review*, p. 40.

Editors can take several steps to develop these qualities:

Read hungrily. Reading helps develop the ear for good writing, and for bad writing. The editor who learns to "hear" the copy will occasionally get a timely nudge from the subconscious that something is out of whack. Similar nudges also clue editors to cases where copy should go untouched even when it appears to violate some rules.

Know yourself. As an editor, make a mental checklist of your own trouble areas, of the structural flaws you most often overlook. Then compensate by spending more effort in areas where you seem weakest.

Develop routines. Some items should be checked every time they occur: subject–verb agreements, pronoun references, tense, and number. Even in the writing of professionals, you will spot enough such errors to pay for the time spent.

Forget the third grade, or at least that part of it where teachers encouraged you to read rapidly, comprehending entire lines and thoughts at once. That facility betrays you in editing. It leads your eyes to see, not what is actually in front of them, but what they expect. For example, the quick reader tends to overlook the error in the phrase, *the Pananamian Canal,* because the error does not prevent easy comprehension of the overall meaning. In structural editing, reading slowly is more productive than reading rapidly, but you probably will find that doing so takes conscious effort.

Conduct an editor's final fact check. Many writers make their last step a methodical examination of every fact and assertion for accuracy, evidence, sourcing. Editors can take a similar step, by reviewing each change they have made. Modern computer programs, which often highlight the differences between the writer's and editor's versions of copy, can make this easier.

Read backward. When all else is done, many editors read copy backward, from the last word through to the first. This process, which seems agonizingly tedious the first time you try it, works because it breaks down the logical connections. Instead of reading for sense (and therefore taking in entire phrases and ideas at a time), you force yourself to read item by item. Consequently, you see small errors you might otherwise read past.

One Final Read

As the last step, read the copy one final time. Does it add up to a successful story? Have any problems or careless errors been added during editing? Amazingly, you will routinely find that your final trip through a story unearths something you had overlooked all along.

CONCLUSION

Make no mistake: both content and structure influence meaning.

With experience, editors may learn to examine many content areas automatically. But it normally proves safer and more thorough to do so explicitly, thinking through each issue and consulting with the writer.

Once content seems secure, the editor can move confidently to structure. Far more than a preoccupation with technicality, structural editing seals the final impressions copy will leave. Writers connect, or misfire, because of scores of accumulated decisions about spelling, grammar, punctuation, and usage. That explains why careful attention to structure is a culmination of good editing.

SIDEBAR 7
10 STEPS TOWARD BETTER EDITING

By Carl Sessions Stepp
Washington Journalism Review

Here are 10 tips toward better editing, based on interviews with writers and editors around the country:

1. *Remember that the editor's job is to help the reporter, not to take over the story.* "The biggest mistake I made as an editor," according to the *Chicago Tribune*'s Jim O'Shea, now reporting again, "is that I tried to edit every story as I would have written it." Gene Miller, legendary writer and now associate editor/reporting for the *Miami Herald,* expressed it this way: "As an editor, you are deprived of the exquisite ecstasy of doing it your way."

2. *Don't change copy without consulting the writer.* Many writers consider edited-in errors to be journalism's capital offense. Barry Bearak of the *Los Angeles Times* still would like to hand-chop the editor (at a previous paper) who changed every "martial arts" in his story to read "marshall arts."

3. *Coach, don't fix.* Roy Peter Clark and Don Fry of the Poynter Institute, both admired writing coaches, have pointed out that "coaching builds confidence; fixing undercuts confidence. Coaching brings writers and editors together as partners; fixing divides writers and editors as adversaries."

4. *Make time to treat every reporter and story as special.* A story that may be one small part of a full day to an editor is an all-consuming passion to a reporter. And writers remember. One reporter told me glowingly how an editor had helped revise a recent story. "I'd forgotten that," the editor said. "Stories are so intensively important to reporters, but I've got 10 of them at any given moment." Reporters shouldn't be passive; they must take responsibility for engaging their editors' attention. One way, of course, is by handing pieces in on time.

(Continued)

Sidebar 7 (*Continued*)

5. *Stay involved.* Andrew Schneider, two-time Pulitzer winner at the *Pittsburgh Press,* saluted his editors Flora Rathburn and Madelyn Ross for not shrinking from round-the-clock marathons on tough stories. "You really know what kind of editor you have," he said, "if he or she is sitting across the desk from you at 4 a.m. and still cares what the hell you're trying to do."

6. *Find ways to say yes.* "I try very hard not to say no very often," said Kristin Gilger of the *New Orleans Times-Picayne.* "I know some editors who don't feel like they're doing their jobs unless they say no a lot. People come with an idea and they find something wrong with it. Well, that suffocates people and they stop coming with ideas."

7. *Treat writers like colleagues, not flunkies.* Flora Rathburn, now metro editor in Pittsburgh, remembers being a reporter. "One thing I always appreciated," she said, "was an editor who treated me like a professional—who seemed to believe that I wasn't mentally retarded, that I wouldn't deliberately go out and screw up a story, that I had a capacity for thought."

8. *Be tough without being mean.* Reporters want skeptical, challenging editors, but want them to be fair and open-minded. "When you've stepped on as many land mines and lost as many toes as I have," said Miami's Gene Miller, "you learn to be careful. I know very few good editors who are tin-hearted tyrants."

9. *Do your homework.* "There is nothing that makes a writer feel worse," said Bearak, "than turning in a bad story and having an editor think it's good because the editor is ignorant of the subject or what has been written before."

10. *Make reporters feel they can come to you for help.* Milton Coleman, now a *Washington Post* editor, appreciated the support he got from his editors in 1984 when, as a reporter, he drew death threats for reporting Jesse Jackson's use of the term "Hymie" for Jewish people. Coleman said Post executive editor Ben Bradlee told him, "If you ever get in trouble, let me know right away; I'm very good at getting out of trouble because I've been in a lot of it myself."[20]

[20]Stepp, C. S. (1987, December). 10 steps toward better editing. *Washington Journalism Review,* p. 32. (Reprinted with permission.)

8

Making Decisions About Design

Once, newsrooms divided fairly neatly into "word people" and "picture people," who got along about as well as the Montagues and the Capulets. Word people issued assignments, reported, made news judgments, and determined play. Picture people took photos and laid out pages, generally under the direction of word people. Occasionally, when more exotic illustration was called for, picture people provided locator maps to accompany news of foreign coups or supplied drawings of enlarged fruits for the Thursday food pages.

All this took place back in the Neanderthal age of newspapering, when editors assumed unshakeable audience loyalty, hardly ever fretted about declining readership, and scorned television as an upstart, pesty playtoy. That is to say, it all was going on until a decade or so ago.

Then panic erupted. Editors (and, more menacingly, publishers) noticed that (a) readership and penetration were drooping, (b) specialty publications and splashy new suburban papers were cutting into circulation and advertising, and (c) television and its visual images were displacing typography as the central form of audience experience.

So, like adolescents suddenly discovering the opposite sex, newspapers scurried to spruce up appearances, catch up with fashion, and woo the newly fickle audience. Design arrived. A process once left mainly to printers (and known as *makeup*) and later handled by harried editors scribbling furious diagrams on dummy sheets (a process known as *layout*) was transformed into a rejuvenated art form. *Design* came to denote the conception, coordination and execution of an overall artistic and journalistic plan for the newspaper. Advancing technology (particularly innovations in color photo usage and the advent of computers) further spurred the rush toward brighter, sharper, more orderly, more attractive newspapers.

For editors, this sudden change brought new demands as well as new opportunities. It mortally undermined (although it has not, so far, actually eradicated) the division between journalists who are word people and those who are picture people. Today's journalists, and certainly tomorrow's, must be both. No longer can editors delegate design and artistic decisions to a small corps of specialists. No longer can designers isolate themselves from the mainstream rush of producing the paper.

The new editor must work toward integrating both word and visual elements, understanding the fundamental role of design in both the form and the substance of journalism. Not only is design a pleasant cosmetic for enhancing appearance, but it is becoming an increasingly useful device for conveying some substantive information more effectively and powerfully than traditional typography.

The new editor, like a television producer or movie director in many ways, oversees and coordinates an increasingly elaborate process. It begins, as it always has, with ideas and assignments. It ends, these days, with the use of computer technology to blend text, headlines, photos, and artwork into coherent packages.

Magazines recognized earlier than most newspapers that words and images were not adversaries jostling for page position but, instead, were allies in unifying communication. Newspapers only now are moving with any speed to integrate the processing of copy.

In many newsrooms, it remains common for one person (say, the editor in chief) to have a story idea, another (say, the features editor) to be asked to assign it, another (the reporter) to report and write it, another (the photo editor) to assign art for it, another (the photographer or artist) to prepare the art, another (the assistant features editor) to edit it when it arrives late in the day, another (the design editor) to place the copy and related material on a page, and another (the copyeditor) to fine-tune it and write a headline. Seven or eight people may be involved, many of whom do not even talk to the others or appreciate what effects the others were seeking.

This system has several predictable consequences.

First, the final product, after passing through so many hands, may barely resemble the original concept. This is not always bad, because sometimes the evolution improves the original. But it does point up how the system makes it fairly difficult to steer an idea all the way from conception to publication.

Second, it is largely luck if the various elements—article, artwork, headline, design—work together in tone, style, and effect, because no one hand has coordinated them all. Projects done by committee may well lack the artistic integrity and flair of those that reflect one individual's vision.

Third, the cumulative impact of such packaging throughout the newspaper can thwart readership. Although the ideal might be a carefully planned paper skillfully tailored to attract, engage, interest, and inform the audience, the reality is more likely a hodgepodge hastily assembled as attractively as possible under deadline. This may be enough for many loyal readers, but such a system is unlikely to entice marginal consumers or passive audience members who need special incentives to become regular readers.

The new editor, then, faces the important challenge of using design as a powerful instrument in improving the effectiveness of communication and in helping produce more desirable, interesting, understandable, and competitive newspapers.

Although a detailed technical discussion of typography and design is not intended here, every editor should be exposed to at least some key issues and techniques. In the sections that follow, we examine several elements related to design: headlines, photos, illustrations and graphics, and page layout.

HEADLINES

Recall your own newspaper-reading style. You probably do not read everything. Few of us do. Instead, you select from the dozens, sometimes hundreds, of choices. Typically, you flip through the paper page by page, glancing at headlines, stopping when they capture your attention, breezing on hurriedly when they fail to arouse you. And notice, next time, how often you fail to stop at all or glance away after a few moments. In this pattern, headlines can become the leading determinant of what the audience reads and avoids.

More than probably any other element on a page, headlines serve both content and design functions. They summarize stories, set a tone, help distinguish news and features, and provide a dollop of information for readers just looking for a quick summary. In their design role, headlines provide visual variety, dress up pages, and act as a kind of carnival barker calling attention to special attractions waiting in the small type.

Nothing influences readership more than headlines. Yet far too little attention is paid to how headlines look and read. Consider the following scene, common in every newsroom: Deadline nears. A frantic reporter paces the floor, struggling with the lead on a major project. The story has been in the works for days. Leads have been written, discarded, revised, rewritten. Fellow reporters have been consulted. The city and managing editors have weighed in with suggestions. The lead is *almost* there, and the writer is whirling in the final fevered stages of creativity.

Now ask yourself this question: How often have you seen a similar scene featuring the headline writer?

For most journalists, the answer would be seldom, if ever.

Sweating for hours, even days, over a lead is common, even routine in some newsrooms. Unfortunately, headline writing more typically takes place at the last minute, under excruciating time and space constraints. The copyeditor may spend 15 or 20 minutes pondering a head for a project that has taken weeks. The slot person may help, and occasionally on extremely big projects senior editors may get involved in head writing. But those instances are exceptions.

Yet, is the headline any less important than the lead? Of course not.

Too often editors see headlines as mostly a design convenience, not as the all-important gateway leading the reader into, or away from, the entire package. The result can be stark one-column, three-line heads with such flat, obvious messages as "President/to speak/Wednesday" or "Big storm/causes havoc/on highways."

Other times, whether because of time pressure or other reasons, headline writers simply fail to focus on an interesting point. In a column called "In Search of the World's Most Boring Headline," Michael Kinsley once cited such jewels as "U.S. Leadership Needed," "Thoughts at Graduation Time," "Surprises Unlikely in Indiana," and "Dramatic Changes Fail to Materialize on Hill" (p. A23).[1] On vacation one summer, I clipped such headlines as "Panel seeks probe of allegations," "Governors OK waste figure examination," and "Soviet foreign policy in hands of party." Would you stop to read any of those stories?

Good headlines sell their stories and enhance their pages without any compromise in accuracy and without resort to sensationalism. They stress what is most interesting, important, and special about their stories. They give readers a reason to slow down and enjoy an unusual article. "Will You Go Out With Me?" read the plaintive head on a young woman's *Newsweek on Campus* column about dating.[2] "Read This Article—Or Your Kids Will Be Stupid" was the headline for an essay on parenting in the *Washington Post*.[3] "How To Eat More and Weigh Less" introduced an *American Health* piece on how exercise affects weight.[4]

Granted, writing headlines can be arduous. Strong editors go pale at the very idea of reducing a 2,000-word, 6-month investigative project to six or seven words—which, of course, must be scrupulously accurate, irresistibly clever, and sculpted to fit within two counts of the designer's maximum.

Although some editors take to this task with an apparently congenital genius, most learn through practice, practice, practice.

---

[1]Kinsley, M. (1986, May 14). In search of the world's most boring headline. *Washington Post*, p. A23.

[2]Ullman, L. (1984, April). Will you go out with me? *Newsweek on Campus*, p. 32.

[3]Edmondson, B. (1986, March 2). Read this article—Or your kids will be stupid. *Washington Post*, p. C1.

[4]Silver, N. (1985, March). How to eat more and weigh less. *American Health*, p. 110.

Among the common guides in the practice of headline writing are the following:

- Use a subject and verb in every headline.
- Try not to split verbs, phrases, or nouns and modifiers between lines. Avoid splits such as "District Judge Rules Boy/Scouts Can Play Around/ City-Owned Parkland."
- Use action verbs, active voice. A headline, like a lead, should express action, change, or movement.
- Avoid the verb "to be" and its forms.
- Build on key words and thoughts from the story but do not mimic the exact language of the lead or give away a good punchline.
- Be specific. Say "Man robs downtown bank/to get money for Christmas" instead of "Downtown bank robbed/of undetermined amount."
- Be precise.
- Don't exaggerate.
- Avoid headlines that state a continuing condition ("Meetings planned," "Mayor to speak") or fail to single out what is unusual about a particular story ("Defense spending criticized").
- Avoid double meanings and double entendres, as chronicled regularly by *Columbia Journalism Review* in such examples as "Rape classes planned" and "Police can't stop gambling."
- Take care with words that can be used as both nouns and verbs (loves, races, moves, plays). In a headline such as "U.S. hopes/dashed in Olympics," readers may be confused by whether "hopes" is meant as a noun or verb.
- Avoid contrivances or words used in ways you would not normally use or accept ("Solons flay prez").
- Use words that have high visual or descriptive power (grandmother, tax increases, flash fire) and avoid words that do not summon any image at all (process, system, activity).
- Do not waste words. Make every word in a headline add to the reader's visual image.

Because headlines double as design devices and information blocks, headline writers and designers should not hesitate to negotiate to achieve both goals. The copyeditor needs a sufficient count to write an accurate, appealing, and understandable head. The designer needs sufficient size to catch the reader's eye and add variety to the page. If either one fails, the headline fails, and the reader may be lost.

The new editor cannot reform overnight a newspaper system that tends to save headlines to the last minute. But it is a reasonable goal to move toward a system that decides on headlines earlier in the processing of stories, that allows more time for copyeditors to ponder, write, and rewrite them, and that recognizes the vital role headlines play in achieving any paper's number one goal: to communicate with the audience.

PHOTOS

Photos have many uses. They often tell a story better, more dramatically, more profoundly than words. Such classic photographs as the young woman kneeling over a fallen student at Kent State University in 1970 or President John F. Kennedy's young son saluting his father's passing coffin linger in our minds years after we first see them.

Photos also add color, capture moods, make pages more inviting, and intensify reader interest. Surveys show that illustrations increase the readership of text by about one third. For example, the Newspaper Readership Project reported that 42% of those in one survey had read text accompanied by illustrations; only 31% had read text-only material.[5]

Like other elements we discuss, photos have a role in both the form and substance of journalism. Just as editors must consider the structure and the content of news articles, they so must judge photos.

Where does photo editing begin?

It does not begin with processing film or handling prints or cropping or sizing photos for the layout sheet. Photo editing begins with the *assignment*.

Photo assignments should be clear and complete, reflecting the vision and coordination of an editor thinking ahead.

In fact, thinking ahead has become one hallmark of contemporary design. As design advances, it requires more and earlier decisions by editors. A vital one these days (which, for production reasons, must be made early) is whether and where to use color in the daily paper. Other decisions include:

- Whether to tell a story as text only, as photo only, as graphic only, as text with photo, or as text with graphic.
- Whether, in view of staff limitations, it is wiser to commission complicated artwork for an early story or wait for later but possibly more important developments.
- Whether to gamble on long-distance, on-deadline transmission of key art.

[5]Bogart, L., & Gollin, A. (1983, May 9). *How do your papers rate with readers?* Paper presented to the American Society of Newspaper Editors, Denver, CO.

Especially given the relatively small photo and art staffs of most newspapers, editors must direct their forces carefully, or risk wasting resources on projects that fall through or that do not merit special handling.

These decisions underscore the role of the new editor as coordinator and planner. Therefore, with photos as with other aspects of design, good editing should begin at the point of conception:

- As an editor, you should make clear assignments. Make your intentions fully known (do you want a feature shot, a news shot, a stand-alone, an illustration for a specific point in a story?).
- Give the photographer as much information as possible about the story, its tone, any preliminary plans for packaging.
- Ensure that writers, photographers, artists, and editors consult and coordinate.
- And follow up to see that plans get carried out and that all parties get alerted if conditions change.

As with so much else in journalism, the editor's initial investment often proves crucial to the outcome. When the work arrives on your desk, you have little remedy if a fundamental early miscommunication has sent the reporter and photographer out with divergent views on the nature of their assignments.

Once a photographer shoots an assignment, the next editing decision concerns which shots will be made into prints. Typically, photographers take numerous shots (often using several rolls of film) for each assignment. But for reasons of time and money, relatively few prints can be made. Choosing which shots to print is an editing decision that should be made by someone who is informed and current on intentions for the project. That person can be a photographer, a photo editor, a designer or a coordinating editor. Papers have many systems that work well, and many systems that do not. The point is that selecting which negatives to make into prints should not be left to guesswork but should be regarded as an important *editing* decision and delegated accordingly.

Finally, a print or series of prints will arrive at the editor's desk. This calls for a new round of decisions: choosing which prints to publish, then *cropping, sizing,* and *shaping* them.

Cropping involves marking a print to show what portions an editor wants actually published. Typically, photos can be cropped from the top (eliminating, for instance, vast expanses of sky), the bottom or the sides to focus attention on the key point of the shot. *Sizing* means determining how wide and deep to display a photo. *Shaping* means considering whether a vertical, horizontal, or square photo works best.

Traditional design rules say that in general, bigger photos are more effective than smaller ones. Strong horizontal and vertical shapes are more pleasing than squares. Cropping should focus viewer attention on the central element of a photo but not so tightly as to eliminate or distort perspective.

As do words, photos have content that must be considered. Because of their inherent power, photos often trigger deeper, more emotional reactions from readers than articles that describe the same events in words. Shots of bodies, gore, and nudity cause some readers to recoil and to protest. Scenes that seem to embarrass or disregard the dignity or privacy of their subjects call for judicious handling. The editor must anticipate such problems and make considered, defensible decisions about how to proceed.

Cutlines or *captions,* the brief explanatory material accompanying a published photo, must also receive the same attention as any other copy. Cutlines should be double-checked for accuracy (and, in particular, cross-checked for consistency with the story), fairness, and tone.

In 1983, the Associated Press transmitted a photo of Secretary of State George Shultz with his hands over his face as he sat at a congressional hearing beside Marine Corps Commandant Paul Kelley. The cutline explained that Shultz had reacted to an embarrassing misstatement by Kelley, who had referred to a recent case of U.S. Marines being sent to "Vietnam"; he meant to say Lebanon. Later analysis of television footage revealed, however, that Shultz's gesture had actually come 7 seconds after Kelley's slip and had been a reaction to fatigue, not to Kelley's slip.[6] The moment the camera caught was not what the cutline made it appear.

GRAPHICS

From the moment that newspapers began using "dingbats," or small typographic devices, to break up columns of type, editors have known that artwork improves pages. Two recent developments—the bold graphic style of *USA Today* and the introduction of computer graphics technology—fueled a trend toward increasing use of non-photographic art on newspaper pages.

Like photos, these illustrations, which are commonly called *graphics* or *informational graphics,* go far beyond the cosmetic. They can highlight information contained within an article, serve as "sidebars" by presenting information beyond what the article contains, or stand alone, as do the daily "Snapshots" on *USA Today* front pages. The editor's job has expanded into making decisions about which single element or set of elements—text, photo, drawing, chart, graph—works most appropriately with each topic.

Graphics have marched quickly forward from the days of primitive locator maps. Today most newsrooms have a Macintosh or similar computer with the ability to generate complex, multicolored illustrations for everything from the

---

[6]AP's seven-second gap. (1983, November). *Washington Journalism Review,* p. 9.

explosion of the space shuttle Challenger to the intricacies of a heart transplant. Graphics services, in the manner of wire services, transmit daily menus of available computer illustrations. "Graphics director" or "graphics editor" may be the fastest-growing title in the business, as newsrooms search for expertise in this relatively new field.

Computer technology makes drawing infinitely faster and quicker than it was just a few years ago. Importantly, it also liberates the editor. In the old days, revising or correcting an illustration could necessitate time-consuming redrawing, resetting type, and reconfiguring overlays. Today, editing a computer graphic happens in seconds, with a few keystrokes.

As with photos, editing graphics begins at the conceptual stage. Editors, along with reporters, artists, designers, and others, must plan carefully and communicate regularly. Old systems must be remodeled. For example, as we have noted already, it once was typical for the "word" team and the "art" team to work parallel on a project without overall coordination. What resulted, too often, was a mishmash of related but poorly coordinated activities.

Today's editor often must plan, pull together and oversee both tracks of the production. For a complex package to have unity and maximum effect, it needs an editor's attention at every stage.

For instance, just as stories and photos can produce both structural and content problems, so can graphics. Structurally, graphics must be correct and in clear, appropriate, easily grasped form. Their content, often necessarily simplified or abstracted, must not distort or exaggerate. Because graphics often deal with statistics and other mathematics, editors must show extra care in examining them for careless or logical errors.

Even the nature of a graphic device can raise fairness issues. For example, consider the "black Monday" in October 1987 when the Dow Jones stock market average plunged more than 500 points. One way to illustrate such a drop would be with a "fever line" charting the course of the average over several weeks, as it rose to near 3,000, then dropped into the 1,700s. But does one draw the chart with a base point of, say, 1,500, which will show a steady increase followed by a dramatic plunge almost to the bottom of the chart? Or does one use a base of 0, which will seem to show a much smaller decrease with a much less dramatic falling line?

Barely over the horizon waits an entire new classification of ethical dilemmas involving photos and graphics. Computerization now allows every photo and graphic to be reduced to a computer code and then stored within the computer's memory. To put it in simplest form, a photo or graphic is merely a series of millions of tiny dots; the printed image is determined by which dots receive ink and which ones do not. What the computer code does is record the location of each dot and indicate a "yes" if the dot should have ink and a "no" if it should not.

In many ways, this so-called digitizing of photos is a remarkable advance.

It allows photos to be shipped quickly over very long distances by transmitting the precise codes from one computer to another. But this system also raises serious ethical issues. Once a photograph or graphic is encoded in computer memory, then an editor can change the code, and therefore alter the photo, merely by pressing some keys in much the same way as editors can make insertions and deletions in written copy.

This may make it easy, and tempting, for editors to rearrange photos electronically, for example to delete unwanted background scenes or to move two people closer together for a tighter shot or even, at extremes, to add elements that were not in the original picture. To take an obvious example, a photo could be doctored to show, say, a political candidate in the same room as a prostitute.

Where journalists draw the lines between appropriate "editing" of photos and unethical "doctoring" will be negotiated over the next few years. And the ubiquity of graphics raises the stakes of such decisionmaking. It illustrates again how outmoded is the distinction between word people and picture people.

Noted graphics editor Rob Covey offered several words of advice for journalists coping with this new world of graphics[7]:

- "Decide what is important," through collaboration among reporters, artists and editors. "That doesn't mean just turning over a 50-inch rough draft of a story to an artist and saying, 'See if you get any ideas from this.' . . . You jointly make the first key decisions."
- Make sure the graphic makes a point, is kept brief and contains an explanatory caption.
- Expect an added workload. Reporters, artists and editors all may need to do additional research and reporting to gather material for graphics.
- Learn the color production process so you will know what to expect and what is possible.
- Edit graphics carefully, double-checking facts and making certain the overall presentation will make sense to someone not familiar with the subject.

LAYOUT

For our purposes, we define layout more narrowly than design. Where *design* is the overall planning and coordination of a newspaper's look, *layout* refers to the actual dummying of each page.

Some editors specialize in layout, others lay out pages occasionally, and still

---

[7]Covey, R. (1988, Winter). Eight ways to improve graphics for your projects. *IRE Journal*, p. 5.

others never touch a dummy sheet or computer pagination screen. But, as part of their overall understanding of design, all of today's editors should become familiar with the essential principles and techniques. The new editor should (a) understand and appreciate design and layout, (b) feel comfortable working with design and designers, and (c) know how to lay out attractive pages.

Professional designers often have specialized training in art and aesthetics, as well as journalism, and this book cannot duplicate that material. What follows, instead, is an overview of some basic concepts, intended as an introduction to the newcomer or a review for the editor with some previous exposure.

Design can be both highly subjective and highly technical. It is subjective because, like other aesthetic judgments, design choices can be rooted in personal, debatable ideas about style and beauty. And it is technical because designers use a host of methods and devices, both large and small, to create subtle, cumulative impressions. Ultimately, a reader sees a page in its entirety, and may seldom notice individual techniques such as the size of rules, the space between headlines, or the careful matching of colors. The designer, however, begins with a collection of parts, and must blend them one by one into a coherent, orderly and attractive whole.

A successful page is not one that induces a reader to exclaim, "What a beautiful newspaper layout!" Instead, it is a page that the individual is attracted to, reads and enjoys. Likewise a poor page does not cause readers to comment on its ugliness. It simply causes them to turn away.

Mario R. Garcia, a leading teacher and theorist in design, reported being struck by how readers notice "content and how it is organized, more so than typographic styles and aesthetic considerations." Garcia added:

> Much more research is needed in the area of graphics and design—especially to gain insight into eye movement, color preferences and, of course, reader perception of all the subtleties of design. (p. 56)[8]

Some Principles of Layout

1. The goal of layout is to attract and assist readers. Layout editors try to package material in a neat, considered way that invites attention, makes it easy to understand and read the material, and encourages reading as much of a page as possible.

2. A successful page layout should be orderly, easy to follow, visually exciting, and consistent with the general tone of a newspaper.

3. Page layouts tend to employ similar aesthetic values to those used in

---

[8]Garcia, M.R. (1988, June 25). Redesign and readers. *Editor & Publisher*, p. 56.

other areas, such as fashion, decorating or art: grace, neatness, imagination, symmetry, order, cleanliness, elegance.

    4. Three key principles to keep in mind are *balance, variety,* and *proportion.*

Balance refers to the arrangement of elements (art, body type, headline type, and white space) on the page. A page should be somewhat top heavy, with the most important items above the fold. But the bottom should not be ignored, and the page should not seem right-heavy or left-heavy, or very heavy in one area and very light in another. Each quadrant should have some appealing visual item.

Variety, or contrast, means mixing elements to avoid monotony. Variety can be achieved in size (e.g., using headlines of different point sizes), shape (mixing horizontals and verticals), and weight (incorporating blacks, whites, grays, and where available, colors). Notice that most newspaper pages use two or three widths of body type, both one-line and multiline headlines, and several different rectangular-shaped packages (known as *modules*).

Proportion rests on the assumption, supported by research, that strongly rectangular shapes are more pleasing than squares and that several different shapes on a page are preferred to several similar ones.

    With these principles in mind, an editor can turn to the detailed process of creating pages.

Some Techniques of Layout

Here is a step-by-step work flow for laying out a page. We assume it is a news page, although the process is similar for feature pages and others:

    1. List available articles, photos, illustrations, and other elements. Develop a general idea of what should go at top of page (generally the most important material) and what at bottom (lesser material, but at least one unusual or eye-catching element). Do not try to cram too much on a page. For a news page, using five to nine elements works well. For a feature page, use two to four elements.

    2. Begin with your most important illustration and most important story. Decide where you want them, and how much space they should get. Usually, these two items should be clearly dominant, and they should go near the top of the page. They should be arranged so a reader naturally focuses first on them.

    3. Place an item of interest at the bottom of the page: a package that can be attractively boxed, a story that can be "stripped" across all columns, a feature with a small piece of art.

    4. Note what elements you have remaining. Think of your page as having

three sections: top, middle, bottom. Working toward the middle, find places for each remaining element.

5. Work with *modules* (blocks of material that form rectangles). Make each package, whether text only or text with art, "square off" at the bottom to form a rectangle. This gives unique status to each module, prevents items from interfering with one another, and makes pages seem clean and uncluttered.

6. *Wrap* as little copy as possible, except for strongly horizontal modules. A wrap is copy that is continued from one column to the next. Do not require more than 4 or 5 inches of vertical jump for the reader's eye from the bottom of one leg of type to the top of the next.

7. Use photos large, and strongly horizontal or vertical. Give special stress to one piece of art per page.

8. Use a variety of shapes, most horizontal, some vertical. Do not stack similar shapes, and do not divide page in half either horizontally or vertically.

9. Avoid massive areas of gray type (a massive area is defined as one where you can put down a hand on the page and hit only body type). Use white space to add contrast and to let a page "breathe."

10. Use boxes, rules, screens, colors, small typographical devices, and white space to call attention to special stories and to provide variety.

11. Try not to bump headlines. That has the same effect as having two people shout for your attention at exactly the same time.

12. Vary headline sizes and shapes: bold/italics, one-line and multiline, one column and wider. Use kickers, hammerheads, and other devices where appropriate.

13. Do not run a story out from under its headline. The headline should be an "umbrella" that covers the entire package, making the boundaries clear to the reader.

14. Use biggest headlines at top of page, and one fairly large headline at the bottom. Use smallest headline sizes in the middle.

15. For one-column headlines, use three lines. For two-column headlines, use two lines. For wider headlines, use one line. Make sure to provide adequate room for an informative, compelling headline.

Many newsrooms already experiment with computerized page design, and within a few years this process (known as *pagination*) should be quite common. It lets editors use a computer to assemble and fit all elements for a page. Like the advent of computer editing terminals, the arrival of pagination technology should not alter fundamental philosophies or principles. It should, however, add speed, flexibility and artistic capabilities far beyond what many editors now possess.

Laying Out Specialty Pages

The previous suggestions apply directly to *news pages,* including front pages and section fronts. Although the overall principles do not change, some specialty pages call for different wrinkles.

Inside News Pages.   Inside pages usually contain ads as well as editorial content. The ads are positioned first, leaving the editor with designated space to fill. Because the ads take up room and limit flexibility, inside pages usually contain fewer and shorter stories, and fewer and smaller pieces of art. Do not crowd too many tiny stories onto a page. Keep it clean and simple by not bumping headlines and not using too many clashing typographical devices. Try to avoid bumping photos and boxes up against ads, which also may contain artwork.

Feature Pages.   Feature pages may be designed more like magazine pages, using fewer elements than news pages and striving to be bold, innovative and eye-catching. Often, one huge element will consume half the page or more. Art may be stylized or staged for effect (using models, posed scenes, collages, and other combinations, as long as they are not presented as reality). Drawings and other non-photographic illustrations appear more often than on news pages. More variety is expected in type style, sizing and shaping of art, and the use of effects (such as enlarged letters, unusual boxes, special screens) that would not be considered dignified in the news columns.

Sports Pages.   Sports pages serve as both news and feature pages. Typically, they resemble the former in presenting information in an orderly way based on its news value, and the latter in the use of large art and striking packaging. In fact, sports designers enjoy one key advantage over their colleagues from other sections: the almost daily presence of strong, dramatic, action photographs. Use them, and use them big.

Overall, specialty pages begin with the fundamental precepts of design, such as balance, variety, proportion and the use of modules, and then adapt them to suit particular audiences and tastes. As always, the goal is to create clear, interesting, creative pages that will lure and serve readers.

CONCLUSION

Design links the newspaper to its audience. Like translators, designers stand in the middle. They are connectors. As journalists, designers must appreciate the subtleties and sensitivities of the news. As friends of the audience, they must recognize the needs and tastes of potential readers. Then they must shape the content into forms that hurried readers find engaging and meaningful, without letting those forms misshape or overwhelm the substance.

Without doubt, design decisions are editing decisions, fully intertwined with judgments about news, content and structure. No longer does it make any sense to tolerate segregation of "word people" and "picture people." In these days, to be a complete editor demands the ability to travel in both those worlds.

SIDEBAR 8
THE NEW AGE OF GRAPHICS

By Bill Steinauer
Gannetteer

I suspect that the new age of graphics has caused many a traditional "word" editor or reporter to break out in a cold sweat.

But there is no need to be overwhelmed. Relax. And then treat photos and graphics like stories. Just make sure you are passing information on to readers, and that it is presented in a simple, readable way.

When I worked in Reno a few years ago, our publisher would always react the same way when he saw that we were becoming too gimmicky. We thought we were being clever; he thought we were being confusing. He was right. "Keep it clean and simple," he would tell us . . . and tell us . . . and tell us.

Those aren't bad words to live by. But it may not be as simple as it seems, to be simple. A lot of editors are having a rough go of it. At least those were my thoughts after I studied what some Gannett newspapers are doing graphically.

The best graphics I saw were clean and simple. They were edited, easy to read and easy to understand. That's basically how we gauge the value of stories. That's how we—and I think readers—gauge the value of photos and graphics.

But there were problems. A commitment to simplicity would have solved many of them. For example, some photos lacked a clear focal point or center of attention. They were poorly cropped with too much unneeded information left in the photo.

I remember one photo with a cutline that told me this was a picture of John Doe on a piece of equipment that was going to tear down a building. It took me five minutes to find John Doe. Instead, I, the reader, received a wide-angle view of the surroundings. I didn't know what I was supposed to look at. Without the focal point, I was lost and inclined to just forget the picture and go onto something else. Does that remind you of some long stories you've read lately?

It was much the same way with graphics. Some were too big and confusing. They weren't edited. Some maps didn't direct but confused. They weren't edited. Some graphics and maps were informational, only to be ruined by heavy dark gray or color screens. They weren't readable.

And then there were those newspapers that did very little. Many of their editors

(Continued)

Sidebar 8 (*Continued*)

wrote letters explaining that they had no artist, or that their only artist was off during the week of the newspapers we reviewed.

Those editors feel overwhelmed and believe that providing graphics is a lot of work. It's not. It's just thinking of the reader. It's just a matter of looking at each story and asking yourself: "Is there some additional information that would help the reader that I can present in a quick, readable way?"

More often than not, you don't have to have an artist. Or, for that matter, a Macintosh computer. You just need a commitment to help your reader through the newspaper, to be as useful and as meaningful as you can.

And then find the focus. Concentrate on what you are communicating.

Remember: "Keep it clean and simple."

Frequently Asked Questions About Photos and Graphics

How Should I Use an Artist?

As a journalist. Make sure your artist understands your role as a newspaper—to give readers information. If an artist understands that, there should be a minimal amount of decorative art (merely drawings without information). The same hold true for photographers. Make sure photographers know their roles: to tell a story, to produce information.

For example, a food feature on tomatoes could be illustrated with a pretty picture, but a drawing or picture that included information would be better.

With almost all stories, there is potential work for an artist. Whether it's to explain graphically how water gets from the river to your kitchen (to go with a water-shortage story), or a map and demographic chart to go with a trend story about a nearby town, an artist can be involved. It's a matter of setting priorities. The production of cute drawings to go with Page One promos should be low on the priority list. Graphics, maps and informational pullouts that help the reader should be high on the list.

What If I Don't Have an Artist?

That's OK. Somebody (or as many staffers as possible) can be trained on your Macintosh so that simple pie charts or fever-line graphs can be produced. But most of the work can be done by putting statistical lists or consumer information in at-a-glance boxes. Make sure the type is legible and that it has a headline. Keep the information short and to the point and set it off with rule or a box. Anyone can create a "fact box" with a newsroom computer system—and the "fact box" can help readers.

How Do You Come Up With Graphic Ideas?

(*Continued*)

Sidebar 8 (*Continued*)

By planning and communicating. Make sure photographers and artists are involved in planning meetings. Brainstorm. Talk to each other. City editors should have good issue and trend stories that lead to good graphics and photos. Plan early. Feature editors especially need to plan for exciting-looking pages. If you want a graphic on a story that can be published at any time, let the artist read the story first. Then, it's a good idea to have a brainstorming session with as many staffers as possible.

Come up with a headline for the story first. That will help put the story in focus; play off the head—think of a way to visually express the idea. And remember to include information.

Also, try not to be satisfied with your first idea. Try to build on it. As with a lead of a story or a headline, challenge yourself.

What About Projects?

Often, an enormous amount of time is spent on writing and editing a series, but not nearly enough time is devoted to producing and editing photos and graphics for it. Get artists and photographers involved at the outset. Make sure they see the drafts of the stories. Good graphics and photos are essential. Give photographers and artists time to research and to do the job right.

How Do You Plan Good Photos?

Too many photos are static and don't show action or expression. Too often we are relying on what some editors call "environmental portraits." In these photos, a person or a group of persons is photographed in their environment. That can be OK, especially if the environment is an important part of the story and really shows readers something. But too often, it's the easy way out.

It might be better if editors tried to think like TV assignment editors when planning. TV editors are forced to think of movement—they can't have their subjects standing in one place. Thinking that way could lead to better planning in your newsroom.

When Should We Think About Using Graphics?

Almost anytime. Some kind of "fact box" can be expected from the following:

- Profiles on places (Some ideas: how to get there, places to stay, demographic information, maps).
- Profiles of people (biographical facts, quotes on a variety of subjects not mentioned in story).
- Fashion (costs, where you can buy locally).
- Events (time and place, ticket information, telephone numbers).

(*Continued*)

Sidebar 8 (*Continued*)

- Almost anything that's consumer oriented, whether it's the latest in sunglasses or where to buy the best hamburger in town (how to get to places, suggestions on what to buy, costs).
- Medical and scientific information (visually explain technical advances or what causes air pollution or acid rain).
- Business stories (statistics, company highlights).

How Do You Edit Graphics?

Just as you do with a story: Does it make sense? Is it accurate? Is it simple and easy to understand? Is it readable?

Let a lot of staffers read the graphics. If it's a chart on trapshooting, give it to someone who knows nothing about trapshooting. That person will be a much better judge than an expert who might be too close to the subject to know whether something is missing.[9]

---

[9]Steinauer, B. (1987, November). Editorially speaking. *Gannetteer*, pp. 2–5. (Reprinted with permission.)

Making Decisions About Legal Issues

We live in a litigious society, beset by a fear of lawyers. Few areas of editing have expanded as much in recent times as those dealing with courts and legal concerns.

"Has this story been lawyered yet?" is a modern editing question that ranks along with "What's the lead?" and "How much space can I have?"

Journalists have become masters of defensive editing, striving to anticipate problems, and ward off legal challenges before they develop. Lawyers stand on call for reporters facing subpoenas, or photographers worried about invasion of privacy, or desk people concerned about national security disclosures.

In part, this defensiveness stems from growing professionalism within journalism itself. As standards rise, editors naturally give copy more scrutiny. After all, few if any journalists actually want to violate the law or provoke a lawsuit.

But what is happening today also evidences more troubling conditions. One is journalists' widespread concern about public hostility toward the press. In our large and contentious society, the press may seem, to many people, a big, impersonal, and heartless money machine and, consequently, an inviting target for lawsuits. Fearing an aroused public, journalists tend to watch their step.

In addition, many journalists perceive that the court system, up through the U.S. Supreme Court, has become less friendly to the press. If so, court action is even more to be avoided. For instance, press lawyer Barbara Dill reported to an American Press Institute seminar her evaluation that:

> The Supreme Court has dealt the press a string of losses in the last decade. It has threatened to cut back on legal privileges that have helped to shield the media from libel losses for the last 20 years. It has denied constitutional protection to

various messages and expressions that it considers to be outside the public interest. Chief Justice William Rehnquist has consistently voted against the press. . . . [1]

Whatever the full range of causes, one result is probably more careful, responsible journalism. Another, however, may be excessive self-doubt and self-censorship, editing grown overly defensive. This is called the *chilling effect*.

"There certainly is a chill . . . in the sense that people have to take second, third, and fourth looks at stories," libel lawyer Sam Klein told a journalists' conference. He said the chill affects not only publishers, editors and reporters but even news sources and letters-to-the-editor writers. Consequently, said Klein, papers are "backing away" from investigative reporting and matters that could lead to suits (p. 10).[2]

It isn't just the fear of losing a lawsuit that distresses journalists. It is also the enormous potential expense and inconvenience of being sued at all. At another journalism convention, one publisher told of retracting, under threat of libel suit, a story his paper knew to be true.[3]

No less venturesome a journalist than columnist Jack Anderson has said:

We are hedging a little more than we did to avoid libel. We are not as likely to name names because when you name names, you invite libel suits. I am not a multimillionaire. . . . There's no question that newspapers across the country are avoiding stories that might lead to libel suits. (p. 7A)[4]

More and more, editors find themselves acting almost as paralegal trouble-shooters, sandwiched between gung-ho reporters and photographers on one side and cautious lawyers and publishers on the other:

- A reporter has discovered juicy information after overhearing jury members in conversation. The newspaper's lawyer warns that, if published, it could lead to contempt proceedings against the paper.
- A reporter has sworn herself to secrecy to protect a source. The publisher fears huge fines from an angry judge insisting on the source's name.
- A photographer has shots of a violent police-labor confrontation. Lawyers for both sides demand the film.

Although such dramatic examples are not unusual, they inevitably are accompanied by lengthy deliberations involving lawyers, publishers, editors, and line

---

[1]Dill, B. (1987, October 7). *The courts and the newsroom today.* Reston, VA: American Press Institute.

[2]Stein, M.L. (1987, July 4). The chilling effect. *Editor & Publisher*, p. 10.

[3]Fitzgerald, M. (1985, October 5). Don't give in to libel "hysteria," lawyer says. *Editor & Publisher*, p. 15.

[4]Inquiry. (1985, August 14). *USA Today*, p. 7A.

journalists. What can sometimes be even more dangerous are the routine, everyday legal issues that may arise without fanfare and that may slip past less-than-alert reporters and editors. In fact, it is something of a truism among lawyers and editors that legal trouble may arise as much in the small items and back-of-the-paper tidbits as in the high-profile projects that get painstaking scrutiny.

But wherever they come from, legal problems create turmoil.

Eugene Roberts of the *Philadelphia Inquirer* bluntly summarized the worries of many colleagues when he wrote the following:

> We, as a society, have now delivered into the hands of government officials the nation over—indeed, the world over—a simple but effective weapon against freedom of expression. It is the capability of using protracted litigation to harass, intimidate, and punish the press and private citizen alike for views and reports that officials do not like.[5]

In view of such an environment, what is the editor's role? How can editors balance the tension between their duties as law-respecting citizens and as unfettered journalists?

According to editor Bill Schultz: "Our challenge as editors is to respond to (these) concerns—to teach our reporters and editors how to be careful without becoming timid" (p. 11).[6]

Needless to say, editors should increase their understanding of potential legal problems. In addition, they should try to develop a philosophical framework for analyzing their obligations and expectations. Before getting to some specific trouble spots, then, we should try to delineate a strategic overview for editors confronting legal issues. It might begin with the following major tenets:

1. *The editor's job is to edit:* to gather and publish material of value to the readers. It is not to solve crimes, serve the state, protect government secrets, or prosecute cases. Those are worthy roles, and editors seldom oppose them, but fulfilling them is a task assigned to others.

2. *The editor must respect courts but see them in context.* Unlike police and lawyers who swear to uphold the law, journalists do not do that. Certainly, they are not exempt, but extreme circumstances may lead them to challenge current readings of the law, as editors have done from John Peter Zenger to the publishers of the Pentagon Papers.

3. *Editors should learn about the law, but never try to be lawyers.* Do not try to outguess lawyers. They do not think like other people. When you need

---

[5]Roberts, E. (1985, April). On collision course. *Quill,* cover.

[6]Schultz, B. (1985, September). We're consulting with him more often on stories. *ASNE Bulletin,* p. 11.

legal advice, consult a good lawyer with a commitment to First Amendment values.

4. *Editors should listen to lawyers but make their own decisions.* To a lawyer, the judicial process can be an end in itself. To an editor, the end is the best interests of truth and the audience. Sometimes this means taking a chance by publishing investigative material that could spark a lawsuit. Other times it means defying politically motivated efforts at censorship. And still other times it means leaving out risky copy that serves no overriding purpose. Lawyers should offer advice on the law and the risks of certain action. Journalists should decide what course to pursue and what risks to accept.

If editors cannot be expected to fully understand complexities of the law, how can they do their jobs with least risk? As is true with content and structural editing, a start is for each editor to develop a sense of the danger areas, a working understanding of where potential trouble most likely lurks.

Further, editors must not relent on the fundamentals. Carelessness and inattention can bring legal battles just as quickly as irresponsibility. The name you do not double-check may be the one that is misspelled or transposed so as to libel an innocent person. The columnist's work you approve each day with a glance may one day contain plagiarism. The human-interest photo you select at the last minute may depict a disabled child and produce a privacy claim. The secretary barely mentioned in paragraph 19 of an otherwise perfect investigation of a local official may have a case against you even if the official doesn't. Simply put, never take editing shortcuts with even the most innocuous-seeming items.

In the following sections, we briefly examine several areas relating to press law. Remember: This is not a law textbook. It is advice, from journalist to journalist, about how to sense impending trouble.

LIBEL

This is the hardy perennial, the sleeping ogre all journalists tiptoe softly around. Libel has many complex legal definitions, but they boil down to the following: Libel is published, false material that defames someone. Beyond that, what editors need to know is that libel is what a judge and jury say it is. Because it involves issues like reputation and character, libel can be subjective and slippery. That means lots of work for lawyers and lots of confusion for journalists.

Common categories of libel include:

- accusations of a crime
- charges of immorality

- insinuations of insanity or loathsome diseases
- claims of incompetence in business.

Defenses for libel begin with *truth*. You need not worry about libel if you can prove to a jury's satisfaction that what you published is true. Clearly, however, truth is a sticky term. How, for instance, does one prove the truth of concepts such as "immoral" or "loathsome" or "incompetent"? Although truth is an adequate defense, it often is an elusive one.

Two other defenses are important. First is *fair comment,* an individual's right to express an opinion about public affairs (such as politics) and public performances (such as movies or books). An opinion, even a harsh one, is not libelous if it is founded on facts and relevant to a public matter.

Second is *qualified privilege,* the right to report on official proceedings (like city council meetings) and official documents (like most court papers), as long as the reporting is fair and accurate. A key point here is that the material in question must have been uttered or written in an official forum. If a congressman takes to the floor of the House of Representatives and calls a colleague a child molester, you can publish the charge without fear of libel. However, if the congressman makes the same charge in conversation while walking to the chamber, it is unofficial, and publishing it could constitute libel.

Since the landmark 1964 *Sullivan decision* of the U.S. Supreme Court, distinction has been made between *public figures* and *private figures.* In its 1964 decision and follow-ups, the court has ruled under the Constitution the press and public have great freedom to debate controversial public issues, without undue fear of libel suits. For a public figure to collect libel damages, he or she must not merely prove libel but also *actual malice.*

Unfortunately, when the court chose the term *malice,* it did not use it in the ordinary meaning of "bad motives." In libel, actual malice has a much narrower meaning. It generally means either of two things: knowingly publishing untruths (lying) or "reckless disregard for the truth." Motives are not really relevant, although courts do allow some questions about a journalist's "state of mind." What matters most is what journalists knew and did at the time of publication.

Generally, in libel cases involving public figures, the burden of proof lies with those suing the press. That is, they must prove the press acted with malice. But, pragmatically, it makes sense for editors to assume in their own minds that they carry the burden of proof.

When confronting potentially libelous material as an editor, ask yourself this question: Can I convince a jury that I acted without malice and in the public interest? Is the evidence adequate for the assertions being made, and is all conflicting evidence being carefully considered? If not, reconsider.

Finally, several possible misconceptions and pitfalls surrounding libel should be clarified, and some advice given:

1. *Don't depend on the word "allegedly."* It is a hedge word that does not help in fending off libel. You should consider the sentence, "Smith allegedly robbed the bank" to be the same, legally speaking, as "Smith absolutely robbed the bank." Better to say "Smith is *charged with* robbing the bank" (assuming, of course, that charges have been filed). I recommend eliminating "allegedly" from your vocabulary.

2. *Attributing libelous material to a source doesn't necessarily relieve journalists of responsibility for what they publish.* If you quote Jones as falsely saying, "Smith is a drug dealer," you may be as guilty of libel as Jones, and even more likely to be sued because newspapers are easy targets. In many cases, the key distinction is whether your source is a public or private figure. When public figures trade charges on public issues, for instance, courts commonly allow journalists to report the incidents without fear of libel. When private individuals make libelous statements, however, journalists should be very wary about quoting them. Veteran First Amendment lawyer Bruce W. Sanford has written that most states allow the press to report on "public people . . . hurling accusations or epithets at each other." But the publication of "unsubstantiated gossip-mongering by private individuals" carries risk of libel (p. 14).[7]

3. *Beware of headlines and cutlines.* They can libel too. In fact, big type can exacerbate libel problems. Do you know how often papers spend months on investigative projects, only to have the headlines and cutlines slapped on minutes before deadline? That can be very dangerous.

4. *Beware of big problems in small places.* Libel can occur, for instance, in the agate-type police roundup column, or in a paragraph mentioning a bit player in an otherwise perfect story focused on someone else. Precision is important. One paper lost a judgment after using the term *testimony* when *affidavit* was correct (p. 35).[8]

5. *As in every legal matter, recognize that state and local laws aren't all alike.* Learn the peculiarities of your own state's laws. In some places, for instance, a newspaper can reduce or eliminate libel liability by publishing a correction or retraction as soon as an error comes to its attention.

6. *As an editor, remember your quality-control function.* Insist that copy have satisfactory evidence, documentation and sourcing for any potentially damaging charge. Do not fear challenging a reporter or source. Better to argue out tough points in the newsroom than in the courtroom. And do not shrink from getting legal advice when you need it.

---

[7]Sanford, B.W. (1984). *Synopsis of the law of libel and the right of privacy.* (3rd ed., p. 14). New York: World Almanac Publications.

[8]Massing, M. (1985, May/June). The libel chill: How cold is it out there? *Columbia Journalism Review,* p. 35.

7. *Use common sense and common courtesy.* Surveys have shown that people tend to sue for libel *after* they have tried vainly to get satisfaction more informally. Some sue after being treated rudely or being patronized when they call the newspaper to complain. An easy but appallingly overlooked point: Train people who answer your newsroom telephones to be respectful to callers (even angry ones) and to pass complaints along to someone with authority. When I was a supervisor, I always told them to assume that every caller was the publisher's cousin.

Gilbert Cranberg, through the Iowa Libel Research Project, interviewed 164 libel plaintiffs and analyzed hundreds of complaints and cases.[9] He reported that "virtually all" the plaintiffs said their "post-publication experiences with the press had influenced them to bring suit."

Cranberg also found that few papers have clear procedures for handling complaints, that callers often get transferred endlessly around a newsroom, that news organizations have a "siege mentality" that resists all pressures including legitimate requests for retraction, and that newspeople, like everyone else, hate to admit their mistakes. His recommendations, as he outlined them in *Columbia Journalism Review*:

• Impress on employees the great power the press has to hurt people— and, as a corollary, insist upon courtesy in dealing with complaints.

• Center responsibility for dealing with complaints in a person with good human-relation skills who is not responsible for news coverage.

• Develop policies and procedures for addressing complaints, put them in writing, and emphasize their importance.

• Make sitting on serious complaints a firing offense. (p. 41)[10]

The press also might benefit by helping educate the public in the difficulties of journalism. Reporting is a complex and imperfect craft, where the truth is elusive and often deliberate obscured. It would help if the public showed more patience with the inevitable errors and abuses that get into journalism, and supported open records, public meetings, and the general forthrightness needed to bolster fair and accurate reporting.

Then, journalists should stop being such know-it-alls. They should remember how much there is, on nearly every story, that they do not know. They should distinguish between fact, and opinions, inferences, or hunches. They should

---

[9]Cranberg, G. (1986, January/February). The libel alternative. *Columbia Journalism Review*, pp. 39–43.

[10]Cranberg, G. (1986, January/February). The libel alternative. *Columbia Journalism Review*.

acknowledge when evidence is conflicting. And, of course, they should give their critics ample opportunity to comment and to respond.

With such steps on both sides, the desire to resort to libel suits might abate.

INVASION OF PRIVACY

This is a relatively new, confusing area of press law, but editors should keep in mind one bit of perspective: Whereas libel law has evolved in ways deliberately calculated to protect journalists, privacy law contains much less built-in respect for the press. Although editors should not let themselves be intimidated by our society's newfound concern with privacy, they must take it into consideration and operate accordingly.

Privacy actions divide into four categories: *intrusion,* or the common-sense definition of invasion of privacy as an infringement on someone's solitude or property; *disclosure of embarrassing private facts,* such as medical or sexual records; *placing someone in a false light,* making an individual appear (through a photo or a docudrama technique, for example) to be something different from what is true; and *misappropriation of likeness,* using someone's name or likeness for commercial advantage without permission.

Defenses begin with *permission.* Individuals can waive their privacy claims by inviting you onto their property or signing consent forms for your use of certain material.

Otherwise, privacy cases tend to turn on issues such as *newsworthiness* and *relevance.*

For example, if an individual was convicted 20 years ago of child abuse, reporting on the case now, for no good reason, might constitute invasion of privacy. If the individual chooses to run for the local school board, however, the old conviction might gain renewed newsworthiness.

Unlike libel, where the Supreme Court has spelled out important doctrines (such as that of actual malice), privacy law is less developed. So the editor's best defense is to stand alert for any privacy issues, to consider them in light of permission or relevance standards, and to seek legal advice anytime potential privacy claims arise.

Managing editor Tim J. McGuire of the *Minneapolis Star Tribune* has suggested that editors have a further duty: to defend the First Amendment from creeping restrictions spawned by privacy concerns. "There is no constitutional right to informational privacy, but it is becoming more and more difficult to convince citizens, lawyers and even judges of that," McGuire wrote. He advised editors that:

> media defendants and media advocates should concentrate on challenging the very idea that a right to be free from embarrassment should exist. . . .

This alleged right to be let alone must be challenged and questioned. Inherent in that argument is the belief that for some reason persons do not have to be fully accountable for everything they are and do. That argument does not seem consistent with the realities of modern life. (p. 32)[11]

In privacy as in libel and other issues, the editor is not expected to fully comprehend the legal intricacies. The editor's clear duty, however, is to know enough to spot potential problems and then get whatever expert help is needed to solve them.

COURTS AND CONTEMPT

Red hot just a few years ago, court-related issues have cooled a bit lately. However, they remain areas where editors must exercise vigilance.

Subpoenas.   Perhaps the most common ways editors encounter potential contempt of court occur when reporters and their notes are subpoenaed. Historically, journalists have firmly opposed this practice, claiming that it makes them arms of law enforcement and discourages nervous sources from taking reporters into their confidence.

Although the courts have been reluctant to accept this argument, they have tended to set strict conditions on when journalists can be subpoenaed. Two typical conditions are that (a) the material being subpoenaed must be central to a case and (b) every effort should be made to get it elsewhere so that subpoenaing a journalist becomes only a last resort.

Tactically, editors who resist having their staff subpoenaed can take several actions.

First, all staff members can be instructed to volunteer nothing. If contacted by a prosecutor or lawyer, they should make no agreements and immediately refer the inquiry to their editors. I have known reporters who, in a naive willingness to be helpful, have volunteered on the spot to testify in court or cooperate in a case. Despite the good intentions, they should know that such actions have serious implications; for example, once a reporter has been subpoenaed in a controversy, he or she may become a part of the story and therefore no longer free to cover it. Newspapers should develop policies for these occasions, and editors should explicitly instruct reporters in them.

What should a reporter do if subpoenaed while in court? This occasionally happens when a reporter is covering a case he or she knows a great deal about.

---

[11]McGuire, T.J. (1986, December). Don't let the "right" to privacy overtake the first amendment. *ASNE Bulletin*, p. 32.

In such an event, reporters can be directed to ask for a brief recess in order to consult their employers and attorneys. Judges usually will honor such a request.

However, reporters often find themselves tongue-tied when forced, under such pressure, to interrupt a court proceeding. So it may help if editors provide, in advance, wallet or purse cards with an appropriate statement written out. As a city editor, I once devised such a statement with help from the newspaper's lawyer. It read as follows:

> Your honor, I am _____, a reporter for (the local newspaper). I request that the court allow a brief recess in order for me to consult with my editor and with the paper's legal counsel.
>
> I have been advised by my editor and the paper's legal counsel to seek a brief recess if ordered to testify on short notice because I may be asked to provide information that is privileged.

Once a request for notes or testimony has been referred to editors, how should they respond? That will vary, depending on the editor, the nature of the issue, and the policy of the paper. Often, editors will try to explain the First Amendment concerns in a way that causes a lawyer to back off. Other times, editors will refer the inquiry to the paper's lawyers.

How should the lawyers respond? Several things help. Often, when the newspaper's lawyers explain the legitimate journalistic concerns involved, the inquiring lawyers will yield. Most lawyers have more important things to do than to bog down in time-consuming First Amendment battles. So delay and determination can be important allies for the newspaper. If these tactics fail, challenging subpoenas in court may come next.

What if all this fails? My experience is that the vast majority of subpoena cases can be deflected. But a few cannot be. If such cases, editors should explore every option. In some cases, for instance, a court may settle for a sworn statement vouching for the accuracy of information in a story. This limits the extent of the disclosure and prevents a reporter from having to testify.

If a journalist has agreed to keep material confidential, then professional ethics hold that the agreement must be kept, even to the point of the reporter's going to jail if necessary. Reporters and editors should show extreme reluctance to make such confidentiality agreements, as we discuss in chapter 10. But, once made, they should be honored.

Usually, it is a line reporter threatened with jailing, not an editor. But editors (and publishers) can certainly stand with their reporters, to the point of demanding to be held accountable *instead* of their staff members. Matters tend to go far better if the entire newspaper—including publisher, editor and reporter—is perceived as standing side by side before the court.

It should be noted that some states have *shield laws,* which grant journalists protection from some court-ordered disclosures. However, these laws vary greatly and almost always, in my view, contain too many loopholes to be dependable. For example, *Washington Post* reporter Loretta Tofani was threatened with jail for refusing to testify about her Pulitzer Prize-winning series on rapes in a Maryland county jail. Although Maryland has a shield law, it protects *confidential* sources only. Tofani, ever the scrupulous journalist, had named the sources at issue, and thus her case fell outside the shield law.

While all editors should become familiar with the pertinent laws in their states, I would stop short of depending on shield laws for protection.

Defiance. Rarely, journalists will provoke contempt of court by outright violation of a judge's orders. Obviously, snubbing court orders is not a course to be lightly undertaken, and no editor should do so without extensive consultation with superiors and attorneys. There have been times, however, when newspapers chose defiance. One widely publicized case involved the *Providence Journal,* which in 1985 published an article based on FBI wiretap transcripts despite a judge's order not to do so. The paper argued the judge's action violated the First Amendment. The judge fined the paper $100,000 and gave executive editor Charles Hauser an 18-month suspended sentence, on grounds that— even if the order had been unconstitutional—the paper should have obeyed it pending appeal. However, a federal appeals court overturned the conviction and sentences, calling the ban on publication "transparently invalid." Even so, the appeals court did add that appealing the judge's ban, instead of ignoring it, would have been "a far safer means of testing the order."[12]

Access and Court Coverage. Recent Supreme Court rulings have strengthened the nation's commitment to open court hearings and trials, but some lawyers and judges still occasionally push for secrecy. In such cases, reporters should immediately contact their editors and newspaper lawyers. Some editors also instruct their reporters to protest to the judge on the spot. Again, the best course is to prepare the reporter, in advance, with whatever wording and procedures are appropriate when a judge threatens to close court.

Similar action is called for when officials attempt to close public meetings or forbid access to public documents. Editors should see that they and their reporters learn state and local laws regarding open meetings and records. In fact, many reporters carry copies of the laws with them, and pull them out in protest when officials try to halt access. Often, such challenges are sufficient to make bureaucrats and politicians reconsider.

Free Press Versus Fair Trial. This longstanding issue hinges on whether news stories and editorials, particularly in spectacular criminal cases, can preju-

---

[12]See "Media May Violate Clearly Unconstitutional Gag Order," *News Media & The Law,* Spring 1987, pp. 19–20, and "Newspapers Get Two Big Victories in Court," *Editor & Publisher,* January 10, 1987, p. 9.

dice the public so much that individuals cannot get fair trials. This argument, too, raged more furiously a few years ago than now.

Traditionally, it has been compromised in a way that generally favors freedom to attend trials and publish most material. "Gag orders," or other court-ordered restraints on the flow of information, should be last resorts. Before they are allowed, courts try alternatives such as interviewing large numbers of potential jurors in order to find enough unbiased jurors, delaying trials until public furor cools, moving trials to new locations, and sequestering jurors to prevent their access to press reports.

For its part, the press has tended to voluntarily accept a duty to avoid unduly inflammatory pretrial publicity. Journalists also have contended that, in the words of lawyers Lee Levine and James Grossberg, "scholarly research and other evidence demonstrates that the prejudicial effect of pretrial publicity is largely a myth" (p. 47).[13] According to this view, most jurors can and will decide cases on the evidence, not the advance coverage. More important may be the need to keep courts open so the public can see justice in action.

PLAGIARISM AND COPYRIGHT

Recent years have seen several publicized cases in which journalists were fired or disciplined for publishing, under their bylines, material actually written by someone else.

In an article in *Washington Journalism Review*, Roy Peter Clark cited several examples of such plagiarism, which he defined as to "kidnap the words of other writers without attribution or shame." Among the examples he noted were an *Atlanta Constitution* critic who "borrowed most of a film review from *Newsweek*"; a *Charlotte News* columnist who published as his own an old Art Buchwald column; a free-lance writer who "fabricated a story that appeared in the *New York Times Magazine*"; and a *St. Petersburg Times* artist who copied a color drawing from *Better Homes and Gardens* (pp. 43–44).[14]

As Clark pointed out, newspapering is ripe for plagiarism because reporters are trained to collect masses of information from everywhere possible. They often rely on second-hand sources, and frequently use information from earlier clips, wire service dispatches, or even press releases as background for their own writing. Much of this material is paid for or presented in hopes of being published, so using it is not plagiarism. But, given the vast amounts of information in circulation, such distinctions can be blurred.

---

[13]Levine, L., & Grossberg, J. (1986, October). The myth of pre-trial publicity. *Washington Journalism Review*, p. 47.

[14]Clark, R.P. (1983, March). The unoriginal sin. *Washington Journalism Review*, pp. 43–44.

Therefore, the editor's role in combatting plagiarism is both educational and preventive.

As newsroom teachers, editors should recognize that not all reporters understand what constitutes plagiarism, especially in these days of rampant photocopying, easily accessed databases, and the overall ease with which information flows in a newsroom. So, through staff meetings, stylebooks, memos, and so on, editors should set clear rules that outlaw plagiarism and require attribution of any borrowed information.

In processing copy, editors should watch carefully for copy that sounds familiar, varies dramatically from a writer's usual style, or is not appropriately sourced.

A similar offense is *copyright violation,* the unauthorized use of creative material owned by someone else. Normally, it is considered *fair use* to publish, *with attribution,* brief excerpts of copyrighted material. Sometimes even that causes trouble. For instance, in 1985 the U.S. Supreme Court ruled that *The Nation* magazine had violated copyright laws by publishing an article, including 300 words of direct quotations, about a book that had yet to be published. The court ruled that use of the copyrighted material, before the book went on sale, hurt its market value.[15]

In recent years, Congress has tightened federal laws regarding copyright infringement, in light of the proliferation of photocopy machines and broadcast taping equipment. Again, the editor's role remains one of watchfulness for any material that is not original.

NATIONAL SECURITY

In 1690, the first American newspaper, Benjamin Harris' *Publick Occurrences,* was put out of business after one issue because it ran afoul of government licensing laws.

Ever since, government and press have argued about what limits, if any, can be placed on journalism. Typically, government invokes the concept of national security to defend efforts to restrict press content.

Traditionally, these have been regarded as ethical rather than legal questions. Restrictions on releasing secret government information, for instance, generally apply to government employees, not journalists. Publishing such material isn't by itself illegal. The press has presumed a freedom from prior restraint (with the exception of formal, wartime censorship) but it has accepted a moral obligation to respect legitimate national interests. "The ground rules are com-

---

[15]Roper, J.E. (1985, May 25). A copyright infringement. *Editor & Publisher,* p. 9.

mon sense," Rick Atkinson of *The Washington Post* once explained. "You don't put people in jeopardy, particularly American servicemen" (p. 34).[16]

However, recent years have seen the issue thrust dramatically into the legal arena.

In 1985, Samuel Morison became the first person ever convicted under espionage laws of leaking classified government information to the press. Morison, a former naval intelligence analyst, was convicted of giving three secret satellite photos to *Jane's Defence Weekly*. At the time, journalists worried whether the case signaled government willingness to begin applying espionage laws against the press.[17] In upholding the conviction, a federal appeals court ruled:

> The mere fact that one has stolen a document in order that he may deliver it to the press, whether for money or for other personal gain, will not immunize him from responsibility for his criminal act. To use the First Amendment for such a purpose would be to convert the First Amendment into a warrant for thievery. (p. 20)[18]

In 1986, then-CIA Director William Casey threatened to prosecute several media organizations, including *The Washington Post* and NBC, for publishing information about top-secret intelligence operations. No journalists were prosecuted, but some journalists felt Casey had succeeded in intimidating the press into self-censorship.[19]

CBS correspondent David Martin told of being warned by an intelligence official about a clause in the 1917 Espionage Act forbidding the publication of classified information about codes and communications. Martin was quoted in *Washington Journalism Review* as saying:

> The way it was explained to me is that they wouldn't prosecute the news organization but that they would come after the individual reporter. They'd say it's a crime to report communications intelligence . . . I think it's fair to say their threats had a chilling effect. (p. 37)[20]

---

[16]Wines, M. (1986, November). Should reporters keep state secrets? *Washington Journalism Review*, p. 34.

[17]Ruhga, V. (1987). Morison case: Testing the waters? *Freedom of Information 1986–1987*, p. 5.

[18]Garneau, G. (1988, April 9). Conviction of classified photo leaker upheld. *Editor & Publisher*, p. 20.

[19]Ruhga, V. (1987). Casey goes to bat against press. *Freedom of Information 1986–1987*, p. 4.

[20]Wines, M. (1986, November). Should reporters keep state secrets? *Washington Journalism Review*.

It seems reasonable to conclude that the uneasy press–government relationship represents still another way in which the legal climate has cooled noticeably for journalists. This chill puts still more strain on editors. They must not shirk the responsibility of standing up to the partisan pressures of politicians and press baiters. But bravado and bravery are not enough. Besides an unflinching commitment to news, the new editor must have an informed, thought-out appreciation of the operative political and legal issues and risks. Every step, every decision requires care.

CONCLUSION

"In today's newsrooms," *Dallas Morning News* editor Burl Osborne wrote in 1985, "editors are spending less and less of their time editing and more and more of their time acting like lawyers or watching lawyers act like editors" (p. 2).[21] In such an environment, the watchword must be: Take care but don't give up.

Journalists must not leave the field to the politicians or the lawyers, but they must respect the law and the public concerns underlying it. They must act with understanding and principle.

As a matter of substance, all journalists should actively assert and defend the First Amendment and the values it represents. Otherwise, it might as well not exist. Editors share in this obligation.

As a matter of process, editors' top priority goes to identifying potential legal issues and raising them for discussion and decision. Every editor should feel duty-bound to sound such alarms. But individual editors should not feel obliged to settle legal quandaries alone. Top editors, as well as publishers and lawyers, must be supportive and closely involved. Debate should be extensive, and decisions should be reasoned.

In summary, given today's chilly climate, editors should be sentinels on watch for potential legal problems. They should know how to get them resolved. And they should do so with both a commitment to the public's right to know and an understanding of legal limits.

Then, as we see in chapter 10, they should be ready to move from the legal arena into ethics.

Having determined, as best they can, what "can" or "cannot" be done under the law, the next, perhaps even harder step is to ponder what "should" be done by news professionals.

---

[21]Osborne, B. (1985, September). Contents. *ASNE Bulletin*, p. 2.

SIDEBAR 9
AN EDITOR'S READING LIST

Editors, like writers, should read and read and read. Read the Great Books and detective whodunits. Newspapers and magazines. Academic journals and trade newsletters. Church bulletins and comic books. Annual reports and speech collections. Ad copy and movie scripts.

Reading tunes the mind and educates the ear. Everything helps. The editor's reading list begins with billboards and matchbook covers and runs through Proust and Plato.

As for books directed specifically at editors, the list is relatively short, enough to fill maybe a good-sized book shelf. Following are some of what I consider the best:

Baskette, F.K., Sissors, J.Z., & Brooks, B.S. (1986). *The art of editing*. New York: Macmillan. My favorite of the many beginning-editing textbooks. Comprehensive and clear.

Berg, A.S. (1978). *Max Perkins: Editor of genius*. New York: Pocket Books. Insight-filled biography of one of the few pure editors to either be called a genius or have a book written about him.

Clark, R.P., & Fry, D. (in prep.). *The human side of editing*. Two excellent writing and editing coaches share experiences, anecdotes, methods.

Gans, H. (1979). *Deciding what's news*. New York: Vintage Books. A sociologist's study of how major media organize themselves to gather and shape the news. An analysis that rings very true.

Garcia, M. (1987). *Contemporary newspaper design*. Englewood Cliffs, NJ: Prentice-Hall. Good specialized textbook by one of design's leading figures.

Giles, R.H. (1987). *Newsroom management*. Indianapolis: R.J. Berg. Elaborate discussion of management theories and practices as applied to newsrooms.

Levy, M., & Robinson, J.P. (1986). *The main source*. Beverly Hills: Sage. Study of what people comprehend in news coverage and of how journalists help or hurt. Geared to television but applicable to print editors as well.

Murray, D. (1983). *Writing for your readers*. Chester, CT: Globe Pequot Press. Sage, witty, insightful, and inspirational. Based on Murray's coaching at the *Boston Globe*.

Newsroom Management Handbook. (1985). Washington: American Society of Newspaper Editors Foundation. Loose-leaf pointers on everything from hiring and firing to coping with your boss.

Plotnik, A. (1982). *The elements of editing*. New York: Collier Books. Not up to Strunk and White and not really newspaper oriented, but savvy and helpful.

(Continued)

Sidebar 9 (*Continued*)

Scanlan, C. (Ed.). (1986). *How I wrote the story*. Providence, RI: Providence Journal Co. Editors and writers discuss specific works and share some secrets.

Strunk, W., Jr., & White, E.B. (1935). *The elements of style*. New York: Macmillan. An all-time gold medalist. Graceful and wise, with charming advice and examples. Aimed at writers, but a must for the desk as well.

Wardlow, E.M. (Ed.). (1985). *Effective writing and editing*. Reston, VA: American Press Institute. Useful compilation of tips, experiences, good sense; unusual in that it takes both writing and editing seriously and separately.

Zinsser, W. (1985). *On writing well*. New York: Harper & Row. Lyrical and deeply thoughtful. A classic.

10

Making Decisions About Ethics

Actor Richard Dreyfuss was discussing his drug problems before about 850 people at the University of Maryland when he noticed reporters in the audience.

Even though he was giving an open speech at a public university, the Oscar-winning star of *The Goodbye Girl* and other films declared the evening a "nonquotable experience." As the campus newspaper reported, Dreyfuss demanded that journalists abide by this "gentlemen's agreement."

Of two reporters present, one left the auditorium. The other stayed and took notes.

Which did the right thing?

Questions like this arise hundreds of times every day for journalists from campus weeklies to metropolitan dailies. They do not involve legal issues. In the Dreyfuss incident, leaving the auditorium or remaining to report both were perfectly permissible under the law. Instead, they involve ethics and values: what *should* be done in difficult situations. Should reporters insist on their right to cover public events, or accede to the privacy wishes of a celebrity talking to students about personal matters?

For many reasons, ethics has become a growth industry in journalism. As reporters and editors become increasingly professional, they naturally spend more time pondering standards for appropriate and inappropriate behavior. As society becomes more complex and contentious, journalists' decisions invite sharper public scrutiny.

The result has been rising concern both inside and outside newsrooms about what constitutes journalistic ethics, who decides what standards apply, and what, if anything, happens when journalists transgress the rules.

151

In the ongoing rhythms of the newsroom, it is of course the editors who must take the lead in resolving these issues. Indications can readily be found to demonstrate how much attention, of editors as well as others, is being devoted to ethics:

- One survey, to which 225 newspapers responded, showed that 30 journalists had been suspended and 48 fired for ethics violations during a three-year span.[1]
- The Society of Professional Journalists produces an annual journalism ethics report examining both national and regional issues from the preceding year. For several years, the society has been debating whether members should be subject to discipline for violating the group's code of ethics.
- Such institutions as the Poynter Institute for Media Studies in St. Petersburg, Florida, regularly conduct ethics seminars involving journalists and others from around the country.
- Numerous books have been published on journalism ethics in recent years. Three excellent examples are *Media Ethics* by Clifford Christians, Kim Rotzoll, and Mark Fackler; *Committed Journalism* by Edmund Lambeth; and *Ethical Journalism* by Philip Meyer.

Although in most cases cited in these books, studies, and reports, editors have a central role in determining, applying, and enforcing newsroom ethics, precise rules remain elusive. As Philip Meyer pointed out, "Defining ethical behavior is a little bit like defining art, and most of us follow the I-know-it-when-I-see-it rule" (p. vii).[2]

Neither journalists nor readers can agree among themselves about many relatively common ethical matters. For example, consider this hypothetical case presented to both readers and journalists in several cities:

A mayor is a hard-liner on crime. He has made drug enforcement a major issue. You learn that his 19-year-old son, who lives at home and attends junior college, has been arrested for possession of a small quantity of marijuana, a misdemeanor if convicted. (p. 5)[3]

When readers and editors were asked if they would publish the arrest story, here are some results from several newspaper markets:

---

[1]Ethics violations. (1986, April 26). *Editor & Publisher*, p. 50.

[2]Meyer, P. (1987). *Ethical journalism*. New York: Longman.

[3]Oppel, R. A. (1984, October). Readers "In the Editor's Chair" squirm over ethical dilemmas. *ASNE Bulletin*, p. 5.

Charlotte, NC:

| Readers | Yes 61% | No 39 |
| Editors | Yes 42 | No 58 |

St. Paul, MN:

| Readers | Yes 58 | No 42 |
| Editors | Yes 48 | No 52 |

Miami, FL:

| Readers | Yes 64 | No 36 |
| Editors | Yes 75 | No 25 |

Given such divergent views, what models can editors follow in wrestling with ethics dilemmas? Are there universal standards, or is each case unique? To help examine these questions, we consider several common categories of ethical problems that accompany editors as they rise through the newsroom structure. Reporters and line editors face daily battlefield questions involving methods of news gathering and the use and misuse of sources. Supervising and assigning editors bear policymaking responsibility for how their reporters treat people and for many other issues involving the newsroom and staff. Managing editors and other top-ranking executives confront the further dilemmas of hiring and firing, and must also monitor the overall ethical reputation of their newspapers.

At every level, from their first day in an editor's chair to the crowning command posts of upper management, editors must be prepared to deal with the realm of ethics.

THE ETHICS OF DAY-TO-DAY JOURNALISM

Case: You are a sports editor for your campus newspaper, investigating tips that star athletes are performing poorly in classes. As you and a reporter interview an athletic department official, she refers occasionally to a form apparently listing each athlete's grades. When you ask to see the report, she replies that it is private. Suddenly, she is called out of the room. She leaves the report in open sight on her desk. The reporter turns to you for guidance. Do you ignore the form? Sneak a quick peak? Read it carefully and take notes? Take it and leave the office?

In considering ethical issues concerning their methods of news gathering, journalists often frame the issue this way: Under what circumstances (if any) would you lie, cheat, or steal to get a story?

Although reporters commonly must make on-the-spot decisions about such issues as snooping around a source's desk, it is editors who set the tone for ethical behavior in a newsroom. The editor who looks the other way, reflexively defends reporters against all complaints, and demands "get the story or else" projects a message of permissiveness that no reporter will miss. By contrast, the editor who constantly second guesses reporters' conduct, kills stories over the tiniest lapses and tries to promulgate strict guidelines for every contingency sends an opposite signal.

How do editors decide these things?

There is no one way, of course. Most editors try to avoid rigidity and inflexibility. The best articulate high overall standards and then encourage, expect, and reward adherence to them. Reporters who want to bend, or break, the rules bear a high "burden of proof" for persuading editors to acquiesce.

Thus, in most cases editors would argue that lying, cheating, and stealing are improper ways of acquiring stories. Deception taints the final product. It alienates sources, outrages readers, clouds both the reporter's and the paper's credibility in all matters, and undermines future access to sources and information. And, simply but importantly, deception is wrong, and most of us know it.

Yet, as most of us also know, the line between deception and ingenuity can be hard to discern. For example, I once obtained an interview after a source, who had refused in advance to see reporters, mistook me for a cab driver as he left a hospital. For a minute or two, I did not correct him. In fact, I even walked with him in the general direction of a cab. Then, after some brief warming-up conversation, I introduced myself as a reporter, and the source courteously granted an interview.

Strictly speaking, I had not lied. Had I deceived? Is there a difference ethically between blatantly lying and simply neglecting to set straight a mistaken source?

In an earlier chapter, I mentioned a reporter who staked out a grand jury that was considering allegations of misconduct against a public official. The reporter happened to be standing outside the room when the grand jurors took a break. As several jurors talked, he sidled up and listened quietly. Apparently assuming that he was a court official, they talked openly about the case they were hearing.

Did my reporter have a responsibility to identify himself? Or is it sources' responsibility to determine to whom they are speaking?

Most editors, I suspect, clearly believe that it is unethical to break the law or breach ethics most of the time. But almost every editor can cite exceptions.

Take breaking the law. I know of no editor who would condone committing murder to get a story. But I also cannot imagine any editor complaining if a reporter jaywalked to reach a breaking news event.

Furthermore, we can regard suppressing or neglecting the truth to be just as unethical as violating standards to get the truth. That means journalists must match *means* and *ends*, a tricky but inescapable reality in the news business. In so doing, they learn to examine situations systematically and to outline the issues at stake, the potential good and harm, all available options, and the likely response from everyone involved.

Too often, however, reporters make such decisions by themselves and under pressure. They may not trust their editors, may fear them, or simply may be conditioned to operating as lone-wolf individualists.

Almost as important as *what decision is made* is *how the decision gets made*. It is a basic duty for editors to create an environment in which reporters understand the importance of discussing ethical matters, in advance wherever possible, with their editors. Cultivating an air of trust and mutual dependence can prevent many ethical dilemmas from flaring into disaster.

When faced with these everyday ethical conundrums, editors often can foster a cool, systematic, rational analysis, by suggesting such questions as:

- How important is the information being sought? Is it crucial to an important story, or of secondary importance?

- Is there any other way to get it besides breaching ethics? For example, can documents be demanded under Freedom of Information laws rather than pilfered or surreptitiously copied?

- Will the information be made public eventually anyway? Is there any real advantage to be gained by cheating to get it early?

- How do the consequences of an ethical violation compare with the consequences of not getting the story? An oft-cited hypothetical: Suppose a reporter, by stealing documents, could have gained access to plans for murdering Jews during World War II? Wouldn't the theft be outweighed by the lives that might have been saved? On the other hand, the benefits of a routine story that involved theft of documents might be more than offset by ensuing ethical, and even legal, controversies.

- How would you explain your actions in print? How would you defend yourself if your methods were challenged?

- How would you feel is the story involved you or your family? Would you condone the questionable methods?

- How would a court or jury or a panel of subscribers react to borderline actions by a journalist? Would they understand and consider them reasonable under the circumstances?

- And, in a common way of formulating the question: How would your mother respond if she knew what you were doing?

Ethicists cite more formal methods of analysis. One popular textbook recommends considering Aristotle's Golden Mean (finding the appropriate location between extremes); the Judeo-Christian principle (loving your neighbor as yourself); Kant's Categorical Imperative (acting in a way that you think should be universal law); and Mill's Principle of Utility (seeking the greatest happiness for the greatest number of people).[4] Others often suggest applying the Golden Rule (doing unto others as you would wish them to do unto you).

More particularly, journalists can examine where their obligations lie. Reporters and editors have duties to themselves as individual professionals, to clients and subscribers paying for their services, to employers, to the overall profession, to sources and subjects of their copy, to the law, and to society. Ethical dilemmas often involve choosing between competing obligations.

In my view, the highest journalistic obligation is to the truth. In fact, the Code of Ethics of the Society of Professional Journalists begins, ". . . the duty of journalists is to serve the truth."

Ethical conduct, then, lies in following the spirit of service to truth: in representing the truth, pursuing the truth and publishing the truth whenever possible.

Lying, cheating, and stealing to obtain stories do not, in most cases, serve the truth. It is only when the value of a story is so urgent. its good ends so overwhelming, the harm from not publishing so clear, that the truth of the ultimate story may redeem questionable methods employed to get it. And direct involvement in making such judgments constitutes a prime duty of editors as they operate daily in the newsroom.

> *Case:* President Lyndon B. Johnson, a crafty old gamesman, once upbraided a reporter for not publishing information Johnson himself had leaked. "But, Mr. President," the reporter protested, "you told me that was off the record." Replied Johnson, "I know that. But why didn't you use it?" (p. 72)[5]

That anecdote, related by journalist James Deakin, reveals much about the concept of "off the record"—a confusing and often dishonored technique that provides endless opportunity and controversy for journalists. It exemplifies a category of ethical issues that line editors and reporters face routinely: the use and misuse of sources.

Most of journalists' information, by far, comes from sources. And most sources, including presidents, have their own reasons for using and abusing the journalistic process.

At stake is the very nature of "the record" that sources are perpetually sliding onto and off of.

"The record" is not, as some might assume, a faithful snapshot of reality. It is instead subject to revisions, deletions and manipulations in a process governed by byzantine codes that are applied inconsistently and self-servingly. Sources

---

[4]Christians, C., Rotzoll, K., & Fackler, M. (1987). *Media ethics*. New York: Longman.
[5]Deakin, J. (1984). *Straight stuff*. New York: William Morrow.

employ constant propaganda. Journalists face time and access limits. Most "news" is pieced together, second hand, by journalists trying to catch up after the fact.

What we read and hear, then, is not reality, but a reconstituted reality. The struggle to control "the record" becomes a battle to shape what consumers are offered as "reality"—the common information base of our society.

As journalists and sources jockey to produce "the record," they affect one another in many ways.

Journalists can "burn" their sources my misquoting them, taking remarks out of context, or violating agreements about confidentiality. Sources can undermine journalists by lying, exaggerating, distorting or omitting information, failing to divulge conflicts of interest, and refusing to stand behind the information they provide.

Numerous surveys have shown public annoyance with the widespread practice of using anonymous sources, but journalists persist in so doing.

Over the years, a semiformal collection of rules has evolved to govern attribution of information to sources:

On the record means information can be published and attributed to a source by name.

Background means information can be reported but without identifying the source.

Deep background means information can be reported but without referring to any source at all (such as, "It was learned that . . .").

Off the record means information is not to be published at all.

In my experience, several categories of sources routinely seek shelter behind some form of background or off the record agreements: *front people*, such as press secretaries or political aides whose job is to publicize their bosses not themselves; *celebrities and titans of industry*, who often are accustomed to giving orders and having everyone scurry to obey; *policymakers*, such as high officials who may want to advance information unofficially, to avoid the complications of formal announcements; *politicians*, who as a class are notorious gossips but do not like having a reputation for it; and *laypeople*, who often simply are shy or do not want to get involved in the publicness that attribution brings.

In most of the cases just mentioned, anonymity is neither necessary nor desirable. Anonymous information is as suspicious and lacking in credibility as a new car would be if its manufacturer's name were kept secret. Editors should insist that their reporters try extremely hard to persuade reluctant sources to talk on the record.

Several arguments can be made. Some sources, particularly public officials, can be shamed by a hard-headed reporter who insists on public accountability.

Many sources will respond to reporters who say, "My editor won't allow me to take off-the-record information" or "I really need your help to get this right and do my job properly." Other sources will agree to attribution if they feel their story will not be fairly told in any other way. Sometimes editors can help, by contacting a wavering source and explaining the importance of on-the-record attribution.

Even so, some reporters all too easily accept spurious rationales for sources remaining unidentified. As an editor, you can save yourself many headaches by making clear to reporters, in advance, that you must approve any grant of anonymity and that you require a heavy burden of proof to do so. The more important or sensitive the information, the higher the need for attribution.

For one key group, confidentiality can be crucial. That group consists of sources with important information and with *specific* reason to fear for their jobs, lives or families if they are associated with it. This includes employees exposing corruption and government whistle blowers. But even if such sources remain confidential, their information should be checked and double-checked thoroughly. Many editors require at least two independent sources for any disputable assertion.

Reporters, therefore, should hesitate to grant anonymity to a source. If anonymity is necessary, they at least should try to limit its scope. For instance, a reporter might agree to withhold a crucial source's name from a story but get the source's permission to divulge the name if the story results in court action.

In short, editors should prod reporters to resist anonymity, to hold sources accountable, and, when deals are necessary, to make the best deal possible. Blanket confidentiality is seldom necessary.

Once a deal is made, its terms should be absolutely clear to both parties. Many sources, for example, do not know the difference between "off the record" and "background." Reporters should make clear their precise understanding of where confidentiality begins and ends. Then, they are duty bound, under the ethics of the profession, to honor any such deal, even to the point of going to jail if necessary. That, of course, is a big reason why granting confidentiality is risky and undesirable in the first place.

Good editors will confer with reporters in advance about these issues, so reporters can operate with the clearest possible understanding of their paper's policies and expectations.

THE ETHICS OF NEWSROOM POLICYMAKING

Case: Your newspaper receives a tip that the head of a federal agency once was caught cheating at golf in a country club tournament. The club suspended him on the condition that he seek psychiatric help for his compulsion to cheat. In an interview, the official acknowledges the episode but insists he doesn't cheat in any business or government activity. Do you publish the story? Mention it as part of a profile? Omit it?

The *Washington Post's* Bob Woodward raised this real-life example in an ethics discussion sponsored by Investigative Reporters and Editors. It typifies cases in which the press weighs publishing articles about the private or semi-private conduct of public figures. And it helps illustrate a continuing ethical concern for editors: What policies govern how your newspaper treats people?

A standard rationale for publishing such information is that it sheds light on the character of people entrusted with public policymaking. A leading argument against publishing is that individuals should retain their privacy unless their conduct can be shown to directly affect public issues. In Woodward's illustration, the *Post* came close to publishing but did not because, he explained, "we held our breath and it didn't seem right" (p. 17).[6]

Clearly, gray areas abound here, and editors frequently must referee such situations. In many cases, either decision—to publish or to suppress—will anger a large segment of your audience and newsroom. Earlier in the book, I mentioned once receiving a call from the mother of an individual being investigated by my newspaper. She argued that what we had unearthed was private and that publishing it might drive her son to suicide. Later the same day, I was called by the reporter on the story, who said his sources were questioning whether we planned to "cave in" and "cover up" the man's dubious activity. A decision either way was certain to antagonize a substantial constituency.

As life constantly reminds editors, newspapers hold awesome power over people's lives and work. Bad reviews can close plays and restaurants. Investigative reporting can cost people their jobs and point them toward prison. Careless mistakes can ruin reputations.

Sometimes, even innocuous material can bring unwanted and even dangerous public attention to individuals and families. A few years ago, the *Charlotte Observer* published a simple feature photo of a young mother walking her daughter to school. The woman subsequently reported horrifying phone calls and letters of sexual harassment to both herself and her child.[7]

Regularly these days, we hear complaints about journalistic insensitivity, discourtesy, and disrespect. From microphones shoved at grieving parents to questions yelled at political officeholders to mob scenes when prominent defendants enter court, journalists often seem hellbent to corner their prey at any price. The rise of invasion of privacy as a legal concern further underscores public dismay at press conduct.

What guidelines govern how the press treats people?

---

[6]Investigative reporting roundtable. *IRE Journal*, p. 17.

[7]Ring, G. (1986, February). Are exact addresses always part of the news? *ASNE Bulletin*, pp. 20–22.

The question naturally divides itself into two areas: first, how journalists treat people during the reporting process and second, what they publish about people. Editors have responsibility in both areas.

How Journalists Treat People During Reporting.   Editors should make their views clear on how they expect reporters to deal with the public. Some editors still adhere to the "story-at-any-price" philosophy. More often these days, editors can encourage reporters to be persistent and tough without belligerence. Simple courtesy and respect remain good standards. And editors can distinguish between public and private figures.

I see nothing wrong, for example, with approaching the proverbial grieving parents, politely identifying oneself as a journalist, and asking if they wish to talk about their children. Many such parents do want to talk, and gentle encouragement seems appropriate. If they decline, then I think reporters should leave them alone.

On the other hand, reporters are entitled to much more aggressively bulldog public figures who refuse to return phone calls or to hold press conferences or to otherwise discuss public issues. In those cases, the disrespect is not on the part of the press, but on the part of the officials dodging their responsibilities. The *Washington Post's* managing editor, Leonard Downie, has said:

> I'm very sympathetic to what it means to be thrust into the public eye. It changes your life and it's difficult to live with, and we must be sensitive to that. At the same time, I'm impatient with people who thrust themselves aggressively into public positions—and that includes senior executives in private corporations who have sway over people's lives. It is quite unreasonable for these people to not be held publicly accountable. (p. 40)[8]

What Journalists Publish.   Editors have long espoused *relevance* and *newsworthiness* as standards. But as we have seen, they can be hard to apply. It surprises many people that, despite the conflicts over what papers do publish, papers routinely choose not to publish much juicy material.

In a report for *Washington Journalism Review*,[9] I asked several editors to share examples of hot items they had withheld. Among the illustrations they gave were:

• A story about a Michigan politician who showed up at a campaign rally soon after his son had committed suicide.

---

[8]Stepp, C. S. (1986, December). When a public figure's private life is news. *Washington Journalism Review*, p. 40.

[9]Stepp, C. S. (1986, December). When a public figure's private life is news. *Washington Journalism Review*, pp. 39–41.

• Details about a prominent figure in an Oklahoma criminal case seen cavorting nude at a hotel swimming-pool party.

• Persistent rumors of homosexuality involving a well-known television personality in a Northeast city.

In all cases mentioned, editors determined the information was not sufficiently germane to public issues.

In other cases where they did choose to publish, they offered several reasons, beginning with relevance. The *Wall Street Journal* reported on a federal official who had confessed to beating his wife. "What the story did was raise a number of questions about (the official) that were relevant to his job," Washington bureau chief Albert Hunt explained.

Sometimes, even stories about an individual's family are deemed newsworthy. Janet Sanford, of the *Visalia (CA) Times-Delta,* said her paper reported that a county supervisor's husband was arrested for drunken driving. The paper went public, Sanford said, "because he was so often seen with her, because the family was so well known."

It is not unusual for competing media to act differently on the same case.

In the Twin Cities of Minnesota, a high school athlete hanged himself in a school building. The *St. Paul Pioneer Press and Dispatch* withheld the boy's name. "This was a private act. I could not see any major public value to be served," said editor John R. Finnegan.

Across town, the *Minneapolis Star Tribune* named the youth. Managing editor Tim J. McGuire said the decision was influenced by the fact that it was the second similar event in a short time and by "the extremely public nature of what he had done and where he had done it."

Nothing can anticipate every situation for editors who must raise, debate and decide such issues, but it can help to develop policy guidelines in advance and to distribute them to staff members. (As examples, see the excerpts from the *Seattle Times'* policies accompanying this chapter.)

As with so many other aspects of editing, an editor's insistence on care, thoughtfulness and broad consultation can help produce wise, defensible decisions.

Case: One of your general-assignment reporters is a 40-year-old father of three school children. He has lifelong ties to the community. One day he tells you he has decided to run for the city school board. How should the paper respond? Approve his civic-spirited gesture? Forbid it as a conflict of interest for a journalist covering community events? Allow him to remain at the paper but move to a job where his political activity would not be considered a conflict? Ignore it, on the grounds his personal time is beyond his employer's control?

Ethical conflicts arise within the newsroom as well as outside it, and editors must encode and then enforce the standards. Sometimes, the conflicts are purely internal (should the paper hire relatives of current staff members?). Occasionally, they pit the interests of different divisions of the paper against each other (should the paper print a marginal feature about a new business whose account the advertising department wants to win?). Often, they involve both the paper and the general public (should the publisher chair the local united charities drive?).

Often newspapers evaluate such issues in terms of *conflict of interest* and *perceived conflict of interest.*

Actual conflict of interest occurs when a staff member stands to benefit personally from professional behavior. Accepting money or gifts from a source in exchange for favorable coverage is a direct conflict of interest and a firing offense. Buying stock on the basis of inside information gained while covering a corporation falls into a similar category. Newspapers routinely forbid conflict of interest, and relatively few cases of it come to light. Simply put, it is wrong, and everyone should know it.

Editors, however, should never take for granted that everyone does know, or heed, it. They should spell out, particularly to new staffers, the importance the newspaper places on strictly upright conduct. Consequences of unethical behavior, including demotion and dismissal, also should be as explicit as possible.

Perceived conflict causes more problems. Newspapers must worry constantly about how people outside the paper will view their actions. Would the public feel coverage of city schools was neutral if a newspaper reporter sat on the school board, even if the reporter was scrupulously honest?

Sometimes such dilemmas extend into journalists' families. Suppose the reporter assigned to cover city hall decides to marry the mayor's press secretary. Would the public have reason to suspect conflict if the reporter remained on the beat? Almost certainly. Yet is it fair to penalize an employee because of his or her spouse's occupation?

Editors frequently must mediate between the paper's desire to appear totally aboveboard and employees' rights as individuals. Written policies help. From the moment of employment, journalists need to know what their papers expect. Another useful vehicle is a newsroom committee established to monitor conflict of interest. If staff members understand that potential conflict issues should be raised and discussed in advance and in a fair setting, then touchy questions can be debated and resolved early.

THE ETHICS OF UPPER MANAGEMENT

Case: You have a vacancy for a beginning reporter. Your newsroom contains fewer minority staff members than you want, and you have committed yourself to an affirmative hiring plan. Because of market demand, you find that hiring a minority reporter will cost you 30% more than hiring a nonminority. The minority reporter would begin with a salary higher than nonminority staffers recently hired. Do you make the hire?

In an earlier chapter, we discussed hiring and recruiting in a management context. A word remains to be said about such practices in an ethical context.

Fair hiring, training, and promotion contribute to a newspaper's overall ethical standing, as policed by its top editors.

As institutions that attempt to cover their total communities and that critically examine the personnel practices of other institutions, newspapers should serve as models.

In my view, aggressive affirmative action plans for women and minorities are as important ethically as clean conflict-of-interest records.

According to 1987 figures, a majority of U.S. daily newspapers had no minority news staffers at all, and minorities composed only 7% of news staffs.[10] While employment totals for female journalists are higher, women, like minorities, have yet to sufficiently crack upper management jobs. Recent figures showed that women held 13% of top editing jobs in U.S. dailies. Of 941 jobs titled "editor" or "editor-in-chief," only 10% belonged to women.[11]

In hiring and developing their staffs, editors should consider that the fair treatment of women and minorities deserves a high place on a paper's ethics agenda.

Terri Dickerson-Jones, manager/minority affairs of the American Newspaper Publishers Foundation, offered several recommendations that can help:

• Maintain a professional work environment and don't tolerate ethnic or sexist jokes.

• Make fairness part of every manager's job, not the responsibility of one department or individual.

• Encourage individualism. Don't expect all employees to look, dress, talk and think alike.

• Train managers to resolve complaints involving discrimination or harassment.

• Have specific grievance procedures.

• Don't make sex and race issues unless they are germane. Learn to separate personality problems from racial and sexual problems.

• Lead by example. (pp. 2–3)[12]

---

[10]Garneau, G. (1988, April 23). Minorities in the newsroom. *Editor & Publisher*, p. 28.

[11]Wilson, J. G. (1988, January). Women make up 13 percent of directing editors at dailies. *ASNE Bulletin*, p. 14.

[12]Dickerson-Jones, T. (1988, June/July). A common sense guide to reducing bias. *Minorities in the Newspaper Business*, pp. 2–3.

Case: Your religion reporter proposes to investigate how a local television ministry collects and spends its money. The reporter has heard rumors of wrongdoing but has no evidence. In fact, she concedes, the investigation may take several weeks and produce nothing at all. In the meantime, you will be short-staffed and have trouble making up for her absence from daily news writing. Do you agree to her proposal?

Too often, journalists confine their thinking about ethics to the narrowest context, dwelling on individual incidents that force tough decisions on whether to lie, cheat or steal for a single story. Such occasions provide provocative fodder for newsroom, classroom, and barroom conversation.

But editors should not neglect their duty to approach ethics more broadly. More profound than the individual episodes are the ethics lessons that flow from the continuing policies and priorities of a newspaper.

Ethics is cumulative. Decisions about how to finance, organize, and operate newsrooms have an ethical dimension that publishers and editors should not overlook.

The following sections give some examples where patterns of behavior have ethics consequences.

The Selection of Stories to Cover. Coverage is a function of staff, time, and money. As those resources tighten, it is tempting to push for higher percentage assignments, sure-shot stories done quickly. The premium may be lowered on chancy, time-consuming investigative projects. Editors and reporters may grow wary of proposals such as the one cited at the beginning of this section. If the press takes its watchdog role seriously, then a commitment to investigations cannot be shoved aside by short-term calculations.

The Messages Editors Send to Reporters. Most editors regularly prod reporters to press hard for stories. These days, however, many editors also spring quickly to second-guess a reporter's methods, often on grounds of ethics. The newshound who stretches the limits to get at a source, a document or a news scene may well face an editor's wrath. Much of today's scrutiny is well-intentioned and overdue, the natural outgrowth of higher standards and a desire to reduce arrogance and warm up to consumers.

But editors should realize that this increasing defensiveness may have unspoken, unexpected consequences. Reporters may react by becoming less aggressive, by not pushing hard enough, for fear of chastisement. Long-term service to readers could suffer. The answer is not necessarily to stop criticizing the ethics lapses, but to reaffirm, at the same time, that hard-nosed journalism has a place and will be rewarded when appropriate.

The Resources Spent on Newsrooms and Salaries. Good journalism is not cheap. For too long, newspapers have taken advantage of the idealistic nature of many recruits by offering low salaries and tolerating unreasonable working conditions. One result is a drain of talent to such places as law school and public relations. Another result is the high stress complained about in every newsroom. How the newspaper industry treats its workers is an ethics issue equivalent to any that reporters face in their daily activities.

CONCLUSION

Because individual cases do vary, editors resist the notion that ethical standards can be codified in advance and applied universally. Nonetheless, some guidelines can assist editors in making decisions about ethics. The decision-making process should encourage honesty, openness, fairness, and broad deliberation, both within the newsroom and with readers. The direction should be toward truth.

For editors, ethics means more than advising reporters on how to resolve the tough calls. Journalists make important ethics statements every day but vastly more important ones over time. Good editors monitor their long-range performance as well as referee the daily dogfights.

More than their response to isolated ethical predicaments, how they deal with the broad issues has a cumulative effect on how staffs perform and readers are served.

In part, papers do assert their ethics by applying codes to individual situations. But even if they are blemish-free by those standards, there remains an overriding judgment, based on the collective amount and depth of coverage and the overall behavior of newspapers and newsrooms. By those standards, editors, and all journalists, are more than the sum of their situational ethics.

SIDEBAR 10
EXCERPTS FROM "NEWSROOM POLICIES AND
GUIDELINES"

Seattle Times

News and Editorial Philosophy

The purpose of the *Seattle Times* is to inform and enlighten readers about what is important to them—what they want to know, need to know or ought to know. We provide an honest view of the world that is accurate, timely, insightful, provocative and entertaining. It is delivered with thought, fairness, perspective, determination and goodwill. Because we stay in touch with readers, we are useful

(*Continued*)

Sidebar 10 (*Continued*)

and vital to them. We challenge them to look deeper, think harder and be involved. We accept the responsibility of searching for truth, ever mindful that it is elusive and we are imperfect.

The style of the *Seattle Times* is balanced. We are thoughtful and thought-provoking, aggressive yet fair, consistent yet compelling, deliberate yet lively, friendly yet authoritative. Excellence is the standard by which we measure our efforts. . . .

How Do We Deal With Crime Victims and Their Families?

Violence in society is an unfortunate reality. As we cover crimes and other events that result from violence we must constantly remind ourselves—and our readers— of the impact on individuals as well as on the community. In our pursuit of a story, we must be sensitive to the plight of the victims. We must avoid victimizing a victim a second time by our coverage. That doesn't mean we don't try to talk to victims if that seems to be an important aspect of the story. But we must remember that victims have no obligation to talk to the press and do have a right to refuse to be interviewed or photographed.

Do We Use Unnamed Sources?

The use of unnamed sources should be limited to the very unusual and most compelling cases where an important story can be told no other way. There usually is another way. Avoid using the terms "unnamed source," "sources say," "a source who asked not to be identified." That is like waving a red flag and calling attention to the lack of a name. Newspapers lose credibility with their readers through a habitual or even occasional use of unnamed sources. If a story must be written without using the name, at least provide some identification, such as "a member of the senator's staff," as a way for readers to judge the credibility of the information.

Reporters should not grant confidentiality lightly to a source. It is a commitment that in some instances a reporter may not be able to honor. Ask the source for an escape clause—an agreement that if the reporter is called to testify, the source will release the reporter from the pledge. And the reporter must be willing to tell an editor when a pledge of confidentiality has been granted and who the confidential source is.

What Is Our Definition of "Good Taste"?

Stories often must be edited for taste—good taste. Although it is difficult to determine the appropriate standards of taste for a mass audience such as Seattle-area newspaper readers, it's fair to assume that our personal notions of taste are more liberal than those of many, probably most, of our readers. So our general guideline on matters of taste should be a conservative one. Err on the side of

(*Continued*)

Sidebar 10 (*Continued*)

caution. A newspaper should have personality, vitality, good humor, but not at the expense of offending a large segment of its readers.

For instance, we would refrain from reporting details of a crime scene that are so graphic as to be labeled gory. In medical stories we should be clinically accurate, but avoid using gratuitous references to body parts or bodily functions. In reporting on issues having to do with obscenity or pornography we should avoid descriptive details.

Ask yourself this question: Is an important journalistic purpose served by the use of the graphic detail?

That same question can apply in the use of profane, obscene, vulgar or blasphemous language. Is an important journalistic purpose served by use of the questionable language?

Questionable language should be limited to material in quotations. The more prominent the person being quoted and the more public the occasion, the more likely a journalistic purpose would be served.

Decisions involving use of questionable language should be referred to the associate managing editor or managing editor.

In feature sections somewhat more latitude on these issues may apply, although here, too, editors and reporters need to carefully weigh the risks in each case. Offensive racial, ethnic or sexist references are never acceptable.

How Do We Avoid Sexism in Our Reporting of the News?

Women and men should be treated alike in the news columns unless their sex is relevant to the news. If a story includes a description of a woman—"attractive mother of three"—ask yourself if the same kind of description would be useful if the subject was a man—"handsome father of two." If the answer is "no," the reference is sexist.

Avoid terms that specify sex. Use police officer and firefighter rather than policeman, policewoman, fireman, firewoman.

We should also, however, avoid using contrived titles, such as waitperson, chairperson. Waitress is acceptable. It is simple to avoid calling a woman a chairman by saying "she heads the committee."

Avoid references such as male nurse, male secretary, woman doctor, woman lawyer. That suggests we think it is unusual for a person of a certain sex to hold a certain job and, in so doing, we perpetuate sexist stereotypes.

When the Offspring Or Other Relative of a Public Figure Gets in the News, Do We Report the Connection?

We draw the readers' attention to the relationship only if it bears directly on the newsworthy incident. Editors also should be asking themselves if the story would be worth telling if the person involved were not related to a well-known figure.

Here are two examples that were published and should not have been:

(*Continued*)

Sidebar 10 (*Continued*)

The director of transportation for the Tacoma School District was arraigned on charges of stealing from the district. Our story noted that the man was the father of a well-known high school and UW football player who had been cut by an NFL team. That fact had nothing to do with the story and should not have been included.

The son of a King County Superior Court judge testified on a pretrial hearing of a case having to do with a car bombing. The story noted the father-son relationship even though it had nothing to do with the case or the son's testimony.

What Is Our Procedure for Corrections?

It is the policy of the *Times* to correct the factual errors that we publish. Typos and misspellings that do no harm and cause no confusion do not need to be corrected. But errors of fact that leave a mistaken impression in readers' minds or harm a person named in a story should be corrected.

Whenever possible, the reporter or editor responsible for the error should write the correction.

Corrections should be run in as timely a fashion as possible in all editions that contained the original error. In writing a correction try to avoid repeating the error while explaining what is being corrected. All corrections are run on page A2.

The editor who handles the correction should determine how the error was made and attach a memo with that explanation to a copy of the correction. City desk corrections should be routed to the city editor, associate managing editor, managing editor and editor. In newsfeatures the correction should be routed through the section editor, newsfeatures editor, assistant managing editor, managing editor and editor. (*Seattle Times*. Reprinted with permission.)

Toward Excellence in Editing

"Is editing a job," a young editor asked me once, "or a lifestyle?"

A good question.

Like priests or police officers, good editors never really go off duty. One reason, as the young editor had surmised, is that editing is not simply a mechanical regimen that one turns on and off at will. It is a way of thinking and an ability to analyze. It is an ever-sharp eye and a tuned-in ear. It is a capacity for leadership and direction. It is, in some sense at least, a way of life.

And it is a rare one. As every newspaper manager knows, trustworthy editors are far scarcer than good reporters and writers. They are harder to find and harder to keep.

Yet, as we have seen, they matter so much. What most often separates weak publications from strong ones is the quality of the editing. Through good editing, the finishing touches get applied and the raw edges get smoothed. Without good editing, the final polishing seldom happens.

While reporters and writers can take a publication much of the way to excellence, it is the editors' work that accounts for the remaining distance— the difference between good and excellent, or between good and mediocre.

As William Zinsser wrote, in a passage cited earlier, editors can be "gods who save us from our sins or bums who trample on our poetic souls" (p. 234).[1] The deciding factors, often, are the attitude, ability, and professionalism of the editors, along with the environment they work in and the support they receive from their own superiors.

Preceding chapters have shown that becoming a good editor today requires

[1]Zinsser, W. (1985). *On writing well*. New York: Harper & Row.

diligence and drive. Although editing has never been easy, we have discussed several reasons why the job is becoming more and more complex as journalism undergoes important transitions. We can summarize as follows:

• Editing is hard work, calling for special capabilities distinct from those of reporting and writing. Too often incoming editors are selected on the basis of outstanding performance as reporters, without regard for whether they have the qualities editors really need. These editors seldom receive sufficient training for their new roles, and they face trouble from the start.

• The editing environment grows increasingly complex and stressful. Newspapers more and more operate as part of big business, aiming to sustain profits in the face of unprecedented competition for readers' attention and good will. In such a climate, editors' journalistic ideals can collide with marketing imperatives.

• Editing increasingly means managing, a job made tougher by the modern work force's unwillingness (understandable as it may be) to submit to the endless hours, low pay, and semi-dictatorial regimes of some traditional newsrooms. The ever-expanding administrative demands of helping run a sophisticated business and lead a volatile staff can overrun the unprepared editor.

• Innovations in graphics and production, sparked by new technology, compel editors to know more than ever about packaging and integrating all aspects of journalism—ideas, assignments, copy, headlines, art, design. The idea of the editor as a "word person" is already quaintly outmoded. Editors need to know more and more every day.

The result is a demand for what we have called the *new editor*, a better prepared and trained specialist in newsroom quality control. Not just "word people," new editors must be comfortable with all phases of editing.

New editors, like their predecessors, take pride in their profession, enjoy working with reporters and copy, and are thoughtful and serious. They know how to use their minds creatively and in different gears. Unlike many of their predecessors, perhaps, new editors see editing as more than a conventional "step up the ladder" after reporting. They see it as a specialized career opportunity, quite distinct from reporting, requiring preparation for a variety of duties, from assigning articles to designing pages, from fine-tuning daily copy to overseeing long-range projects, from hand-holding anguished writers to planning corporate strategy. New editors understand that haphazard, up-by-the-bootstraps, on-the-job training rarely produces, by itself, enough confident, competent editors.

Demand for new editors is high, and supply is not. Throughout this book, therefore, we have been exploring ways of thinking and of working that can foster the age of the new editor. As we look toward the future, we conclude by itemizing some proposals for more effective recruitment, training, and nurturing of editing talent.

In some cases, students can make immediate use of the suggestions. In others, the material may seem more appropriate for those who are teachers and managers, or who hope to assume those positions one day. Because a goal of this book has been to prepare young journalists for editing careers, not simply an introductory editing job, it is hoped they will carry along (and build on) these ideas as they make real the ideal of the new editor.

DEVELOPING NEW EDITORS

One journalist has described old-style editors as "wornout wordsmiths—hard-drinking, hardworking, hard up" (p. 30).[2] Except for the hardworking part, that stereotype seldom prevails any longer, and careful educating, recruiting, and training of new editors can demolish it forever.

For many students and young journalists, editing is an alien art. Although most students practice writing in grade school, few receive exposure to editing. For many, their first editing experience comes in college copyediting classes, which journalism departments often use as ground-level, "weeding-out" boot camps and which consequently loom before students as onerous obstacles. Such courses may concentrate so heavily on drill and structure that students never lift their pencils long enough to appreciate the larger, fascinating context in which most editors work.

Like exercising new muscles, learning to edit can prove painful, especially for the novice. Many students become discouraged at this stage, and depart with the permanent impression of editing as something sour-tasting and medicinal.

More fortunate are those students who study under instructors—and there are many of them—gifted enough to inspire and ignite the editing potential inside many journalists-to-be. When early courses energize rather than squash this dormant talent, young people often awaken to new, exciting career possibilities and turn on to a future of editing.

There, at the moment students first encounter editing, lies the biggest opportunity to identify and develop new editors. To turn them on, and not off, challenges every teacher and journalism school.

Of course, not all journalists attend journalism school or cotton quite so easily to editing. Many reach the profession without a full understanding of editing or a recognition of their own potential as desk people. Many veteran reporters wonder whether editing is for them, unsure even after years in the

---

[2]McMasters, P. (1985, July/August). A dozen ways to fill a gap on the "rim." *ASNE Bulletin*, p. 30.

business of exactly what editing means and requires. So the newsroom, too, plays a central role in the talent search for editors.

Both in the classroom and in the newsroom, changes can take place to spur the development of new editors.

In the Classroom

Teachers and students can help refocus journalism education so that potential editors get more attention. For too long, journalism training has centered nearly exclusively on reporting and writing. Within the past few years, design and graphics have worked their way into more prominence in the curriculum, and deservedly so. Now educators must recognize that students need firmer grounding in editing, too, if they are to be ready for the changing newsroom.

Journalism schools, like newsrooms, must respond to the demand for new and better editors by examining their programs and ensuring that graduates are well prepared for life beyond reporting. Students interested in editing can push to make these changes happen faster.

The following sections round up some specific suggestions for how students, through their education, can prepare themselves to be new editors:

Study Editing.   Knowledge about editing is too important to be restricted to editors. All journalism students, including those who are positive that they want to be lifelong reporters, should study editing. It will make them better at their own jobs, it will help them appreciate good editing, it will prepare them to raise the standards of their editors, and it will equip them for the day when, inevitably, many find themselves bound, to their surprise, for desk work.

As for students who already aspire to editing, study can help reduce the shock of being submerged pell-mell into the job. Some editing skills are instinctive and inbred, but most can be developed and refined through study and practice.

Students, then, should learn writing and reporting, but not neglect courses in editing. Few things will broaden journalism education more importantly than treating editing as a required course. Basic editing courses can pay off not only for potential editors, but also for reporters and others who need, in their jobs, to better understand and appreciate editors' roles. Advanced courses can target those students with special interest or aptitude for editing.

Seek Courses That Teach Editing Broadly.   Too many editing courses stop with language skills. That is where they should *begin*, not where they should *end*. Without neglecting traditional copyediting instruction, today's courses must aim for more. A good editing curriculum should have at least the following qualities:

1. It should underline the basics. It should make students aware of their strengths and weaknesses in grammar, punctuation, spelling, and usage, and see that they address the weak spots. It should make them care passionately about precision and correctness.

2. It should cover the spectrum of editing: structural editing (grammar, style, language), content editing (clarity, completeness, organization, tone, and above all accuracy), news and policy judgments, design, headlines, graphics, photography, management, ethics, and how editing works in other media.

3. It should stress the human and intangible dimensions of editing. Editing involves instincts, analytical skills, respect and sympathy for writers, and a flair for recognizing and solving a variety of puzzles.

4. It should convey that editing requires alertness and resourcefulness. It should foster good reading and newsmonitoring habits, and encourage observation, curiosity, and questioning. Editing demands thinking—and caring.

In summary, students should strive, in their editing courses, to not simply push toward an entry job on the copydesk, but to soak up training for the full range of duties and challenges facing the professional editor at all levels.

Emphasize Management and Human Relations. Much good journalism can be learned outside the journalism school. Students can benefit from courses in areas such as psychology, personnel development and business management, to supplement training in journalism classes.

Stress Critical Thinking. Editors need to be good analyzers and strategic thinkers, advanced concepts that are not easily teachable. In addition to editing courses, classes in math, philosophy, research methods, and problem solving can help immensely and should be sought after by students with editing potential.

Get Editing Internships and Experience. This should not come at the expense of reporting and writing, which editors-to-be need also. But collegiate editing experience can prove invaluable. College newspapers are an obvious and valuable opportunity for young people to edit on the job. Many community newspapers also welcome students as part-time (and occasionally full-time) editors, editing interns, summer fill-ins, or just periodic observers. National programs, including one sponsored by Dow Jones, also offer editing internships.

In the Newsroom

Given the well-documented difficulty of finding and keeping good editors, newspaper managers cannot leave those projects to journalism schools. The profession has its own special interest in taking steps to locate and prepare new editor talent.

In the same way that journalism schools have tended to stress writing over editing, newsroom recruiting and training programs have followed suit. In recent years, the industry has come a long way in recognizing its problem in attracting and holding editors, but there are many more steps that publishers and editors can take to combat the problem.

Recruit Early.   Look for potential editors in journalism schools, at rival newspapers, and within their own newsrooms. Identify potential editors early, and track them.

Broaden the Pool.   Remember the laws of supply and demand. If the supply of good editors has fallen low, then newspapers must move aggressively to expand it. One of the best editors I ever worked with was a former laundry-truck driver whose quick mind and natural genius with words brought him to the attention of the newspaper.

Ask reporters for names of potential editors, because few people can spot good and bad editing more quickly than writers can. Woo reluctant candidates by taking editing seriously and treating editors well. Build a reputation as a well-edited paper, and watch the magnetic effect it has in attracting both editors and writers.

Provide Editing Internships.   Be certain that a paper's internship program makes room for editors as well as reporters and photographers. If possible, offer internships on both the copy and news desks, giving potential editors the widest possible exposure to editorial duties.

Define What is Wanted in an Editor.   Develop an understanding of what qualities good editors have and how they differ from the qualities of good reporters. Many, such as leadership ability, diplomacy, resourcefulness, or teamwork skills, may not show up on resumes or in clips or in tests typically given applicants. *Reference checks* often uncover them.

Interview Reporting Candidates With Editing in Mind.   Most editors begin as reporters. They should; they need reporting experience. But newspaper managers should recognize that a percentage of the reporters they hire will go on to become editors. Try to hire accordingly, placing a premium on hiring some candidates who seem to have long-range editing potential.

Immerse New Editors Gently.   When managers identify reporters as having editing talent, move them along slowly and cautiously. Give them an editing mentor. Assign them to the desk 1 or 2 days a week. Watch their performances closely, treat them as apprentices, and give constructive feedback.

Recognize That Editing and Reporting Differ. Managers should never toss good reporters onto the desk in the assumption that they automatically are ready for the job if they have (a) succeeded as reporters and (b) seen editors in action. This is no more effective than giving a piano to a novice whose only experience is listening to experts play.

Isolate the Real Problems. If a manager's complaints center on poor reporting and lackluster writing, that does not necessarily mean the paper has a reporting and writing problem. It probably has an *editing* problem whose symptoms are poor writing and reporting. The best journalists in the world will look like drudges if their work must pass through lousy editors on the way to the doorstep. Because editors affect so many stories, it is true that hiring, promoting and inspiring one editor has a multiplier effect far more powerful, in most cases, than adding a star reporter.

NURTURING EDITORS

In a recent study of more than 1,200 journalists, a remarkably high 85% called their bosses poor personnel managers. They complained about these editors' inability to work with people, their failure to encourage subordinates, their weaknesses in making assignments and decisions, and their failure to offer helpful feedback.[3]

Notice how many of these complaints can be summarized in the concept of *nurturing*. Editors need to be nurtured themselves, and they need to nurture others. Considering the built-in strains and difficulties of journalism, the work can become overpoweringly frustrating unless superiors share their support, energy and information. One reporter put it this way in a study on job stress: "If a message needs to be sent to managers, editors and supervisors, it's lighten up. Don't kill the spirit that's feeding you" (p. 21).[4]

For newspaper managers, then, the objective cannot be merely to recruit talented editors, as hard as that is in itself. Equally important is keeping good editors, by maintaining the kind of newsroom where good editors are valued, teamwork is rewarded, stresses stay within reasonable check, and the special gratifications of editing are not overwhelmed by exhaustion and exasperation.

The steps that managers can take to help bring about such a newsroom climate are discussed in the following section.

---

[3]*SNPA Bulletin Special Report.* (1988, May 4). p. 6.
[4]Rich, C. (1988, March). Attention newsroom managers: Your staff needs more feedback. *ASNE Bulletin*, p. 21.

Pay Attention.   Much editing is nonglamorous, often invisible. Many editors feel overlooked and alone. So managers and senior editors should carefully monitor subordinates' work, praise, and critique it regularly, and make editors feel that good work is noticed and prized. Small touches can mean a great deal, such as thank-you notes from the managing editor to a copyeditor who has written an unusually good headline or to an assignment editor who has helped a marginal reporter produce unexpectedly sizzling copy. It usually is not hard to determine which editors produce quality work under fire and which need help, and good managers know and respond to both situations.

Teach Editing.   Make editing an exciting topic in the newsroom, through newsletters, critique sessions, markups of the paper, in-house training. Get the newsroom talking about editing the same way it talks about writing. Many papers have internal writing coaches. How many have editing coaches?

Take Advantage of External Resources.   Often it is easier to learn about editing after one has been in the news business for a while. Set against a professional's frame of reference, the subtleties of editing have more impact. Managers can take advantage of this by sending an editor to a college class or a professional seminar at the Poynter Institute, American Press Institute or somewhere similar. Do not overlook training in management, teamwork, and other so-called nonjournalistic areas that might help editors. Periodic outside refreshment is good for the soul—and the newspaper.

Encourage Collegial Relationships Instead of Rigid Hierarchies.   Sharing the responsibilities helps disperse the pressures. Robert Haiman, former executive editor of the *St. Petersburg Times,* told author Robert Giles of taking his first editing job at age 25 and "learning a lesson that probably every young lieutenant has to discover:"

> there are a number of senior staff members who are your single best resource in running the group. Not only is there no shame in asking them for advice as to how the outfit runs, but it is almost essential to do that if you want to avoid giving everybody heart failure, including yourself. (p. 130)[5]

Reduce or Offset Stress Wherever Possible.   Editors are often victims of their own idealism and high expectations. They are perfectionists working under time and space constraints that make perfection impossible. Recognizing those characteristics, managers should act to reduce the tension that inevitably mounts. Have enough editors so that each editor's workload is manageable. Periodically rotate editors out of draining overnight or weekend shifts. Delegate

---

[5]Giles, R. (1987). *Newsroom management.* Indianapolis, IN: R. J. Berg.

enough authority to give editors reasonable control and latitude in their work. Give constructive feedback, but do not second guess so much that editors despair.

Anticipate Burnout and Exhaustion.   Editors handling big stories tend to put in long, hard hours, and then go home burdened by the knowledge that the stories (and the long, hard hours) may go on for days, to be followed by other big stories requiring long, hard hours. For most editors, this scenario produces a combination of exhilaration (big stories are fun!) and exhaustion (big stories are tiring!). Managers should make sure that editors have some relief from this energy-emptying, unending spiral. Insist that they actually take earned vacation time and days off, instead of sending subtle (and not-so-subtle) messages that promotion and success depend on toiling round the clock. Left on their own, editors will overwork themselves to the point of burnout. So, do not leave them on their own.

Reward Editors Fairly.   Providing pay commensurate with responsibility and generous vacation time is obviously important but too often neglected. Managers also should look for other rewards as well. Some newspapers offer paid sabbaticals ranging from a few weeks to several months. Travel to conferences and seminars can be used as rewards. Occasional 1-day special projects (attending a workshop, taking a recruiting trip with the managing editor, running a task force on a current problem) can be timely escape valves. Simple breaks in the routine can go a long way toward heading off potential exhaustion and depression.

Provide Feedback but Also Encourage Dialogue With Editors.   It is a management truism that employees never feel they know enough about what the boss is thinking. Managers should share their thoughts. Level with editors about expectations and performance. Provide periodic formal evaluations, but recognize that ongoing communication is even more important. Do not hold grudges or let sore points fester.

At the same time, feedback should flow two ways. Managers should listen to editors. Editors need regular opportunities to make suggestions, offer advice, issue complaints, define problems, ask for help. Having an open-door policy is not enough. Take the next step to invite editors through the door on a regular basis.

Celebrate Diversity.   John Walter, an editor at *USA Today*, once was asked what he wished he had known before starting life as an editor. He replied:

> I wish I had known earlier that you don't need to do it all. God made some people great reporters, some great copyeditors, some great graphic artists, some good

organizers, some fine idea people. Each job is just one important part of the whole—find what you're really terrific at, and do it. And find a wise manager, who will encourage you to do it, and reward you accordingly. (p. 26)[6]

Help Editors Enjoy Their Work. For all its problems, few jobs beat newspaper editing for fun, excitement, and stimulation. Every day brings interesting, unexpected challenges and opportunities. Good newsrooms reflect this spirit. Maintaining a sense of humor and a good-hearted perspective can make the difference between a newsroom ground down by the pressures or one uplifted by the daily wonders of it all.

SOME SPECIFIC STARTING POINTS

Here, finally, are several specific recommendations that can help reporters, editors, and their newsrooms move immediately and painlessly toward better writing and editing. They cost very little but return championship interest:

• *Create a newsroom writers' and editors' group* to meet monthly and discuss topics such as writing leads that sparkle, writing under pressure, improving relationships between editors and writers, using graphics and headlines to best advantage, and so on.

• *Distribute a newsletter* praising, critiquing, discussing, and generally celebrating writing and editing. Invite everyone in the newsroom to contribute ideas, examples, and observations from your paper and elsewhere. Such newsletters are often produced monthly by someone such as the city editor, news editor, or copy chief.

• *Hold occasional critique sessions* in which you invite people with various points of view to discuss your paper's writing and editing. Some possibilities: a reporter, a copyeditor, the publisher, the circulation director, a local fiction writer or teacher, a reader who's always writing in with gripes.

• *Buy 1-month subscriptions* to newspapers and magazines known for their excellent writing and editing.

• *Publicly praise* good writing, editing, headlines, art, design, using a newsroom bulletin board.

• *Demonstrate from the top down that good editing and writing have priority.* Top editors should read the paper carefully, recognize good writing and editing, encourage and praise it. If they don't notice, the newsroom will stop caring.

• *Coach one another.* Foster a newsroom climate where writers gather

---

[6]Woodhull, N. (1986, January). Things we wish we had known. *ASNE Bulletin*, p. 26.

around to discuss their leads, where editors spend time talking with reporters about writing, where junior and senior editors compare notes about issues and problems.

Overall, nothing will contribute more toward better journalism than better editing. In the classroom and in the newsroom, we should welcome every opportunity to identify, spotlight and build upon the qualities of leadership, sensitivity and aptitude that will be the hallmarks of the best new editors.

CONCLUSION: TO THE FUTURE

Editing will never get easier.

New demands of our ever-changing world will continue to magnify the editor's role as coordinator, quality controller, decision maker. More than ever, newsrooms will require savvy leaders able to promote good journalism and sensitive management in increasingly competitive corporate environments.

The age of the new editor will be an era of unprecedented opportunity and challenge. Well-rounded new editors will need the full arsenal of traditional skills in writing, editing, and design. They will need a flair for analytical thinking and problem solving. They will need adaptability and shrewdness to cope with the nonstop changes in society and in journalism. And they will need the intangible, personal qualities enabling them to juggle so many disparate duties and constituencies with grace and efficiency.

Perhaps most of all, the new editors will need to maintain their trust in themselves, their colleagues and their readers, and in the words, ideas, and images that constitute good journalism.

If there is one lesson to absorb above all, it is that trouble hounds editors who see their jobs as working with *things*, with the sentences, punctuation marks, headline calls, design sheets, and computer printouts that fill their days.

At the heart of good editing are *people* and *ideas*, powerful, living forces worthy of respect and recognition. In the hands of good editors, copy comes alive, journalists flourish, and journalism shines. Few satisfactions, in any field, can top those.

Appendix:
Helping Writers With Form

In chapter 7, we touched on several editing areas that some readers may want to explore in more detail. Following is a further review of some common problems that have stood out in my experience.

SPELLING

Spelling is a universal problem.

John Bremner, in one seminar involving seven newspapers, found 72 misspellings in the issues from a single day. He then went to the board, wrote four possible spellings of a word, and asked for votes on which was correct. "Millenium" got 27 votes, "milennium" 5, and "milenium" 2. "Millennium," the correct spelling, got no votes, and Bremner admitted misspelling it himself in a book manuscript.[1]

Of course, certain letter combinations pose more hazard than others, and they merit repeated dips into the dictionary. They include:

-able, -ible ending (such as permissible and allowable)

-ant, -ent endings (consistent, descendant)

ie, ei (weird, wield)

doubled consonants in the interior of a word (harass, embarrass)

-er, -or endings (regulator, propeller)

---

[1]Simison, R. L. (1984, July 23). Bremner's golden rules for editors. *Wall Street Journal*, p. 19.

words subject to careless misspelling (it's/its, their/they're, who's/whose)
all-time favorites (use mnemonic devices to remember that the princi*pal* is
your *pal*, or that accom*mo*date has two m's just like com*mo*de, or that
consensus relates to consent, or that stationery is with an e when it means
letter and with an a when it means standing.)

Despite its perpetual capacity to bedevil us, spelling is, more than any other
structural consideration, solvable. As I stressed in chapter 7, I have deep sympathy for students, writers, and editors who have trouble spelling, but I have little
sympathy for those who cannot use a dictionary and turn in copy free from
most misspellings. Buy a dictionary. Look up words.

GRAMMAR AND PUNCTUATION

Subject–Verb Agreement.   Many grammatical mistakes stem from carelessness rather than ignorance. Because both kinds of errors occur regularly, checking all agreement makes sense. The basic rule is simple enough: Singular subjects
require singular verbs, and plural subjects require plural verbs. But enforcing
it can be confusing. Frequent errors are cited here:

1. Incorrectly using a plural verb with a subject that is singular grammati-
cally but logically seems to convey the idea of more than one person. Often,
this error involves *collective nouns,* words that are singular in form but that
name a group, such as *team* or *committee.* Such words usually take a singular
verb.
Wrong: "The team *are* winning the game." It is "*is.*"
Right: "The couple *has* two children."
2. Mistakenly letting a prepositional phrase confuse your thinking. In the
sentence, "John as well as Bill is going," the subject is singular (*John*). *As well
as Bill* is a phrase that doesn't affect the subject–verb relationship.
Wrong: "Not one of the 15 students *are* failing." It is "*is.*"

Noun–Pronoun Agreement.   Similar to subject–verb agreement. Check
pronouns to be sure they match their references in number. A typical problem
involves *institutional nouns,* words singular in form but representing an organization composed of many parts. For example, an increasingly common mistake
is to write "The company has begun advertising *their* new product." Again,
the rule for collectives applies. Most take singular pronouns.

Wrong: "The Supreme Court will reveal *their* decision." It is "*its.*"

Comma Usage. Why the tiny comma should so confuse us remains a mystery, but comma problems plague us all. On this issue, more than most others, writers guess, often inserting commas into copy seemingly at random: "Jane, yesterday was planning to visit us today." A good beginning rule for writers: Do not use any comma unless you have a reason and know the reason. The editors' corollary: Check every comma to make certain you know why it is needed.

Among the most common errors are:

1. Confusing *restrictive* and *nonrestrictive* clauses. Restrictive clauses are vital to a sentence and are not set off with commas; "The man that I saw was different from the man that you saw." Nonrestrictive clauses are parenthetical and do need commas; "The man, whom I saw again yesterday, has been visiting us frequently."

2. Using only one comma where a set is needed.
Wrong: "She is driving from Washington, D.C. to Baltimore." A second comma should come after *D.C.*
Wrong: "The player, 42 plans to retire." Commas should come both before and after the parenthetical *42.*

3. Using a comma before *and* in a series. Most grammarians prefer this comma, but journalistic style traditionally has shunned it as unnecessary. The preferred way journalistically: "They own sheep, cows and goats."

Time magazine once devoted its weekly essay to a lyrical tribute to the comma by writer Pico Iyer. He wrote:

> The gods, they say, give breath, and they take it away. But the same could be said—could it not?—of the humble comma. Add it to the present clause, and, of a sudden, the mind is, quite literally, given pause to think; take it out if you wish or forget it and the mind is deprived of a resting place. . . .
> The difference between "Jane (whom I adore)" and "Jane, whom I adore," and the difference between them both and "Jane—whom I adore—" marks all the difference between ecstasy and heartache. . . . A comma can let us hear a voice break, or a heart. (p. 80)[2]

Period Usage. A rule to live by: Use fewer commas and more periods.

Use a period to end a sentence. Use a period, not a comma, between two independent clauses not connected by a conjunction such as *and.*

---

[2]Iyer, P. (1988, June 13). In praise of the humble comma. *Time,* p. 80.

Wrong: "The mayor has been working in favor of the bill's passage, city council members have not." Put a period after *passage*.

Punctuating Quotations. I see several areas where writers seem prone to confusion.

1. Uncertainty over placing quotations marks. Several rules apply.

First, use quotation marks when, and only when, you know for certain that the material within them is directly quoted; that is, when it is exactly what the speaker said.

Second, quotation marks always go *outside* commas and periods.

Wrong: "She enjoyed watching 'Dynasty'." It is 'Dynasty.'"

Third, do not use quotation marks at the end of a paragraph if the direct quote continues into the next paragraph, but do use them at the beginning of every quoted paragraph.

Right: The speaker said, "We will do everything necessary to accomplish our goal.

"We will contact every legislator and every senator. We will write the White House. We will go to court.

"We will march on Washington. We will be heard at the ballot box. We will not be denied."

2. Confusion over use of commas and periods surrounding attribution. To recapitulate briefly: Use commas between the end of a quote and its attribution. Use commas after the attribution if the quoted sentence continues. Use periods after the attribution if the quoted sentence has ended. Examples:

Wrong: "The home team is winning." he reported.

Right: "The home team is winning," he reported.

Wrong: "The meeting will be held next Thursday," she said. "unless you hear otherwise."

Right: "The meeting will be held next Thursday," she said, "unless you hear otherwise."

USAGE

Wordiness. Fat writing abounds. The best editors become sure-footed wordsmiths, constantly sharpening and focusing. Common symptoms of word flab include:

1. Excessive prepositional phrases. "The family was on a boat in the middle of the lake for 3 hours on Sunday." Instead, try replacing the phrases with

single adjectives, adverbs, nouns, and verbs: "The family spent 3 hours Sunday sailing on the lake."

Often an adverbial phrase can be turned into a one-word adverb: "The soldiers fought with great courage" becomes "The soldiers fought bravely." Likewise with adjective phrases: "The golfer with the suntan" becomes "The suntanned golfer."

2. Lame "of" phrases. "All of a sudden" becomes "suddenly." "She is in favor of endorsing the mayor" becomes "She favors endorsing the mayor." Other examples: a number of, in spite of, in process of, each of.

3. Clauses that can reduce to phrases or even words. "We voted at the meeting that was held yesterday" becomes "We voted at yesterday's meeting."

4. Clauses and phrases that can come out entirely. "He is a man who loves peanuts" becomes "He loves peanuts."

5. -ion words. "Take action" becomes "act." "Make a decision" becomes "decide." "Reach a conclusion" becomes "conclude."

6. Weak verb constructions. Whenever it takes several words to form a verb, consider whether one word will do. "Took the witness stand to testify" becomes "testified." "Held a press conference to announce the firing of her deputy" becomes "fired her deputy." "Arrived at a verdict" becomes "convicted" or "acquitted." "Walked haltingly because of the injury" becomes "limped."

7. Tag-along words. These words can trail behind a phrase or sentence, adding nothing. "Here are the latest traffic conditions" becomes "Here's a look at traffic." "Let's plan ahead" becomes "let's plan." "Canned food items" becomes "canned food." "To fight low enrollment problems" becomes "to fight low enrollment."

As editor Jake Highton once pointed out, "The point is not mere word-counting. The point is economy and impact." Sharpening writing reduces interference in communicating. It also saves more space than one might think, as Highton also pointed out, quoting from the *New York Times* publication "Winners & Sinners":

> If in a single night each of 40 copyeditors saved only a single line in each of, say, 10 stories, the total savings would be almost two columns. (p. 23)[3]

Redundancies. A subcategory of wordiness, in which the thought is repeated. Common examples include "dead body," "10 a.m. in the morning," "12 noon," "lift up," "free gift," "male prostate," "female vagina," "between

---

[3]Highton, J. (1971, March). They barely laid a pencil on my copy. *Quill*, p. 23.

the two of us," and "set a new record." Perhaps less obvious are "personal habit," "active productive life," and "the working press."

Jargon.   Journalists, particularly beat reporters, often spend so much time around particular groups that they adopt the groups' vernacular, and forget the rest of us do not speak the language. Sometimes, jargon is merely annoying ("Police apprehended the perpetrator"). Too frequently, however, it poses a barrier to communication.

Abbreviations and Acronyms.   Using abbreviations and acronyms may suggest an intimate acquaintance with the elite. But, to consumers, they can be baffling. Who outside of Washington would recognize such constructions as "FERC" (the Federal Energy Regulatory Commission) or "NIOSH" (the National Institute for Occupational Safety and Health)? One reporter's copy referred to the purchase of MICUs by local government. Careful deciphering revealed that "Mobile Intensive Care Units" were, in fact, ambulances. Editors should root out abbreviations that too many people will not recognize.

A simple test can help here: If most people use the abbreviation in routine speech ("FBI," for example), then editors should accept it. Otherwise, strike the abbreviation, and use a normal term like *agency, organization,* or *commission.*

Gobbledygook.   Many fields, including science, medicine, law, and journalism, contribute their share of pompous verbiage, but government remains the champion. Consider the Defense Department, which labeled temporary coffins as "aluminum transfer cases" and called a hammer a "manually powered fastener-driving impact device." (p. A5)[4] In this way of speaking, a tax increase becomes known as "revenue enhancement" while a bomb goes by the name "nuclear device."

HELPING WRITERS WITH STYLE AND FORM

Editors also can serve writers immeasurably by helping them evaluate and improve the underlying structure of their work.

Here are some ways editors can help with various writing problems.

Helping With Leads

1. Answer the question, "Who cares?" A good lead makes a reader stop and care. It should provoke some kind of emotion: curiosity, anger, amusement, sadness, sympathy. Help the writer identify the element in the story that reflects

---

[4]NASA wins "doublespeak" award. (1986, November 23). *Washington Post*, p. A5.

the main point in the most stimulating way, and you have probably found your lead.

2. Let the writer tell the story to you or someone else. The point the writer seizes on in talking about a story may be best for the lead.

3. Have the writer read the lead aloud. Listening to one's own writing provides insights that merely reading it silently will not supply.

4. Ask the writer to supply a budget line for the article. Most editors compile a daily budget listing each available story and a one-or two-sentence description of it. Having writers produce these descriptions forces them to distill their stories to the essence—and often helps bring the leads into focus.

5. Prod writers to limit their leads to one thought, expressed directly. A common problem is that writers get so excited by all their good material that they want to tell everything first, to cram all the good stuff into the first two sentences. That seldom engages the busy, distracted reader. Do not let writers settle for roundup leads. Force them to focus.

Helping With Clarity

1. Make certain the subject and verb of a sentence express the main point the writer wishes to make. Do not bury key thoughts in dependent clauses and phrases.

2. Reduce the number of words and ideas in a sentence. Slow the pace of information, and it becomes easier to process.

3. Eliminate jargon and cliches. They confuse.

4. Supply examples or illustrative quotes at the key points of the article.

5. Avoid words that do not convey direct meanings. Words such as "mother," "love," "car," "prison" create strong visual images for readers. Words like "program," "proposal," "legislation," "reform" create fuzzy mental pictures and require still more words to make good sense. Good writing specifies.

Helping Pep Up Flat Writing

1. Use a strong quote within the first three paragraphs. Quotes enliven copy by introducing human beings and new voices. But insist on a strong quote, one that adds fact, feeling or insight. Rule of thumb: Use a good quote at each dramatic high point.

2. Use anecdotes, examples and illustrations. Concrete detail does more to make writing sparkle than any other single thing. Many good sentences begin with the words "for example."

3. Use action verbs and active voice, and reduce reliance on the verb "to be."

4. Recommend re-reporting. Very often, a writing problem isn't really a writing problem at all. It is a reporting problem. If the writer does not have sufficient quotes, details, and facts, then it is time to stop writing and do more reporting.

A CHECKLIST

Good editors try to ask relevant questions and to ask them regularly enough so the writers begin anticipating them on their own. Regularly ask if writers:

- use active voice (subject–verb–object writing: "I hit the ball" instead of "The ball was hit by me.").
- use short sentences (17 words being average) and short paragraphs (40–50 words in two or fewer sentences).
- use colorful nouns and actions verbs more often than flowerly adjectives and adverbs.
- use effective anecdotes and meaningful quotations.
- avoid too many "to be" verbs, sentences beginning with *There*, and successive sentences beginning with articles.
- avoid long separations between the subject and verb of a sentence.
- maintain a strong fact-per-paragraph ratio, with few sentences that contain no new information.
- write directly, revealing major points through the central subjects and verbs rather than in subordinate clauses and phrases.
- write with drama in mind, selecting visual imagery and specific details that help readers feel why an article is special.
- revise and revise, as often as necessary.

Revision seems anathema to many students and professionals, who chorus almost universally, "There isn't time." Occasionally time does run out, but in fact most journalism is not written hard on deadline and most writers can find time for reworking. Editors should routinely ask writers, "Does it really make sense to publish your first drafts for all the world to see?"

Good writing is, almost always, rewriting. As John Kenneth Galbraith once said, "There are days when the result is so bad that no fewer than five revisions are required. In contrast, when I'm greatly inspired, only four revisions are needed" (p. 43).[5]

---

[5]Charlton, J. (Ed.). (1985). *The writer's quotation book*. Stamford, CT: Ray Freiman.

Index